Jewish and Hebrew Onomastics

Garland Reference Library of the Humanities (Vol. 92)

Jewish and Hebrew Onomastics
A Bibliography

Robert Singerman

Garland Publishing, Inc., New York & London

1977

Copyright © 1977
by Robert Singerman

All Rights Reserved

Z
6824
.S5

Library of Congress Cataloging in Publication Data

Singerman, Robert.
    Jewish and Hebrew onomastics.

    (Garland reference library of the humanities ;
v. 92)
    Includes indexes.
    1. Names, Personal--Jewish--Bibliography.
2. Bible--Names--Bibliography. I. Title.
Z6824.S5 [CS3010]   016.9294   76-52684
ISBN 0-8240-9881-1

A man is called by three names: one which his father and mother call him, a second which other persons call him, and a third by which he is designated in the book of the generations of his creation.

Midrash Rabbah: Ecclesiastes

Contents

CONTENTS

Introduction

The work presented here is the first attempt at bringing under bibliographic control all significant literature on the etymology, history, and folklore of Jewish and Hebrew personal names. Every effort has been made to provide a comprehensive treatment of the subject throughout history, and to this end, coverage includes Hebrew names in the Bible as well as Jewish names in Europe, Asia, and the Americas. Considerable attention is given to the compulsory adoption of names by Jews in France and Germany as part of the Jewish emancipation process in those countries. My goal throughout this bibliography has been to record and classify research, whether of a scholarly or a popular nature, devoted to historical and linguistic studies of Jewish names, naming practices, and name-changing.

Regretfully, I have excluded from this work published and unpublished indexes, lists, registers, and directories of names that do not have an accompanying discussion or analysis of their onomastic significance. Examples of such name lists are seemingly infinite in their variety. We commonly think of lists enumerating births, circumcisions, marriages, and deaths. In addition, one can profitably scrutinize census, military, and taxation records; immigration, passenger, and deportation lists; school enrollment and voter registration lists; subscription lists; biographical dictionaries; membership directories; and even telephone directories! All of these sources provide the onomatologist with invaluable primary source material for identifying the names borne by persons in a given community or country at a given point in time. The decision to exclude this material was made in the interest of confining this work to the published results of onomastic investigation and research.

Why study Jewish names? One writer, Rabbi Benzion C. Kaganoff, addressed himself to this topic in the following compelling terms:

> . . . Jewish names can serve as clues for deciphering the cultural patterns of Jewish history: from them we can determine whether people's sentiments inclined towards

separateness or assimilation—or Jewish nationalism. We can tell when the Jews were loyal to the Hebrew language, and when indifferent. And names also reveal something about the changing political and economic orientations of Jews through the centuries. (*Commentary*, November 1955, p. 447)

To facilitate the study of Jewish names and their sources, users of *Jewish and Hebrew Onomastics: A Bibliography* will benefit greatly from the exhaustive index of Norbert Pearlroth's "Your Name" column in the weekly paper *Jewish Post and Opinion* (Indianapolis). This index, to be found on pages 81 to 116, contains more than 3,000 names in common use. Next to each name is the date Mr. Pearlroth presented his brief etymology and history of that name. I have indexed every name, together with variant spellings, from the inception of the "Your Name" question-and-answer series on Sept. 7, 1945, through Sept. 24, 1976, when volume 42 was completed. Although the column is prepared with the non-specialist in mind and while some of the interpretations are perhaps fanciful and overly simplistic, I feel that the information contained therein is extremely useful and not readily available elsewhere.

I hope that my bibliography will provide the impetus for the preparation of a complete etymological lexicon of distinctly Jewish forenames and surnames. Such a lexicon, prepared by an international team of scholars, would ideally present the derivation, definition, and development of each name, together with its pronunciation and geographical diffusion. A work of this nature does not now exist. In many ways, this project should not be deferred. It is especially vital and urgent in the light of modern Jewish history. The Jewish communities of Eastern Europe and North Africa, for example, were once flourishing centers of vibrant Jewish culture. Today, they are but shadows of their proud past. As these centers cease to exist, because of extermination, assimilation, or emigration, there will be fewer and fewer informants steeped in the folklore, traditions, and vernacular languages of the Jewish people. As a result, our knowledge of the meanings of uncommon Jewish names will be diminished. The Hebraization of immigrants to Israel only accelerates this process.

Further research is called for in the refinement of sociological techniques for identifying typically Jewish surnames. Many community surveys and studies, it seems, attempt to determine the Jewish population in a locality by somehow sampling the occurrence of "Jewish-sounding" names. While this method may be statistically valid, the haphazard nature of the guesswork involved is readily apparent and is serious cause for alarm in this writer's opinion.

The compiler has endeavored to scan as many monographs and periodicals as possible for relevant material on Jewish onomastics. As such, this bibliography is without any limitations in terms of languages or dates of publication. In the absence of a primary journal and a unified discipline of Jewish onomastics, the published literature on the subject is scattered throughout publications in other fields of specialization. A cursory glance at the bibliography reveals that a considerable amount of material was gleaned from publications devoted to religion, theology, and Bible criticism, Orientalia and the ancient Near East, Jewish studies and Hebrew philology, and local European history and genealogy.

While including a considerable number of items from the journalistic press, I have unavoidably omitted many more articles from the daily and weekly Jewish press that simply never came to my attention or were otherwise unavailable for consultation. This is particularly true of the Hebrew, Yiddish, and German press in the United States, Israel, and elsewhere. The holdings of Cincinnati's Hebrew Union College Library, the University of Cincinnati Library, the Ohio State University Library in Columbus, and the Joseph Regenstein Library at the University of Chicago provided the compiler with a large percentage of the entries in *Jewish and Hebrew Onomastics: A Bibliography*. The author entries throughout this work are generally based on those established by the Library of Congress and published in the *National Union Catalog*.

The bibliography is a classified one and all the material, excluding the appendix, has been organized into twenty-two broad subject categories. No item is entered more than once and a network of internal cross-references guides the reader to related material in other sections. Several book reviews have been cited on a random basis and reprint editions have been recorded whenever this information was known. Generally speaking, only the first edition of a work has been entered when several editions exist. My coverage in the sections on biblical names is not as exhaustive as originally conceived and for this I apologize. Also, I have emphasized critical and scientific literature on biblical names at the expense of doctrinal and devotional works.

Several librarians in the United States and abroad assisted the compiler in verifying entries from materials in their collections. Two individuals in particular deserve a special note of acknowledgment. Mrs. Ruth Tronik, Head, Reference Service, Jewish National and University Library, Jerusalem, and Mr. Myron Weinstein, Area Specialist, Hebraic Section, Orientalia Division, Library of Congress, gave generously of their time in coping with my seemingly endless barrage of requests for reference assistance.

The editor of *Names; Journal of the American Name Society*, Dr. Conrad M. Rothrauff, graciously inserted a full-page announcement in the June 1975 issue, bringing this project to the attention of other researchers. This same appeal for bibliographic data was subsequently translated into German and mysteriously republished in two German-Jewish newspapers without my prior knowledge. The combined responses were most gratifying and I was able to establish friendly contacts with individuals in several European cities as well as Mexico City. A special word of praise is in order for Mr. Theodor Katz of Stockholm for his fine work on my behalf and for Dr. Bernhard Brilling of Münster for his many favors. I wish to thank also Rabbi Leo Lichtenberg of Cincinnati who proofread my typescript with a careful eye and with dispatch.

All corrections, additions, and suggestions for a possible second edition will be eagerly welcomed.

Robert Singerman
Coordinator, Cataloging and Classification
Hebrew Union College Library
Cincinnati, Ohio 45220

December 1976

Jewish and Hebrew Onomastics

Reference and Dictionaries

0001. Brookes, Reuben Solomon, and Brookes, Blanche. A Guide to Jewish Names. Birmingham, Eng., 1967. 44 p.

0002. Colodner, Solomon. What's Your Name? (A Dictionary of Names). New York, 1959. 38 p.
Another ed.: [n.p., c1968]. 63 p.

0003. Goldin, Hyman E. HaMadrikh, the Rabbi's Guide. Rev. ed. New York, 1956. 263 p.
Names of men: p. 253-259; Names of women: p. 260-263.

0004. Kolatch, Alfred J. The Name Dictionary; Modern English and Hebrew Names. New York, 1967. 418 p.
First published in 1948 under title: These are the Names.

0005. Rozen, Dov. Pesok li shimkha. Jerusalem, 1966. 120 p.
In Hebrew.

0006. Sambatyon, Moshe. Shemon 'ivri. Vol. 1. Tel-Aviv, 1938.
In Hebrew.
No more published?

0007. Schechter, Nahum Shemaria. Sefer Bet ha-midrash Shem va-'Ever.
Jerusalem, 1965-   vol.
In Hebrew.

0008. Schulbaum, Moses. Otsar ha-shorashim. Lemberg, 1880-1904. 5 vol.
Vol. 5: Otsar ha-shemot, by Judah Loeb Benze'eb. Lemberg, 1881.
In Hebrew.

0009. Smith, Elsdon Coles. Personal Names; A Bibliography. New York, 1952. 226 p.
Bible names: p. 27-35; Jewish names: p. 86-90.
Limited to books and articles in English.
Reprinted: Detroit, 1965.

0010. Tkacz, B. Sefer Kuntres ha-shemot he-hadash. Tel-Aviv, 1955-60.
6 vol.
In Hebrew.

Encyclopedias

0011. Enciclopedia Judaica Castellana. México, 1948-51. 10 vol.
Nombres: vol. 8, p. 137-40 (unsigned).

0012. Encyclopaedia Judaica. Jerusalem, 1971. 16 vol.
Names in the Bible: vol. 12, col. 803-807 (Johann Jakob Stamm and Harold Louis Ginsberg); Names in the Talmud: vol. 12, col. 807-810 (Louis Isaac Rabinowitz); Medieval period and establishment of surnames; Modern times: vol. 12, col. 810-813 (Robert Chazan).

0013. Encyclopedia of Jewish Knowledge. New York, 1934. 686 p.
Names (Personal, First Names): p. 377-378 (Israel H. Weisfeld); Surnames: p. 378 (unsigned).

0014. Jewish Encyclopedia. New York, 1901-1906. 12 vol.
Names (Personal): vol. 9, p. 152-160 (Joseph Jacobs).

0015. Jüdisches Lexikon. Berlin, 1927-30. 5 vol.
Namen der Juden: vol. 4, col. 383-396 (Bruno Kirschner and Heinrich Loewe); Namensgesetzgebung für Juden: vol. 4, col. 397-402 (Ismar Freund and Josef Meisl); Schinnuj haschem (Änderung des Namens): vol. 5, col. 210-212 (Bruno Kirschner and Samuel Rappaport).

0016. Universal Jewish Encyclopedia. New York, 1939-43. 10 vol.
Names of the Jews: vol. 8, p. 90-98 (Theodor H. Gaster).

0017. Vallentine's Jewish Encyclopaedia. London, 1938. 696 p.
Names, Jewish: p. 453-454 (Albert M. Hyamson).

Periodicals

0018. American Jewish Archives. Vol. 1- (1948-). Cincinnati.
Index: Vol. 1-5 (1948-53). Cincinnati, 1963. 52 p.

0019. American Jewish Historical Quarterly. Vol. 1- (1893-). Waltham, Mass., etc.
Vol. 1-50 (1893-1961) called: Publications of the American Jewish Historical Society.
Index: Vol. 1-20 (1893-1911). New York?, 1914. 600 p.

0020. Archiv für Jüdische Familienforschung, Kunstgeschichte und Museumswesen. Jahrg. 1-2 (1912-17?). Wien.

0021. Gesamtarchiv der Deutschen Juden. Mitteilungen. Jahrg. 1-6 (1909-26). Berlin, etc.

0022. Gesellschaft für Geschichte der Juden in der Cechoslovakischen Republik. Jahrbuch. Jahrg. 1-9 (1929-38). Prag.
Index: Jahrg. 1-9 (1929-38) in Zeitschrift für die Geschichte der Juden, Jahrg. 5 (1968), p. 177-201.

0023. Historia Judaica. Vol. 1-23 (1938-61). New York.
Index: Vol. 1-20 (1938-58) in Vol. 23 (1961).

0024. Jahrbuch für Jüdische Geschichte und Literatur. Bd. 1-31 (1898-1938). Berlin.
Index: Bd. 1-31 (1898-1938) in Zeitschrift für die Geschichte der Juden, Jahrg. 7 (1970), p. 133-153.

0025. Jewish Historical Society of England. Miscellanies. Part 1- (1925-). London.
Part 7- (1971-) issued with the Society's Transactions.
For index, see 0026.

0026. Jewish Historical Society of England. Transactions. Vol. 1- (1893-). London.
Index: Vol. 1-15 of Transactions and Part 1-5 of Miscellanies (1893-1945). London, 1955. 120 p.

0027. Jewish Quarterly Review. Vol. 1-20 (1888-1908); New Series, Vol. 1- (1909-). Philadelphia, etc.
Index: Vol. 1-20 (1888-1908). New York, 1966. 90 p.
        Vol. 1-20 (1909-30). Philadelphia, 1932. 226 p.

0028. Jewish Social Studies. Vol. 1- (1939-). New York.
Index: Vol. 1-25 (1939-64). New York, 1967. 148 p.

0029. Journal of Jewish Studies. Vol. 1- (1948-). London.

0030. Jüdische Familien-Forschung. Heft 1-50 (1924-38). Berlin.
Index: Heft 1-37 (1924-34). Berlin, 1934? 16 p.

0031. Jüdisches Archiv; Zeitschrift für Jüdisches Museal- und Buchwesen,
Geschichte, Volkskunde und Familienforschung. Jahrg. 1-2 (1927-29).
Wien.
Index: Jahrg. 1-2 (1927-29) in Zeitschrift für die Geschichte der
Juden, Jahrg. 6 (1969), p. 97-106.

0032. Leo Baeck Institute of Jews from Germany. Bulletin. Heft 1-
(1957-). Tel-Aviv.
Index: Heft 1-48 (1957-69) in Heft 49 (1974).

0033. Leo Baeck Institute of Jews from Germany. Year book. 1-
(1956-). London.

0034. Leshonenu. Vol. 1- (1928-). Jerusalem.
In Hebrew.
Index: Vol. 1-25 (1928-61). Jerusalem, 1966-67. 72 p.

0035. Mitteilungen zur Jüdischen Volkskunde. Jahrg. 1-32 (1898-1929).
Berlin, etc.
Vol. for 1898-1904 called Mitteilungen des Gesellschaft für Jüdische
Volkskunde; vol. for 1923-25 called Jahrbuch für Jüdische Volkskunde.

0036. Monatsschrift für Geschichte und Wissenschaft des Judentums. Jahrg.
1-83 (1851-1939). Breslau, etc.
Index: Jahrg. 1-83 (1851-1939). Tübingen, 1966. 250 p.

0037. Rassegna Mensile di Israel. Vol. 1- (1925-). Roma.

0038. Revue des Études Juives. Vol. 1- (1880-). Paris.
Index: Vol. 1-50 (1880-1905). Paris, 1910. 430 p.
         Vol. 51-100 (1906-35). Paris, 1936. 70 p.
         Vol. 101-125 (1937-66) in Vol. 132, No. 3 (1973).

0039. Sefarad. Vol. 1- (1941-). Madrid.
Index: Vol. 1-15 (1941-55). Madrid, 1957. 596 p.

0040. Studia Rosenthaliana. Vol. 1- (1967-). Assen.

0041. Tarbiz. Vol. 1- (1929-). Jerusalem.
In Hebrew.
Index: Vol. 1-30 (1929-61). Jerusalem, 1962-63. 80 p.

0042. Zeitschrift für die Geschichte der Juden. Jahrg. 1-11 (1964-74).
Tel-Aviv.
Index: Jahrg. 1-10 (1964-73) in Jahrg. 11, No. 1-2 (1974).

0043. Zeitschrift für die Geschichte der Juden in der Tschechoslowakei.
Jahrg. 1-5 (1930-38). Prag.
Index: Jahrg. 1-5 (1930-38) in Zeitschrift für die Geschichte der
Juden, Jahrg. 5 (1968), p. 177-201.

0044. Zeitschrift für die Geschichte der Juden in Deutschland. Bd. 1-5
(1887-92). Braunschweig.

0045. Zeitschrift für die Geschichte der Juden in Deutschland. Jahrg.
1-7 (1929-37). Berlin.
Index: Jahrg. 1-7 (1929-37) in Zeitschrift für die Geschichte der
Juden, Jahrg. 5 (1968), p. 27-49.

0046. <u>Zion</u>. Vol. 1-6 (1925-34); New Series, Vol. 1- (1935-). Jerusalem.
Index: Vol. 1-6 (1925-34) and New Series, Vol. 1-20 (1935-55). Jerusalem, 1955? 43, 53 p.

II

General Literature: Books

0047. Adler, Bill, and Kogen, Arnie. <u>What to Name Your Jewish Baby</u>. New York, 1966. 118 p.

0048. Ausubel, Nathan. <u>The Book of Jewish Knowledge</u>. New York, 1964. 560 p.
Names, Jewish: p. 311-312.

0049. Babad, J. <u>Etwas über jüdische und christliche Vor- und Zunamen</u>. Wien, 1894. 22 p.
Reprinted from: <u>Oesterreichische Wochenschrift</u>, Jahrg. 10.

0050. Belloc, Hilaire. <u>The Jews</u>. London, 1922. 308 p.
The Jewish reliance upon secrecy: p. 99-108 (false names).

0051. Brasch, R. <u>The Judaic Heritage; Its Teachings, Philosophy, and Symbols</u>. New York, 1969. 437 p.
Origins of Jewish family names: p. 388-403.

0052. Edidin, Ben M. <u>Jewish Customs and Ceremonies</u>. New York, 1941. 178 p.
Naming the boy: p. 50-51; Naming the girl: p. 51.

0053. Feldman, William Moses. <u>The Jewish Child; Its History, Folklore, Biology & Sociology</u>. London, 1917. 453 p.
Naming the child, and other ceremonies: p. 218-228.

0054. Frieman, Donald G. <u>Milestones in the Life of the Jew; A Basic Guide to Belief and Ritual</u>. New York, 1965. 116 p.
Naming the child: p. 10-13; Naming the girl: p. 26.

0055. Gaster, Theodor Herzl. <u>The Holy and the Profane; Evolution of Jewish Folkways</u>. New York, 1955. 256 p.
Names and nicknames: p. 33-38.

0056. Gottlieb, Nathan. <u>A Jewish Child is Born; The History and Ritual of Circumcision, Redemption of Firstborn Son, Adoption, Conversion, and Choosing and Giving Names</u>. New York, 1960. 159 p.

0057. Hervé, Joseph. <u>Israël; ses enfants perdus et son livre d'or</u>. Paris, 1932. 90 p.
Note sur les noms portés par les Juifs: p. 54-57; Liste alphabétique de noms connus, célèbres ou illustres, marquant une origine juive plus ou moins probable: p. 58-90.

0058. Japhet, Saemy. <u>The Romance of Jewish Names in the Light of Jewish History</u>. London, 1926. 40 p.

0059. Klar, Benjamin. <u>Meḥkarim ve-'iyunim ba-lashon, ba-shirah uba-sifrut</u>. Tel-Aviv, 1953-54. 405 p.
In Hebrew.
Shemot Bene Yisrael: p. 47-70.

4

0060. Krause, Konrad. Die jüdische Namenwelt. Essen, 1943. 196 p.
I. Teil: Jüdische Vornamen. II. Teil: Jüdische Familiennamen in Deutschland. III. Teil: Jüdische Familiennamen in anderen Ländern.

0061. Leroy-Beaulieu, Anatole. Israel Among the Nations. A Study of the Jews and Antisemitism. New York, 1904. 385 p.
Jewish names: p. 322-327.

0062. Levene, Moses. Hebrew Names; Their Meaning and Historical Connections. London, 1944. 48 p.

0063. Loew, Immanuel. Die Flora der Juden. Wien, 1924-34. 4 vol.
Pflanzen als Namen: vol. 4, p. 416-430.

0064. Loew, Leopold. Die Lebensalter in der jüdischen Literatur von physiologischem, rechts-, sitten- und religionsgeschichtlichen Standpunkte betrachtet. Szegedin, 1875. 459 p.
Forms vol. 2 of the author's Beiträge zur jüdischen Alterthumskunde.
Namen: p. 92-110.

0065. Löwe, Heinrich. Geschichten von jüdischen Namen, aus dem Volksmunde gesammelt. Berlin, 1929. 18 p.

0066. Löwe, Heinrich. Namen. [Berlin?, 1925?]. 6 p.
Reprinted from: Sammelblätter jüdischen Wissens, Nr. 17-19.

0067. Massoutié, Georges. Les Noms juifs. Macon, 1917. 17 p.
Also 2d ed.: Paris, 1925.

0068. Memmi, Albert. The Liberation of the Jew. New York, 1966. 303 p.
Name-changing: p. 31-42.

0069. Newman, Louis Israel. The Jewish People, Faith and Life. New York, 1965. 277 p.
The names of the Jews: p. 199-203; Hebrew equivalents for contemporary names: p. 239-249.

0070. Patai, Raphael. Tents of Jacob. The Diaspora - Yesterday and Today.
Englewood Cliffs, N.J., 1971. 464 p.
Naming practices: p. 147-149.

0071. Rappoport, Angelo Solomon. The Folklore of the Jews. London, 1937. 276 p.
Change of name (Shinnui ha-Shem): p. 87-90.

0072. Reisner, Hermann. Hebräische Etymologie für den Hausgebrauch.
Ramat Gan, 1947. 190 p.
Jüdische und hebräische Namen: p. 140-144.

0073. Roback, Abraham Aaron. Destiny and Motivation in Language; Studies in Psycholinguistics and Glossodynamics. Cambridge, Mass., 1954. 474 p.
Destiny in names: p. 57-81.

0074. Ruppin, Arthur. The Jews in the Modern World. London, 1934. 423 p.
Discarding of Jewish names: p. 293-295.
Similar text in the author's The Jewish Fate and Future (London, 1940), p. 256-259.

0075. Sacher, Harry. Zionist Portraits and Other Essays. London, 1959. 355 p.
On names: p. 314-315.

5

0076.   Salzer, Moses. "Die Namen der Juden." In: Gossel, Josef, ed.
        Populär-wissenschaftliche Vorträge über jüdische Geschichte und
        Literatur. Vol. 1, p. 348-360. Frankfurt a.M., 1902.

0077.   Schwadron, Abraham. Von der Schande euerer Namen. Ein Ruf an die
        zionistische Jugend. Wien, 1920. 87 p.
        Review:
            Czellitzer, Arthur. Jüdische Familien-Forschung Heft 21 (1930):
            230-231.

0078.   Simonsen, David. "Eigentümliche Namen." In: Festschrift zum 75-
        jährigen Bestehen des Jüdisch-theologischen Seminars Fraenckelscher
        Stiftung. Vol. 2, p. 367-371. Breslau, 1929.

0079.   Smith, Elsdon Coles. Treasury of Name Lore. New York, 1967. 246 p.
        Israeli names: p. 93-94; Jewish names: p. 97-103.

0080.   Tawiow, Israel Ḥayyim. Kitve Y.Ḥ. Tavyov. Berlin, 1923. 346 p.
        In Hebrew.
        Shemot ha-yehudim: p. 306-318; Shemot mishpaḥah 'ivriyim: p. 319-346.

0081.   Thiel, Matthias. Grundlagen und Gestalt der Hebräischkenntnisse des
        frühen Mittelalters. Spoleto, 1973. 449 p.
        Onomastische Listen: p. 53-138.

0082.   Trachtenberg, Joshua. Jewish Magic and Superstition; A Study of Folk
        Religion. Cleveland, 1961. 356 p.
        In the name of...: p. 78-103.

0083.   Trepp, Leo. Eternal Faith, Eternal People; A Journey into Judaism.
        Englewood Cliffs, N.J., 1962. 455 p.
        Jewish names: p. 218-221.

0084.   Vroonen, Eugène. Les Noms des personnes dans le monde; Anthroponymie
        universelle comparée. Bruxelles, 1967. 495 p.
        Noms juifs: p. 249-257; Anthroponymie profane juive: p. 317-323.

0085.   Witkowski, Teodolius. Grundbegriffe der Namenkunde. Berlin, 1964.
        92 p.
        Judennamen: p. 40-41.

0086.   Zunz, Leopold. Namen der Juden. Eine geschichtliche Untersuchung.
        Leipzig, 1837. 125 p.
        Also published in the author's Gesammelte Schriften. Vol. 2, p. 1-
        82. Berlin, 1876. Namen der Juden reprinted: Hildesheim, 1971.
        Review:
            Israelitisches Predigt- und Schul-Magazin 3 (1836): 338-341.

            Littger, Klaus Walter. Beiträge zur Namenforschung (N.F.) 9
            (1974): 276-278.

        See also:

0086A   Grünwald, Moriz. "Additamenta zu Zunz' 'Namen der Juden.'" Jüdi-
        sches Litteratur-Blatt 9 (1880): 182-183; 10 (1881): 41-42, 59-60.

0086B   Grunwald, Max. "Zur jüdischen Namenkunde. Ergänzungen zu 'Zunz'
        Namen der Juden.'" Mitteilungen zur Jüdischen Volkskunde Heft 37
        (1911): 6-25; Heft 38 (1911): 75-79; Heft 39 (1911): 97-121.

III

General Literature: Periodical Literature

0087. Aquilina, Joseph. "A Comparative Study in Lexical Material Relating to Nicknames and Surnames." Journal of Maltese Studies 2 (1964): 147-176.

0088. Benor, Y.L. "The Correct Order in Writing Personal Names." (Hebrew) Leshonenu la-'am 23 (1951): 26-27.

0089. Bergmann, J. "Wie unsere Familiennamen entstanden sind." Jahrbuch für jüdische Geschichte und Literatur 28 (1927): 34-62.

0090. Berliner, Adolf. "Zur Namenkunde." Blätter für jüdische Geschichte und Literatur 1 (1900): 23-24; 2 (1901?): 24.

0091. Bernardini, Armand. "Les Noms hébraïques." L'Ethnie Française no. 7 (1943): 7-14.

0092. Bernstein, Mordehai. "Jewish Surnames Expressing Various Vocations, Occupations and Handicrafts." (Hebrew) Yeda'-'am vol. 2, no. 2-3 (1954): 123-126.

0093. Bitton, Livia Elvira. "Biblical Names of Literary Jewesses." Names 21 (1973): 103-109.

0094. Blumenau, S. "Etwas über jüdische Namen." Allgemeine Zeitung des Judenthums 57 (1893): 65-66.

0095. Bresslau, Harry. "Namen der Juden im Mittelalter." Hebräische Bibliographie 9 (1869): 54-57.

0096. Chance, F. "The Manufacture of Surnames (Especially Jewish Surnames) in Times Past and Present." The Academy 45 (21 Apr. 1894): 329-330.

0097. Clemens, Samuel Langhorne. "Concerning the Jews." By Mark Twain. Harper's New Monthly Magazine 99 (Sept. 1899): 527-535. Jewish names: p. 533-534.

0098. Flesch, Heinrich. "Abbreviaturen als Familiennamen." Jüdische Familien-Forschung Heft 8 (1926): 188-189.

0099. Flesch, Heinrich. "Berufe als Familiennamen bei Juden." Jüdische Familien-Forschung Heft 7 (1926): 158-160.

0100. Flesch, Heinrich. "Jüdische Vornamen als Familiennamen." Jüdische Familien-Forschung Heft 5 (1926): 110-112.

0101. Flesch, Heinrich. "Phantasienamen bei Juden." Jüdische Familien-Forschung Heft 10 (1927): 235-238.

0102. Flesch, Heinrich. "Place Names and First Names as Jewish Family Names." Jewish Forum 8 (Apr. 1925): 134-137.

0103. Franklin, Arthur Ellis. "Jewish Forenames." The Genealogists' Magazine 7 (1936): 244-245.

0104. Glenn, Menahem G. "What's in Your Name?" Jewish Spectator Dec. 1940, p. 25-26 (Abraham, Anna); Jan. 1941, p. 26 (Esther, Chayim); Feb. 1941, p. 26 (Deborah, Benjamin, Bathsheba); Mar. 1941, p. 26 (Judith, Gershon); Apr. 1941, p. 28-29 (Moses, Miriam); May 1941, p. 23-24 (Jacob, Leah); June 1941, p. 24 (David, Naomi); July 1941,

7

p. 22-23 (Nathan, Eve); Aug. 1941, p. 21-22 (Pearl, Isaac); Sept. 1941, p. 26-27 (Rachel, Levi); Oct. 1941, p. 22 (Ida, Solomon); Nov. 1941, p. 20-21 (Samuel, Judah); Dec. 1941, p. 20 (Gittel, Hirsch); Jan. 1942, p. 20 (Reuben, Elijah); Feb. 1942, p. 19 (Obadiah, Zipporah); Mar. 1942, p. 24 (Phinehas, Helen); Apr. 1942, p. 24 (Kalman, Tamar); May 1942, p. 26 (Mendel, Sprinze); Aug. 1942, p. 22 (Zechariah).

0105. Gold, David L. "Jewish Names." Jewish Digest (Sept. 1973): 34-36.

0106. Grünwald, Moriz. "Die Namen der Juden." Jüdisches Centralblatt 3 (1884): 91-97, 156-159.
No more published.
Italian text in: Corriere Israelitico 23 (1884-85): 52-54.

0107. Gumpertz, Yehiel Gedalyahu Friedrich. "On the Names of the Jews." (Hebrew) Tarbiz 25 (1955-56): 340-353, 452-463.
Includes English summary.

0108. H., H. "Hoe ontstonden Joodsche voornamen en familiennamen." Het Joodsche Weekblad, 23 Jan. 1942.

0109. Ha-Reubeni, Ephraim. "Study on Jewish Names." (Hebrew) Leshonenu 2 (1929-30): 381-395; 3 (1930-31): 39-48, 126-142.

0110. Hyamson, Albert Montefiore. "Jewish Surnames." Jewish Literary Annual, 2d and rev. ed. (1903): 53-78.
Also in: The New Era Illustrated Magazine 4 (1904): 290-297, 350-355.

0111. Imber, Naphtali Herz. "The Derivation of Jewish Names." American Hebrew, 14 Feb. 1902, p. 405-406.

0112. "Jewish Names." American Hebrew, 6 May 1898, p. 8-9.

0113. "Jewish Names." Jewish Chronicle (London), 9 July 1880, p. 4.

0114. Kaganoff, Benzion C. "Jewish First Names Through the Ages." Commentary 20 (Nov. 1955): 447-452.

0115. Kaganoff, Benzion C. "Jewish Surnames Through the Ages." Commentary 22 (Sept. 1956): 249-259.

0116. Kamenka, Eugene. "What's in Your Name?" Jewish Affairs (May 1954): 36-39.

0117. Kaufman, Dorothy. "The Romance of Jewish Names." American Hebrew, 18 July 1930, p. 278.

0118. Kaufmann, David. "Zu den jüdischen Namen." Mitteilungen der Gesellschaft für Jüdische Volkskunde Heft 1 (1898): 116-118.

0119. Kober, Adolf. "Jewish Names in the Era of Enlightenment." Historia Judaica 5 (1943): 165-182.

0120. Kolatch, Alfred J. "The Hebrew Name as a Survival Factor." Reconstructionist, 26 Nov. 1943, p. 18-22.

0121. Landau, Marcus. "Zur Geschichte der jüdischen Vornamen." Mitteilungen der Gesellschaft für Jüdische Volkskunde Heft 9 (1902): 1-9.

0122. Lauterbach, Jacob Zallel. "The Naming of Children in Jewish Folklore, Ritual and Practice." Central Conference of American Rabbis. Yearbook 42 (1932): 316-360.

0123. Lewy, Ernst. "Ein jüdisches Namenslexikon!" Jüdische Familien-Forschung Heft 34 (1933): 558.

0124. Link, Pablo. "Nombres y patronímicos judíos." Davar (Buenos Aires) no. 66 (1956): 77-89.

0125. Lippe, Karpel. "Das Ghetto für jüdische Namen." Neuzeit (Wien) 11 (1871): 437-439.

0126. Löwe, Heinrich. "Geschichten von jüdischen Namen." Jüdische Familien-Forschung Heft 12 (1927): 274-280.

0127. Löwe, Heinrich. "Jewish Personal Names Taken From Names of Animals." (Hebrew) Leshonenu 3 (1930-31): 265-272; 4 (1931-32): 32-37.

0128. Markreich, Max. "Notes on Transformation of Place Names by European Jews." Jewish Social Studies 23 (1961): 265-284.
Jewish family names derived from place names: p. 278-284.

0129. Meltzer, Julian. "A Tanenbaum is a Firtree is an Arazi." National Jewish Monthly (Jan. 1972): 10, 12.

0130. Neumann, Joshua H. "Some Acronymic Surnames." Revue Internationale d'Onomastique 17 (1965): 267-274.

0131. Nicolai, Friedrich. "Ueber die jüdischen Namen." Neue Berlinische Monatsschrift 22 (1809): 45-48.

0132. Papperovitch, A.D. "Jewish Personal Names." Current Jewish Record (Apr. 1932): 47-50.

0133. Plačzek, Baruch Jakob. "Bilschon. Benennungen und Redensarten im Dialekt." Allgemeine Zeitung des Judenthums 61 (1897): 257-259.

0134. Pribluda, A.S. "Etiudy iz oblasti evreĭskoĭ antroponimiki." (Russian) Onomastica 20 (1975): 241-251.
On the names Aaron, Aba, Margulis.

0135. Pribluda, A.S. "Familii-abbreviatury evreev." (Russian) Antroponimika (1970): 138-146.
On Jewish family names derived from abbreviations.

0136. Pribluda, A.S. "Toward the History of Jewish Family Names." (Yiddish) Sovetish Heymland (1968, No. 7): 147-150; (1968, No. 12): 139-141; (1969, No. 8): 148-151; (1970, No. 2): 145-147; (1971, No. 12): 173-176; (1973, No. 4): 177-179; (1973, No. 11): 167-168; (1974, No. 10): 177-180.

0137. Rivkai, Israel. "Jewish Surnames Connected with Certain Profane Occupations, etc." (Hebrew) Yeda'-'am vol. 2, no. 1 (1953): 15-17.

0138. Roback, Abraham Aaron. "Jewish Metronymics." Jewish Chronicle (London), 7 Feb. 1958, p. 19, 30.

0139. Roblin, Michel. "De Krämer à Wechsler; les métiers traditionnels d'Europe Centrale et Orientale." L'Arche no. 27 (mars 1959): 31-32.

0140. Romm, Ittamar S. "Origin of Jewish Names." Hebrew Order of David of South Africa (H.O.D.). Journal (Sept. 1964): 53-57.

0141. Samuel, Edgar Roy. "Jewish Naming Customs." The Genealogists' Magazine 14 (1962): 44-47.

0142. Samuel, Edgar Roy. "New Light on the Selection of Jewish Children's Names." Jewish Historical Society of England. Transactions 23 (1971): 64-86; 24 (1974): 171-172.

0142A Sarsowsky, Abraham. "Hebrew Personal Names." (Hebrew) ha-'Olam (Odessa), 2 July 1912, p. 9-10.

0143. Schott, Rabbi. "Etwas über die Vornamen der Israeliten." Jüdisches Volksblatt 1 (1854): 86-88, 100, 182-183.

0144. Singerman, Marianne. "Name Tracing." Jewish Digest (Mar. 1974): 31-32.

0145. Spiegel, Shimon. "Religion and Ritual in Jewish Surnames." (Hebrew) Yeda'-'am no. 28-29 (1964): 16-18.

0146. Steinschneider, Moritz. "Namenkunde." Hebräische Bibliographie 12 (1872): 66; 13 (1873): 64-65; 14 (1874): 81-82; 16 (1876): 132; 18 (1878): 131-132; 19 (1879): 114-115.

0147. Steinschneider, Moritz. ["Namenkunde"]. Zeitschrift für Hebräische Bibliographie 9 (1905): 154-157.

0148. Stern, A. "Die Namen der Juden. Nach Geschichte und Halacha." Ben Chananja 8 (1865): col. 807-815.

0149. Sternberg, L. "Pol' sokhranenii͡a imeni v evreĭskom levirate." (Russian) Evreĭskai͡a Starina 11 (1924): 177-179.

0150. Strasser, L. "Ein Wort über Namensertheilungen der Mädchen." Neuzeit (Wien) 5 (1865): 530.

0151. Sulzbach, Abraham. "Uber Namengebung bei den Juden." Jeschurun (Berlin) 2 (1915): 35-41.

0152. Weinstein, Jacob Joseph. "Shemot: And These are the Names." National Jewish Post and Opinion, 10 Jan. 1958, p. 14.

0153. Yarden, Dov. "Exegesis of Names." (Hebrew) Leshonenu la-'am 50 (1954): 21-26.

IV

Biblical Names: Reference and Dictionaries

0154. Bates, Lucy. Original Meaning of Scriptural Names. New York, 1949.
       222 p.

0155. Copley, Esther Hewlett. Scripture Biography; Comprehending all the
       Names Mentioned in the Old and New Testaments. London, 1835. 632 p.

0156. Creighton, James. A Dictionary of the Scripture Proper Names. Lon-
       don, 1808. 352 p.

0157. Cruden, Alexander. A Complete Concordance to the Holy Scriptures of
       the Old and New Testaments. New ed. With a List of the Proper Names
       in the Old and New Testaments, by Alfred Jones. New York, [190-?].
       757 p.

0158. Fricke, Klaus Dietrich, and Schwank, Benedikt. Ökumenisches Ver-
       zeichnis der biblischen Eigennamen nach den Loccumer Richtlinien.
       Stuttgart, 1971. 144 p.

0159. Hamilton, Ephraim Nelson. Bible Names, Pronunciations and Meanings,
       Alphabetically Arranged; With a Brief History of the Bible. Chicago,
       1939. 128 p.

0160. Harduf, David Mendel. Biblical Proper Names (A Symbolic Interpreta-
       tion). Tel-Aviv, [196-?]. 48 p.

0161. Harduf, David Mendel. Yalkut ha-shemot ha-pratiyim sheba-TaNaKH u-
       midrashehem. Tel-Aviv, 1964. 188 p.
       In Hebrew.
       See also 0596-0597.

0162. Jones, Alfred. The Proper Names of the Old Testament Scriptures,
       Expounded and Illustrated. London, 1856. 382 p.

0163. König, Eduard. Hebräisches und aramäisches Wörterbuch zum Alten
       Testament mit Einschaltung und Analyse aller schwer erkennbaren
       Formen, Deutung der Eigennamen sowie der massoretischen Randbemer-
       kungen und einem deutsch-hebräischen Wortregister. 4. und 5. verm.
       Aufl. Leipzig, 1931. 681 p.

0164. Lemans, Mozes, and Mulder, Samuël Israël. Hebreeuwsch-Nederduitsch
       handwoordenboek. Amsterdam, 1831. 706 p.
       Register der Eigennamen: p. 676-695.

0165. List (A) of the Proper Names Occurring in the Old Testament with
       Their Interpretations. Principally Compiled from Simonis and Ge-
       senius. London, 1844. 221-239, 129 p.

0166. Meister, Abraham. Biblische Namen: kurz erklärt. Wuppertal, 1958.
       176 p.

0167. Potts, Cyrus Alvin. Dictionary of Bible Proper Names. Every Proper
       Name in the Old and New Testaments Arranged in Alphabetical Order;
       Syllabified and Accented; Vowel Sounds Diacritically Marked; Defini-
       tions Given in Latin and English. New York, 1922. 279 p.

0168. Preisigke, Friedrich. Namenbuch enthaltend alle griechischen, la-
       teinischen, ägyptischen, hebräischen, arabischen und sonstigen semi-

tischen und nichtsemitischen Menschennamen, soweit sie in griechischen Urkunden (Papyri, Ostraka, Inschriften, Mumienschildern usw.) Ägyptens sich vorfinden. Mit einem Anhange von Enno Littmann, enthaltend die in diesem Namenbuche vorkommenden abessinischen, arabischen, aramäischen, kanaanäischen und persischen Namen. Amsterdam, 1967. 526 col.

0169. Proper (The) Names of the Old Testament, Arranged Alphabetically from the Original Text ... With an Appendix of the Hebrew and Aramaic Names in the New Testament. London, 1859. 227 p.

0170. Rosenberg, Abraham Ḥayyim. Otsar ha-shemot asher be-kitve kodesh. 2d ed. New York, 1923. 5 vol.
In Hebrew.

0171. Rowley, Harold Henry. Dictionary of Bible Personal Names. London, 1968. 168 p.
"The scripture quotations in this publication are from the Revised Standard Version of the Bible, copyrighted 1946 and 1952"

0172. Scerbo, Francesco. Lessico dei nomi propri ebraici del Vecchio Testamento, con interpretazione del significato etimologico. Firenze, 1913. 147 p.

0173. Schumacher, Heinz. Die Namen der Bibel und ihre Bedeutung im Deutschen. Stuttgart, 1958. 224 p.

0174. Schusslowitz, Judah Loeb. Otsar ha-shemot. Vilna, 1878. 276 p.
In Hebrew.

0175. Walker, John. A Key to the Classical Pronunciation of Greek, Latin, and Scripture Proper Names ... To Which are Added, Terminational Vocabularies of Greek, Hebrew, and Latin Proper Names. 9th ed. London, 1830. 305 p.

0176. Wilkinson, William Francis. Personal Names in the Bible, Interpreted and Illustrated. London, 1865. 556 p.

0177. Williams, Ara. A Universal Vocabulary of Proper Names, Ancient and Modern; Together with Classes of People, Religious, National, and Philosophical, and Titles, Ecclesiastical and Civil, among Christians, Jews, Mahometans, and Pagans. Cincinnati, 1831. 536 p.

0178. Williams, Thomas David. A Concordance of the Proper Names in the Holy Scriptures. St. Louis, 1923. 1056 p.

Encyclopedias

0179. Dictionary of the Bible. New York, 1900-1904. 5 vol.
Name: vol. 3, p. 478-481 (George B. Gray); Names, Proper: vol. 3, p. 481-485 (George B. Gray).

0180. Dictionnaire de la Bible. Supplément. Paris, 1928- . vol.
Onomastique: vol. 6, col. 732-744 (Henri Cazelles).

0181. Enciclopedia de la Biblia. 2d ed. Barcelona, 1969. 6 vol.
Onomástica: vol. 5, col. 642-653 (B.S.J. Isserlin).

0182. Encyclopaedia Biblica. New York, 1899-1903. 4 vol.
Name; Names: vol. 3, col. 3264-3270; 3271-3331 (Theodor Nöldeke, George B. Gray, Emil F. Kautzsch, Thomas K. Cheyne).

See also:

Gray, George Buchanan. "The 'Encyclopaedia Biblica' (Vols. I and and II) and the Textual Tradition of Hebrew Proper Names." _Jewish Quarterly Review_ (O.S.) 13 (1901): 375-391.

0183. International Standard Bible Encyclopaedia. Chicago, 1915. 5 vol. Names, Proper: vol. 4, p. 2113-2117 (John D. Davis).

0184. Interpreter's Dictionary of the Bible. New York, 1962. 4 vol. Name: vol. 3, p. 500-508 (Raymond Abba).

V

Biblical Names: Books

0185. Asner, Moses David. ha-Mazkir. Warsaw, 1900. 256, 10 p. In Hebrew.

0186. Beeston, William. On the Etymology and Prophetic Character of the Proper Names Found in the Old Testament; Being a Key to the Massoretic Punctuation of the Hebrew Scriptures. London, 1843. 110 p.

0187. Berger, Philippe. Essai sur la signification historique des noms des patriarches hébreux. Paris, [1886?]. 7 p. Extrait des Mémoirs de la Société Linguistique, t. 6, fasc. 2.

0188. Bleefeld, Bradley Nelson. Proper Nouns in North-West Canaanite Inscriptions and Their Relations to Old Testament Names. 1975. 180 ℓ. Unpublished rabbinic thesis, Hebrew Union College-Jewish Institute of Religion (Cincinnati).

0189. Brecher, Gideon. Eleh ha-ketuvim ba-shemot. Frankfurt a.M., 1876. 79 p. In Hebrew.

0190. Chajes, Hirsch Perez. Beiträge zur nordsemitischen Onomatologie. Wien, 1900. 50 p. Review: Clermont-Ganneau, Charles Simon. "Sur quelques noms propres juifs." In the author's Recueil d'archéologie orientale. Vol. 4, p. 218-224. Paris, 1901.

0191. Charencey, Hyacinthe, comte de. De quelques idées symboliques se rattachant au nom des douze fils de Jacob. Paris, 1873. 191-292 p. Reprinted from: Actes de la Société Philologique, t. 3, no. 5.

0192. Chotzner, Joseph. Hebrew Humour and Other Essays. London, 1906. 186 p. Curiosities of certain proper names in the Bible: p. 43-46.

0193. Diringer, David. Le iscrizioni antico-ebraiche Palestinesi. Firenze, 1934. 361 p. Nomi di persone: p. 38-50.

0194. Dvir, Jehuda. "The Essence of the Name in the Bible." (Hebrew) In: Gvaryahu, Haim, ed. Sefer Biram, p. 57-73. Jerusalem, 1956.

0195. Dvir, Jehuda. Yi'udah shel ha-shelihut ba-shem ha-mikra'i. Tel-Aviv, 1969. 368 p. In Hebrew.

13

0196. Eissfeldt, Otto. "Gottesnamen in Personennamen als Symbole menschlicher Qualitäten." In: Festschrift Walter Baetke, p. 110-117. Weimar, 1966.

0197. Eissfeldt, Otto. "Renaming in the Old Testament." In: Words and Meanings; Essays Presented to David Winton Thomas ..., p. 69-79. London, 1968.

0198. Eshel, Ben-Zion. "Dialects and Pronunciation of Names in the Bible." (Hebrew) In: Haran, Menahem, ed. Sefer Tur-Sinai, p. 243-278. Jerusalem, 1960.

0199. Eshel, Ben-Zion. "The Ending-ya(h) in Proper Names in Biblical Hebrew - Is it Theophoric?" (Hebrew) In: World Congress of Jewish Studies, 5th, Jerusalem, 1969. Proceedings. Vol. 4, p. 137-149. Jerusalem, 1973.
Includes English summary.

0200. Estienne, Robert. Hebraea, Chaldaea, Graeca et Latina nomina virorum, mulierum, populorum, idolorum, urbium, fluviorum, montium ... Paris, 1537. 542 p.

0201. Fahrenfort, Johannes Jacobus. De betekenis van de namen in de ethnologie en in het Oude Testament. Leuven, 1958. 26 p.
Contains J.J. Fahrenfort's "De betekenis van de namen bij natuurvolken" (p. 1-15) and P.A.H. de Boer's "Enkele opmerkingen over de betekenis van namen in het Oude Testament" (p. 16-24).

0202. Farbridge, Maurice Henry. Studies in Biblical and Semitic Symbolism. London, 1923. 288 p.
The name: p. 239-244.

0203. Friedländer, Moses. Genealogische Studien zum Alten Testament. I. Die Veränderlichkeit der Namen in den Stammlisten der Bücher der Chronik. Berlin, 1903. 64 p.

0204. Gandía, Enrique de. Del origen de los nombres y apellidos y de la ciencia genealógica. Buenos Aires, 1930. 323 p.
Nombres hebreos: p. 125-126.

0205. Gonzalo Maeso, David. "Cuestiones y problemas de la onomástica bíblica." In: International Congress of Onomastic Sciences, 6th, Munich, 1958. Proceedings. Vol. 2, p. 311-316. München, 1961. (Studia Onomastica Monacensia, Vol. 3).
Also published in: Cultura Bíblica, año 16, no. 164 (1959): 18-28.

0206. Gray, George Buchanan. Studies in Hebrew Proper Names. London, 1896. 338 p.
Review:
    Robinson, Andrew Craig. "Gray's 'Hebrew Proper Names' and Hommel's 'Ancient Hebrew Tradition.'" Churchman (N.S.) 13 (1898-99): 245-262.

    Selbie, John Alexander. Expository Times 8 (1896-97): 329-331.

0207. Grünberg, Samuel. Biblische Eigennamen als Quelle jüdischer Kulturgeschichte und Bibelexegese. Berlin, 1936. 12 p.
Sonderdruck aus Zion, 8. Jahrg., 1936.

0208. Grunwald, Max. Die Eigennamen des Alten Testamentes in ihrer Bedeutung für die Kenntnis des hebräischen Volksglaubens. Breslau, 1895.

77 p.

0209. Güdemann, Moritz. "Die superstitiöse Bedeutung des Eigennamens im vormosaischen Israel." In: Festschrift zum achtzigsten Geburtstage Moritz Steinschneiders, p. 1-15 (German Section). Leipzig, 1896.

0210. Hieronymus, Saint. "Liber de nominibus Hebraicis." In: Patrologiae cursus completus ... Series Latina ... Accurante J.-P. Migne. Vol. 23, col. 815-904. Paris, 1883.
See also 0255, 0350.

0211. Hiller, Matthäus. Onomasticum sacrum. Tübingen, 1706. 960, [33] p.

0212. Hölscher, Gustav. "Zur jüdischen Namenkunde." In: Vom Alten Testament Karl Marti ... gewidmet, p. 148-157. Giessen, 1925.

0213. Hohlenberg, Matthias Haquinus. Fragmentum libri nominum Hebraicorum antiquissimum. Copenhagen, 1836. 102 p.

0214. Hommel, Eberhard. "Namenkunde als Zweig der Rechtswissenschaft und Rechtsgeschichte und in der Bibel." In: International Congress of Onomastic Sciences, 6th, Munich, 1958. Proceedings. Vol. 2, p. 350-360. München, 1961. (Studia Onomastica Monacensia, Vol. 3).

0215. Hommel, Fritz. Ancient Hebrew Tradition as Illustrated by the Monuments. London, 1897. 356 p.

See also:

Cheyne, Thomas Kelly. "Hebrew Proper Names: An Explanation." Expository Times 8 (1896-97): 329.

Gray, George Buchanan. "The Character of the Proper Names in the Priestly Code: A Reply to Professor Hommel." Expositor (5th Ser.) 6 (1897): 173-190.

Gray, George Buchanan. "Professor Hommel on the Evidential Value of Hebrew Proper Names." Expository Times 8 (1896-97): 555-558.
See also 0206.

0216. Hunsberger, David Ritchie. Theophoric Names in the Old Testament and Their Theological Significance. 1969. 407 ℓ.
Unpublished dissertation, Temple University.
cf. Dissertation Abstracts 30-A (1969-70): 2607-A.

0217. Inman, Thomas. Ancient Faiths Embodied in Ancient Names; or, An Attempt to Trace the Religious Belief, Sacred Rites, and Holy Emblems of Certain Nations, by an Interpretation of the Names Given to Children by Priestly Authority, or Assumed by Prophets, Kings and Hierarchs. 2d ed. London, 1872-73. 2 vol.

0218. Jacobs, Joseph. Studies in Biblical Archaeology. London, 1894. 148 p.
Animal and plant names: p. 68-74; List of animal and plant names borne by persons in the Old Testament: p. 94-103.

0219. Jacobs, Noah Jonathan. Naming-Day in Eden; The Creation and Recreation of Language. New York, 1958. 159 p.

0220. Jahn, Gustav. Die Bücher Esra (A und B) und Nehemja, text-kritisch und historisch-kritisch untersucht mit Erklärung der einschlägigen Prophetenstellen und einem Anhang über hebräische Eigennamen. Lei-

den, 1909. 289 p.
For supplement, see 0221.

0221. Jahn, Gustav. Die Elephantiner Papyri und die Bücher Esra - Nehemja. Mit einem Supplement zu meiner Erklärung der hebräischen Eigennamen. Leiden, 1913. 106 p.

0222. Jeffreys, Letitia D. Ancient Hebrew Names. Notes on Their Significance & Historic Value. London, 1906. 186 p.

0223. Kaplan, Zevi. Ba-halakhah uva-agadah. Jerusalem, 1959-60. 141 p. In Hebrew. Midrashe shemot: p. 58-141.

0224. Kerber, Georg. Die religionsgeschichtliche Bedeutung der hebräischer Eigennamen des Alten Testamentes von neuem geprüft. Freiburg i.B., 1897. 99 p.

0225. Köhler, Ludwig Hugo. Hebrew Man. London, 1956. 189 p. Hebrew names: p. 63-68.

0226. Kutscher, Eduard Yechezkel. Ta'tikim akadiyim shel shemot-'etsem mikra'iyim. Jerusalem, 1964. 16 ℓ. In Hebrew.

0227. Lagarde, Paul Anton de. Onomastica sacra. Göttingen, 1870. 2 vol. in 1 (304, 160 p.). Also 2d ed.: Göttingen, 1887. Reprint of 2d ed.: Hildesheim, 1968.

0228. Laur, Elred. Die Prophetennamen des Alten Testamentes. Ein Beitrag zur Theologie des Alten Testamentes. Freiburg (Schweiz), 1903. 164 p.

0229. Lauterbach, Selig. Minhat kohen. Drohobycz, 1892. 144 p. In Hebrew.

0230. Leusden, Johannes. Onomasticum sacrum. Utrecht, 1665. 280 p.

0231. Mandelstamm, Ezekiel. Sefer ha-shemot. Warsaw, 1889. 418 p. In Hebrew.

0232. Meier, Arnold. Die alttestamentliche Namengebung in England (mit einem Ausblick auf die alttestamentliche Namengebung in Deutschland und Frankreich). Leipzig, 1934. 55 p.

0233. Milano, Euclide. Come ti chiami? I nomi proprii di persona nella storia, nella lingua e nell'uso. Torino, 1951. 233 p. Dal mondo d'Israele: p. 19-23.

0234. Nestle, Eberhard. Die israelitischen Eigennamen nach ihrer religionsgeschichtlichen Bedeutung; Ein Versuch. Haarlem, 1876. 215 p. Reprint: Walluf (bei Wiesbaden), 1973.

0235. Neuhausen, Simon Avseyewitz. Bene Binyamin. Berehovo, 1938. 15 p. In Hebrew. Reprinted from: Otsar ha-hayyim.

0236. Noth, Martin. Die israelitischen Personennamen im Rahmen der gemeinsemitischen Namengebung. Stuttgart, 1928. 260 p. Reprint: Hildesheim, 1966.

Review:
Bauer, Hans. Orientalistische Literaturzeitung 33 (1930): col. 588-596.

0237. Noth, Martin. "Mari und Israel; Eine Personennamenstudie." In: Geschichte und Altes Testament. A. Alt ... dargebracht, p. 128-152. Tübingen, 1953.

0238. Oort, Henricus. The Worship of Baalim in Israel. London, 1865. 94 p. The composition of Hebrew names with the divine name: p. 86-94.

0239. Oosterhoff, Berend Jakob. Israelietische persoonsnamen. Delft, 1953. 80 p.

0240. Patai, Raphael. Sex and Family in the Bible and the Middle East. New York, 1959. 282 p. Naming: p. 188-192.

0241. Rauschmaier, Anton. Hebräisches Vokabularium für Anfänger. Mit Zugrundelegung semitischer Eigennamen. München, 1893. 37 p.

0242. Reicher, Isaiah. Ketav bet Yisrael. Seini, 1927. [112] p. In Hebrew. No more published.

0243. Salverte, Eusèbe. History of the Names of Men, Nations, and Places, in Their Connection with the Progress of Civilization. London, 1862-64. 2 vol. Names and surnames of the Hebrews: vol. 1, p. 76-80; Names of women among the Hebrews and Arabs: vol. 1, p. 82-86.

0244. Schmidt, Johannes. Die Namendeutungen im Alten Testamente. Kirchhain, N.-L., 1932. 112 p. Teildruck, Dissertation, Breslau.

0245. Simonis, Johann. Onomasticum Veteris Testamenti. Halle, 1741. 644 p., 59 ℓ.

0246. Smith, Henry Preserved. "Theophorous Proper Names in the Old Testament." In: Old Testament and Semitic Studies, in Memory of William Rainey Harper. Vol. 1, p. 35-64. Chicago, 1908. Also published in: American Journal of Semitic Languages and Literatures 24 (1907-1908): 34-61.

0247. Smith, William Robertson. Lectures & Essays of William Robertson Smith. London, 1912. 622 p. Animal worship and animal tribes among the Arabs and in the Old Testament: p. 455-483 (Hebrew names derived from names of animals).

0248. Staerk, Willy. Studien zur Religions- und Sprachgeschichte des Alten Testaments. Berlin, 1899. 2 vol. Zur Geschichte der hebräischen Volksnamen: vol. 1, p. 77-96; vol. 2, 50-82.

0248A Stamm, Johann Jakob. "Eine Gruppe Hebräischer Personennamen." In: Travels in the World of the Old Testament. Studies Presented to Professor M.A. Beek ..., p. 230-240. Assen, 1974.

0249. Stamm, Johann Jakob. "Hebräische Ersatznamen." In: Studies in Honor of Benno Landsberger on his Seventy-Fifth Birthday, April 25, 1965, p. 413-424. Chicago, 1965.

17

0250. Stamm, Johann Jakob. "Ein Problem der altsemitischen Namengebung." In: World Congress of Jewish Studies, 4th, Jerusalem, 1965. Papers. Vol. 1, p. 141-147. Jerusalem, 1967.

0251. Thompson, Thomas L. The Historicity of the Patriarchal Narratives. The Quest for the Historical Abraham. Berlin, 1974. 392 p. The names of the Patriarchs and the "Patriarchal Period": p. 17-51.

0252. Ulmer, Friedrich. Die semitischen Eigennamen im Alten Testament auf ihre Entstehung und Elemente hin untersucht. Theil 1. Leipzig, 1901 44 p. Inaug.-Dissertation, Erlangen.

0252A Van Seters, John. Abraham in History and Tradition. New Haven, 197! 335 p. Personal names, peoples, and places: p. 39-64.

0253. Widmer, Gottfried. "Hebräische Wechselnamen." In: Vom Alten Testament Karl Marti ... gewidmet, p. 297-304. Giessen, 1925.

0254. Widmer, Gottfried. Versuch einer Erklärung der verschiedenartigen Überlieferung einzelner Namensformen im Alten Testament. Bern, 1932. 51 p. Habilitationsarbeit, Bern.

0255. Wutz, Franz Xaver. Onomastica sacra; Untersuchungen zum Liber interpretationis nominum hebraicorum des hl. Hieronymus. Leipzig, 1914-1! 2 vol. in 1. See also 0210, 0350.

0256. Zimmermann, Frank. "Folk Etymology of Biblical Names." In: International Organization for the Study of the Old Testament. Congress Volume (Geneva, 1965), p. 311-326. Leiden, 1966. (Supplements to Vetus Testamentum, Vol. 15).

0257. Zolli, Eugenio (formerly Israel Zoller). Israele; Studi storico-religiosi. Udine, 1935. 415 p. Il rito del cambiamento del nome nel pensiero ebraico: p. 352-360.

VI

Biblical Names: Periodical Literature

0258. Albright, William Foxwell. "The Name Yahweh." Journal of Biblical Literature 43 (1924): 370-378.

0259. Albright, William Foxwell. "Further Observations on the Name Yahweh and its Modifications in Proper Names." Journal of Biblical Literature 44 (1925): 158-162.

0260. Alt, Albrecht. "Menschen ohne Namen." Archiv Orientální 18:1-2 (1950): 9-24.

0261. Avigad, Nahman. "New Names on Hebrew Seals." (Hebrew) Eretz-Israel 12 (1975): 66-71. Includes English summary.

0262. Bardis, Panos A. "Social Aspects of Personal Onomastics Among the Ancient Hebrews." Social Science 47 (1972): 100-109. Italian text in: Rassegna Italiana di Sociologia 11 (1970): 81-98.

0263. Barr, James. "The Symbolism of Names in the Old Testament." John Rylands Library. Bulletin 52 (1969-70): 11-29.

0264. Bartina, Sebastián. "Más sobre los apellidos de la Biblia." Cultura Bíblica, año 17, no. 175 (1960): 348-350.

0265. Bauer, Hans. "Die hebräischen Eigennamen als sprachliche Erkenntnisquelle." Zeitschrift für die alttestamentliche Wissenschaft 48 (1930): 73-80.

0266. Beegle, Dewey M. "Proper Names in the Dead Sea Scroll (DSIa)" Journal of Biblical Literature 72 (1953): xiii-xiv.

0267. Beegle, Dewey M. "Proper Names in the New Isaiah Scroll." American Schools of Oriental Research. Bulletin 123 (Oct. 1951): 26-30.

0268. Berger, Paul-Richard. "Die bisher ältesten keilschriftlichen Äquivalente zu zwei althebräischen Namen?" Ugarit-Forschungen 1 (1969): 216-217.
Isaac, Hosea.

0269. Boehl, Franz Marius Theodor. "Volksetymologie en woordspeling in de Genesis-verhalen." Koninklijke Akademie van Wetenschappen, Amsterdam. Mededeelingen. Afdeeling Letterkunde 59 (1925): 49-79.

0270. Boehmer, Julius. "Sind einige Personennamen I. Chr. 25, 4 'künstlich geschaffen'?" Biblische Zeitschrift 22 (1934): 93-100.

0271. Bonk, Hugo. "Ueber die Verwendbarkeit der doppelformigen mit Jeho und Jo anlautenden Namen im Alten Testament für die historische Quellenkritik." Zeitschrift für die alttestamentliche Wissenschaft 11 (1891): 125-156.

0272. Brandt, Wilhelm. "De tooverkracht van namen in Oud en Nieuw Testament." Teyler's Theologisch Tijdschrift 2 (1904): 355-388.

0273. Canney, Maurice A. "The Significance of Names." Manchester Egyptian and Oriental Society. Journal 9 (1921): 21-37.

0274. Caspari, Wilhelm. "Die kleineren Personenlisten in Samuelis." Zeitschrift für die alttestamentliche Wissenschaft 35 (1915): 142-174.

0275. Caspari, Wilhelm. "Rechtliche Bedeutung von 'Name' im Alten Testament." Theologische Studien und Kritiken 83 (1910): 471-480.

0276. Chilperic (pseud.). "Foreign Names in the Old Testament." The Free Review 1 (1893-94): 150-159.

0277. Chotzner, Joseph. "Hebräische Eigennamen in der Bibel." Jüdisches Literatur-Blatt 23 (1894): 106-107.

0278. Clines, D.J.A. "X, X ben Y, ben Y; Personal Names in Hebrew Narrative Style." Vetus Testamentum 22 (1972): 266-287.

0279. Cuervo, Rufino José. "Acentuación de las voces hebreas en castellano." Instituto Caro y Cuervo. Boletín 1 (1945): 205-211.

0280. Derenbourg, Hartwig. "Les noms de personnes dans l'Ancien Testament et dans les inscriptions himyarites." Revue des Études Juives 1 (1880): 56-60.

0281. Driver, Godfrey Rolles. "The Original Form of the Name 'Yahweh': Evidence and Conclusions." Zeitschrift für die alttestamentliche

Wissenschaft 46 (1928): 7-25.
On Hebrew names derived from the Tetragrammaton.

0282. Eissfeldt, Otto. "'Gut Glück' in semitischer Namengebung." Journal
of Biblical Literature 82 (1963): 195-200.

0283. Eybers, I.H. "The Use of Proper Names as a Stylistic Device." Se-
mitics (Pretoria) 2 (1971-72): 82-92.

0284. Feiler, Wolfgang. "Hurritische Namen im Alten Testament." Zeitschrift für Assyriologie und Vorderasiatische Archäologie 45 (1939):
216-229.

0285. Fichtner, Johannes. "Die etymologische Ätiologie in den Namengebungen
der geschichtlichen Bücher des Alten Testaments." Vetus Testamentum
6 (1956): 372-396.

0286. Galling, Kurt. "Die Ausrufung des Namens als Rechtsakt in Israel."
Theologische Literaturzeitung 81 (1956): col. 65-70.

0287. Gees, F.W. "Das endschwache Zeitwort in hebräischen Eigennamen."
American Journal of Semitic Languages and Literatures 27 (1910-11):
301-311.

0288. Geiger, Abraham. "Der Baal in den hebräischen Eigennamen." Deutsche
Morgenländische Gesellschaft. Zeitschrift 16 (1862): 728-732.

0289. Gibson, Edgar Charles Sumner. "Some Names in Genesis." Expositor
(2d Ser.) 6 (1883): 259-272, 350-362.

0290. Gilbert, Henry L. "The Forms of the Names in 1 Chronicles 1-7 Com-
pared with those in Parallel Passages of the Old Testament." Hebraic
13 (1896-97): 279-298.

0291. Gilbert, Henry L. "A Study in Old Testament Names." Hebraica 11
(1894-95): 209-233.

0292. Ginsburger, Moses. "Les Explications des noms de personnes dans
l'Ancien Testament." Revue de l'Histoire des Religions 92 (1925):
1-7.

0293. Gowen, Herbert H. "The Name." Anglican Theological Review 12 (1929-
30): 275-285.

0294. Gray, George Buchanan. "A Group of Hebrew Names of the Ninth Century
B.C." Expository Times 27 (1915-16): 57-62.
On ostraca from Samaria.

0295. Grunwald, Max. "Zur jüdischen Namenkunde. Die Gottesnamen in den
Eigennamen des Alten Testamentes." Mitteilungen der Gesellschaft für
Jüdische Volkskunde Heft 8 (1901): 122-153.

0296. Heller, Jan. "Namengebung und Namendeutung. Grundzüge der alttestamentlichen Onomatologie und ihre Folgen für die biblische Hermeneu-
tik." Evangelische Theologie 27 (1967): 255-266.

0297. Hogg, Hope W. "The Ephraim Genealogy." Jewish Quarterly Review
(O.S.) 13 (1901): 147-154.
1 Chronicles 7:20.

0298. Honeyman, Abraham Mackie. "The Evidence for Regnal Names Among the
Hebrews; The Practice of Metonomasia." Journal of Biblical Literature 67 (1948): 13-25.

0299. Jacob, Benno. "'Im Namen Gottes.' Eine sprachliche und religionsge-schichtliche Untersuchung über shem und onoma im Alten und Neuen Testament." Vierteljahrsschrift für Bibelkunde 1 (1903-1904): 128-149, 171-195.
No more published.

0300. Jastrow, Morris. "The Element bosheth in Hebrew Proper Names." Journal of Biblical Literature 13 (1894): 19-30.

0301. Jastrow, Morris. "Hebrew Proper Names Compounded with iah and iahu." Journal of Biblical Literature 13 (1894): 101-127.

0302. Jean, Charles-François. "Les Noms propres de personnes dans les let-tres de Mari et dans les plus anciens textes du Pentateuque." Revue d'Histoire et de Philosophie Religieuses 35 (1955): 121-128.

0303. Jong, P. de. "Over de met ab, ach enz. zamengestelde Hebreeuwsche eigennamen." Koninklijke Akademie van Wetenschappen, Amsterdam. Verslagen en Mededeelingen. Afdeeling Letterkunde 2:10 (1881): 54-68.

0304. Joüon, Paul. "Trois noms de personnages bibliques à la lumière des textes d'Ugarit (Ras Shamra): Terach, Issachar, Daniel." Biblica 19 (1938): 280-285.

0305. Key, Andrew F. "The Giving of Proper Names in the Old Testament." Journal of Biblical Literature 83 (1964): 55-59.

0306. Klawek, Aleksy. "Onomastyka biblijna." Onomastica 7 (1961): 403-416.

0307. Klein, Samuel. "Kleine Beiträge zur Erklärung der Chronik Divre Ha-Yamim." Monatsschrift für Geschichte und Wissenschaft des Judentums 80 (1936): 195-206.
1 Chronicles.

0308. Köhler, Ludwig Hugo. "Eine Rechtssitte in einem Eigennamen." Zeit-schrift für die alttestamentliche Wissenschaft 36 (1916): 27-28.
Jehoiachin, Jehoiakim.

0309. Köhler, Ludwig Hugo. "Syntax zweier hebräischer Namengruppen." Vetus Testamentum 2 (1952): 374-377.
Names beginning with jo and names ending with iah.

0310. Lewy, Heinrich. "Jüdische Namen." Allgemeine Zeitung des Judenthums 62 (1898): 333-335.

0311. Löwy, Albert. "The Elohistic and Jehovistic Proper Names of Men and Women in the Bible." Society of Biblical Archaeology. Proceedings 11 (1888-89): 238-247.

0312. Löwy, Albert. "Jewish Names. The Meaning of Biblical Patronyms and Hebrew Surnames." Reformer and Jewish Times (New York), 27 Dec. 1878, p. 2.

0313. McCaffery, Ellen Conroy. "The Names of the Archangels." Open Court 41 (1927): 278-287.

0314. McKnight, George Harley. "Scriptural Names in Early Middle English." Modern Language Association. Publications 19 (1904): 304-333.

0315. Marmorstein, Arthur. "Die Namen der Schwestern Kains und Abels in der midraschischen und in der apokryphen Literatur." Zeitschrift für die alttestamentliche Wissenschaft 25 (1905): 141-144. See also 0328.

0316. Marmorstein, Arthur. "Zu den traditionellen Namenserklärungen." Zeitschrift für die alttestamentliche Wissenschaft 25 (1905): 368-374.

0317. May, Herbert Gordon. "An Interpretation of the Names of Hosea's Children." Journal of Biblical Literature 55 (1936): 285-291.

0318. Milhokez. "Namen und Namensänderung." Jüdisches Jahrbuch für die Schweiz 3 (1918-19): 64-68.

0319. Montgomery, James Alan. "Some Hebrew Etymologies." Jewish Quarterly Review (N.S.) 25 (1934-35): 261-269.

0320. Nestle, Eberhard. "Some Contributions to Hebrew Onomatology." American Journal of Semitic Languages and Literatures 13 (1897): 169-176.

0321. Nöldeke, Theodor. "Bemerkungen über hebräische und arabische Eigennamen." Deutsche Morgenländische Gesellschaft. Zeitschrift 15 (1861): 806-810.

0322. Nöldeke, Theodor. "Kleinigkeiten zur semitischen Onomatologie." Zeitschrift für die Kunde des Morgenlandes 6 (1892): 307-316.

0323. Noth, Martin. "Gemeinsemitische Erscheinungen in der israelitischen Namengebung." Deutsche Morgenländische Gesellschaft. Zeitschrift 81 (1927): 1-45.

0324. Penna, Angelo. "I nomi propri dei primi due libri dei Maccabei nella Peshiṭta." Rivista degli studi orientali 40 (1965): 13-41.

0325. [Philippson, Ludwig?]. "Ueber die biblischen Namen." Allgemeine Zeitung des Judenthums 22 (1858): 239-241, 281-283.

0326. Pilter, William Turnbull. "Some Amorite Personal Names in Genesis XIV." Society of Biblical Archaeology. Proceedings 35 (1913): 205-226; 36 (1914): 125-142, 212-230.

0327. Poole, Reginald Stuart. "The Date of the Pentateuch; Theory and Facts." Contemporary Review 52 (Sept. 1887): 350-369. Levitical names: p. 364.

0328. Poznański, Samuel. "Zu den Namen der Frauen Kain's und Abel's." Zeitschrift für die alttestamentliche Wissenschaft 25 (1905): 340-342. See also 0315.

0329. Praetorius, Franz. "Ueber einige Arten hebräischer Eigennamen." Deutsche Morgenländische Gesellschaft. Zeitschrift 57 (1903): 773-782.

0330. Rabin, Chaim. "Archaic Vocalisation in Some Biblical Hebrew Names." Journal of Jewish Studies 1 (1948): 22-26.

0331. Radin, Max. "Technonymy in the Old Testament." Harvard Theological Review 15 (1922): 293-297.

0332. Rafel, Dov. "Remarks on Personal Names and Genealogies in Numbers." (Hebrew) Bet Mikra no. 28 (1966): 87-90.

0333. Ruska, Julius Ferdinand. "Zur Umschrift der syrischen und hebräischen Eigennamen." Archeion 21 (1938-39): 99-102.

0334. Scholz, Anton. "Die Namen im Buche Esther." Theologische Quartalschrift 72:2 (1890): 209-264.

0335. Skipwith, Grey Hubert. "Hebrew Tribal Names and the Primitive Traditions of Israel." Jewish Quarterly Review (O.S.) 11 (1899): 239-265.

0336. Sukenik, Eleazar Lipa. "Inscribed Potsherds with Biblical Names from Samaria." Palestine Exploration Fund. Quarterly Statement (1933): 200-204.

0337. Tomkins, Henry George. "Biblical Proper Names, Personal and Local, Illustrated from Sources External to Holy Scripture." Victoria Institute or Philosophical Society of Great Britain. Journal of the Transactions 16 (1883): 132-169.

0338. Tsevat, Matitiahu. "Ishbosheth and Congeners: The Names and Their Study." Hebrew Union College Annual 46 (1975): 71-87.

0339. Utley, Francis Lee. "The One Hundred and Three Names of Noah's Wife." Speculum 16 (1941): 426-452.

0340. Wächter, Albert. "Israelitische Namen." Zeitschrift für Wissenschaftliche Theologie 49 (1906): 153-193.

0341. Wilson, Philip Whitwell. "Names in the Bible." Bibliotheca Sacra 108 (1951): 315-322.

VII

Biblical Names: Septuagint

0342. Brønno, Einar. "Einige Namentypen der Septuaginta. Zur historischen Grammatik des Hebräischen." Acta Orientalia 19 (1943): 33-64. English text in: Classica et Mediaevalia 3 (1940): 180-213.

0343. Flashar, Martin. "Das Ghain in der Septuaginta." Zeitschrift für die alttestamentliche Wissenschaft 28 (1908): 194-220, 303-313.

0344. Isserlin, B.S.J. "The Names of the 72 Translators of the Septuagint (Aristeas, 47-50)" Columbia University. Ancient Near Eastern Society. Journal 5 (1973): 191-197.

0345. Köhler, Ludwig Hugo. "Septuaginta-Eigennamen und ihre Entartung." In: Festgabe Adolf Kaegi von Schülern und Freunden dargebracht zum 30. September 1919, p. 182-188. Frauenfeld, 1919.

0346. Könnecke, Clemens. Die Behandlung der hebräischen Namen in der Septuaginta. Stargard, 1885. 30 p. Programm des k. Gymnasiums zu Stargard in Pommern.

0347. Lisowsky, Gerhard. Die Transskription der hebräischen Eigennamen des Pentateuch in der Septuagint. Basel, 1940. 154 p. Inaug.-Dissertation, Basel.

0348. Muneles, Otto. Die Transskription der hebräischen Eigennamen in der Septuaginta in ihrem Verhältnis zum masoretischen Text. 1925. Dissertation, Prague.

cf. Sebastian P. Brock and others. A Classified Bibliography of the Septuagint (Leiden, 1973), p. 40.

0349.   Sperber, Alexander. "Hebrew Based Upon Greek and Latin Transliterations." Hebrew Union College Annual 12-13 (1937-38): 103-274. Hebrew proper names in the Septuagint: p. 106-107.

0350.   Wutz, Franz Xaver. Die Transkriptionen von der Septuaginta bis zu Hieronymus. Stuttgart, 1933. 569 p. Eigennamen: p. 10-36.

VIII

Biblical Names: New Testament

0351.   Bammel, Ernst. "What is Thy Name?" Novum Testamentum 12 (1970): 223-228.
On the Hebrew names of Jesus' disciples.

0352.   Cadbury, Henry J. "Some Semitic Personal Names in Luke-Acts." In: Amicitiae Corolla; A Volume of Essays Presented to James Rendel Harris ..., p. 45-56. London, 1933.

0353.   Harris, James Rendel. "On Certain Obscure Names in the New Testament." Expositor (6th Ser.) 1 (1900): 161-177.

0354.   Ingholt, Harald. "The Surname of Judas Iscariot." In: Studia Orientalia Ioanni Pedersen ..., p. 152-162. Hauniae (Copenhagen), 1953.

0355.   Logan, Innes. "The Article Before Proper Names." Expository Times 33 (1921-22): 520-521.

0356.   Schwen, Paul. "Die syrische Wiedergabe der neutestamentlichen Eigennamen." Zeitschrift für die alttestamentliche Wissenschaft 31 (1911): 267-303; 32 (1912): 155.

0357.   Torrey, Charles Cutler. "The Name 'Iscariot.'" Harvard Theological Review 36 (1943): 51-62.

See also 0155, 0157, 0167, 0169, 0272, 0299.

IX

Biblical Names: Miscellaneous

0358.   Tur-Sinai, Naphtali Herz. "Some Explanations of Hebrew Names by the Church Fathers." (Hebrew) In: Mazkeret Levi, p. 15-20. Tel-Aviv, 1953.

0359.   (Ambrose) Wilbrand, W. "Die Deutung der biblischen Eigennamen beim hl. Ambrosius." Biblische Zeitschrift 10 (1912): 337-350.

0360.   (Augustine) Altaner, Barthold. "Augustinus und die biblischen Onomastica." Münchener Theologische Zeitschrift 4 (1953): 34-36.

0361.   (Josephus) Cardona, Giorgio R. "I nomi dei figli di Tôgarmāh secondo il 'Sēpher Yôsêphôn.'" Rivista degli Studi Orientali 41 (1966): 17-27.

0362.   (Josephus) Schlatter, Adolf von. Die hebräischen Namen bei Josephus Gütersloh, 1913. 132 p.

Reprinted in the author's Kleinere Schriften zu Flavius Josephus. Darmstadt, 1970.

0363. (Josephus) Shutt, R.J.H. "Biblical Names and Their Meanings in Josephus' Jewish Antiquities, Books I and II, 1-200." Journal for the Study of Judaism in the Persian, Hellenistic and Roman Period 2 (1971): 167-182.

0364. (Origenes) Hanson, Richard Patrick Crosland. "Interpretations of Hebrew Names in Origen." Vigiliae Christianae 10 (1956): 103-123.

0365. (Philo) Amir, Joshua. "Explanations of Hebrew Names in Philo." (Hebrew) Tarbiz 31 (1961-62): 297.

0366. (Philo) Belkin, Samuel. "Philo's Interpretations of Names." (Hebrew) Horev 12 (1956): 3-61.

0367. (Philo) Hanson, Anthony. "Philo's Etymologies." Journal of Theological Studies (N.S.) 18 (1967): 128-139.

0368. (Philo) Kahn, Jean-Georges. "Did Philo Know Hebrew? The Testimony of the 'Etymologies.'" (Hebrew) Tarbiz 34 (1964-65): 337-345.

0368A (Philo) Rokeah, David. "A New Onomasticon Fragment from Oxyrhynchus and Philo's Etymologies (P Oxy 2263, saec. 2, graeca)" Journal of Theological Studies (N.S.) 19 (1968): 70-82.

X

Biblical Names: Individual Names

0369. Ball, Charles James. "Four Biblical Names." (Jezebel, Job, Abigail, Ahikar) Expository Times 19 (1907-1908): 473.

0370. Cheyne, Thomas Kelly. The Veil of Hebrew History. London, 1913. 161 p. Jephthah: p. 145-146; Nahash, Hagab, Ah'ab, and other strange names: p. 147-151; Ephraim, Yoseph, Yehudah: p. 153-154.

0371. Dvir, Jehuda. "Nabal the Carmelite; A Study in the Nature of Biblical Personal Names." (Hebrew) Leshonenu 20 (1956): 97-104. Nabal, Avigail, Daniel.

0372. Glaser, Eduard. Jehowah-Jovis und die drei Söhne Noah's. Ein Beitrag zur vergleichenden Götterlehre. München, 1901. 28 p. Names beginning with am, ham, shem: p. 9-12.

0373. Gray, George Buchanan. "Nebo as an Element in Hebrew Proper Names: Machnadebai and Barnabas." Expository Times 10 (1898-99): 232-234.

0374. Mulder, Martin Jan. Ba'al in het Oude Testament. 's-Gravenhage, 1962. 211 p. Academisch-Proefschrift, Vrije Universiteit, Amsterdam. Ba'al in persoonsnamen: p. 169-173.

0375. Yaure, L. "Elymas - Nehelamite - Pethor." Journal of Biblical Literature 79 (1960): 297-314.

(Aaron, see 0380, 0472)

(Abigail, see 0369, 0371)

0376. (Abraham) Albright, William Foxwell. "The Names Shaddai and Abram." Journal of Biblical Literature 54 (1935): 173-204.

0377. (Abraham) Bacher, Wilhelm. "Contribution à l'onomastique juive." Revue des Études Juives 36 (1898): 103-105.

0378. (Abraham) Breasted, James Henry. "The Earliest Occurrence of the Name of Abram." American Journal of Semitic Languages and Literatures 21 (1904-1905): 22-36.

0379. (Abraham) Condamin, Albert. "Lettres de Larsa, vers 2100. Le nom 'Abraham.'" Recherches de science religieuse 9 (1919): 257-262. Review of H.F. Lutz, Early Babylonian Letters from Larsa (New Haven, 1917).

0380. (Abraham) Fraenkel, Meir. "Abraham und Aron. Zwei Beiträge zur biblischen Namensforschung." Bibliotheca Orientalis 19 (1962): 213-216.

0381. (Abraham) Guenzburg, David. "Le Nom d'Abraham." Revue des Études Juives 47 (1903): 7-22.

0382. (Abraham) Langdon, Stephen. "The Name Abraham in Babylonian." Expository Times 21 (1909): 88-90.

0383. (Abraham) Margoliouth, David Samuel. "The Name 'Abraham.'" Expository Times 9 (1897-98): 45.

0384. (Abraham) Pilter, William Turnbull. "The Personal Names Abram and Abraham." Society of Biblical Archaeology. Proceedings 37 (1915): 175-191.

(Abraham, see also 0251, 0252A, 0414)

(Abram, see Abraham)

(Achikar, see Ahikar)

0385. (Adam) Middelkoop, P. "A Question." Bible Translator 6 (1955): 30-31.

0386. (Adam) Sayce, Archibald Henry. "The Name of Adam." Expository Times 17 (1905-1906): 416-417.

0387. (Adam) Walker, Norman. "'Adam' and 'Eve' and 'Adon.'" Zeitschrift für die alttestamentliche Wissenschaft 74 (1962): 66-68.

0388. (Adlai) Lévy, Isidore. "Adlai." La Nouvelle Clio 7-9 (1955-57): 465-467.

0389. (Agee) Köhler, Ludwig Hugo. "Alttestamentliche Wortforschung. Der Personenname Age." Theologische Zeitschrift 4 (1948): 153-154.

0390. (Ahab) Boehmer, Julius. "The Name 'Ahab.'" Expository Times 17 (1905-1906): 564-566.

(Ahab, see also 0370)

0391. (Ahikar) Margoliouth, David Samuel. "The Name Achikar." Expository Times 31 (1919-20): 329-330.

(Ahikar, see also 0369)

0392. (Amminadab) Derenbourg, Joseph. "Sur le nom d'Amminadab." Revue des Études Juives 2 (1881): 123-124.

0393. (Ariel) Feigin, Samuel Isaac. "The Meaning of Ariel." Journal of Biblical Literature 39 (1920): 131-137.

(Asaph, see 0454)

0394.	(Ashur)	Reider, Joseph. "The Name Ashur in the Initials of a Diffi-
cult Phrase in the Bible." (Nahum 1:12)	American Oriental Society.
Journal 58 (1938): 153-155.

0394A	(Balaam)	Scheiber, Alexander. "War der Name Balaam gebräuchlich
bei den Juden?" In: The Muslim East; Studies in Honour of Julius
Germanus, p. 35-37. Budapest, 1974.

0395.	(Barnabas)	Brock, Sebastian P. "Barnabas." Journal of Theological
Studies (N.S.) 25 (1974): 93-98.

0396.	(Barnabas)	Hitzig, Ferdinand. "Etymologisches zu biblischen Eigen-
namen." Archiv für wissenschaftliche Erforschung des Alten Testaments 1 (1869): 106-108.
On the names Barnabas, Barsabas, Bartimaeus.

(Barnabas, see also 0373)

0397.	(Bartholomew)	Geiger, Abraham. "Thalmai, Bartholomäus, Ptolemäus."
Deutsche Morgenländische Gesellschaft. Zeitschrift 16 (1862): 732.

0398.	(Barzillai)	Poznański, Samuel. "Zu dem Namen Barzillai." Oriental-
istische Literaturzeitung 21 (1918): col. 155; 23 (1920): col. 128-
129.

0399.	(Bildad)	Albright, William Foxwell. "The Name of Bildad the Shu-
hite." American Journal of Semitic Languages and Literatures 44
(1927-28): 31-36.

0400.	(Bildad)	Speiser, Ephraim Avigdor. "The Name Bildad." Archiv für
Orient-Forschung 6 (1930-31): 23.

0401.	(Cain)	Budde, Karl Ferdinand Reinhardt. "Die Erklärung des Namens
Ḳajin in Gen 4,1." Zeitschrift für die alttestamentliche Wissenschaft 31 (1911): 147-151.

0402.	(Caleb)	North, Robert. "Caleb." Bibbia e Oriente 8 (1966): 167-171.

0403.	(Daniel)	Kohler, Kaufmann. "Die chaldäischen Namen Daniel's und
seiner drei Freunde." Zeitschrift für Assyriologie 4 (1889): 46-51.

(Daniel, see also 0304, 0371)

0404.	(David)	Compston, Herbert Fuller Bright. "The Name 'David' in
O.T." Expository Times 22 (1910-11): 140-141.

0405.	(David)	Hoffmann, Adalbert. David; Namensdeutung zur Wesensdeutung.
Stuttgart, 1973. 269 p.

0406.	(David)	Pákozdy, Ladislas Martin von. "'Elḥanan - der frühere Name
Davids?" Zeitschrift fur die alttestamentliche Wissenschaft 68
(1956): 257-259.

0407.	(David)	Stamm, Johann Jakob. "Der Name des Königs David." In: In-
ternational Organization for the Study of the Old Testament. Congress Volume (Oxford, 1959), p. 165-183. Leiden, 1960. (Supplements to Vetus Testamentum, Vol. 7).

0408.	(Deborah)	Dvir, Jehuda. "The Study of Biblical Names." (Hebrew)
Sinai (Jerusalem) no. 237 (1956): 374-383.

0409.	(Deborah)	Margulies, Heinrich. "Das Rätsel der Biene im Alten

Testament." _Vetus Testamentum_ 24 (1974): 56-76.
Deborah: p. 71-76.

(Elhanan, see 0406)

0410.   (Elihu) Montgomery, James Alan.   "The Hebrew Divine Name and the
Personal Pronoun hu." _Journal of Biblical Literature_ 63 (1944): 161-
163.

0411.   (Elizabeth) Golde, Max.   "Wandlungen eines altbiblischen Namens."
Jüdische Familien-Forschung Heft 35 (1934): 585-589.

(Ephraim, see 0370, 0498, 0855)

(Ephron, see 0498)

0412.   (Esau) Jenner, J.K.   "Die Etymologie des Namens 'Esau' (Gen 25,25)"
Theologische Quartalschrift 71 (1889): 649-651.

0413.   (Esther) Yahuda, Abraham Shalom.   "The Meaning of the Name Esther."
Royal Asiatic Society of Great Britain and Ireland. Journal (1946):
174-178.

(Esther, see also 0334)

0414.   (Eve) Eitan, Israel.   "Two Onomatological Studies. 1. The Name Eve.
2. The Name Abraham."   _American Oriental Society. Journal_ 49 (1929):
30-33.

0415.   (Eve) Halévy, [Joseph?].   "Le Nom d'Eve."   _Journal Asiatique_ (10e
Sér.) 2 (1903): 522-524.

0416.   (Eve) Heller, Jan.   "Der Name Eva."   _Archiv Orientální_ 26 (1958):
636-656.

(Eve, see also 0387)

(Hagab, see 0370)

0417.   (Hanani) Tuland, C.G.   "Hanani - Hananiah."   _Journal of Biblical
Literature_ 77 (1958): 157-161.

(Hananiah, see 0417)

(Hosea, see 0268, 0317)

0418.   (Isaac) Heller, Jan.   "Der Name Isaak."   (Czech)   _Křest'anká Revue_
22 (1955): 102-104.
cf. _Zeitschrift für die alttestamentliche Wissenschaft_ 69 (1957):
256.

0419.   (Isaac) Pinches, Theophilus Goldridge.   _The Old Testament in the
Light of the Historical Records and Legends of Assyria and Babylonia._
2d ed. London, 1903. 591 p.
Isaac, Jacob and Joseph: p. 242-245.

0420.   (Isaac) Stamm, Johann Jakob.   "Der Name Isaak."   In: _Festschrift für
Albert Schädelin_, p. 33-38. Bern, 1950.

(Isaac, see also 0268)

0421.   (Ishmael) Dahood, Mitchell.   "The Name Yišmā''ēl in Genesis 16,11."
Biblica 49 (1968): 87-88.

0422. (Israel) Albright, William Foxwell. "The Names 'Israel' and 'Judah', with an Excursus on the Etymology of 'Tôdâh' and 'Tôrâh.'" Journal of Biblical Literature 46 (1927): 151-185.

0423. (Israel) Caspari, Wilhelm. "Sprachliche und religionsgeschichtliche Bedeutung des Namens Israel." Zeitschrift für Semitistik und Verwandte Gebiete 3 (1924): 194-211.

0424. (Israel) Chajes, Hirsch Perez. "Der Name Israel." Jewish Quarterly Review (O.S.) 13 (1901): 344.

0425. (Israel) Coote, Robert. "The Meaning of the Name Israel." Harvard Theological Review 65 (1972): 137-142.

0426. (Israel) Danell, Gustaf Adolf. Studies in the Name Israel in the Old Testament. Uppsala, 1946. 334 p.

0427. (Israel) Feist, Sigmund. "Die Etymologie des Namens Israel." Monatsschrift für Geschichte und Wissenschaft des Judentums 73 (1929): 317-320.

0428. (Israel) Fraenkel, Meir. "Israel - eine Namensdeutung (Israel, Sarah)" Die Liberale Rundschau (Tel-Aviv), Apr. 1965, p. 12.

0429. (Israel) Hulst, A.R. "Der Name 'Israel' im Deuteronomium." Oudtestamentlische Studiën 9 (1951): 65-106.

0430. (Israel) Kahn, Jean-Georges. "Israel - videns Deum." (Hebrew) Tarbiz 40 (1970-71): 285-292.

0431. (Israel) Marcus, Ralph. "The Hebrew Sibilant śin and the Name Yiśra'el." Journal of Biblical Literature 60 (1941): 141-150.

0432. (Israel) Mihalik, Imre. "Some Thoughts on the Name Israel." In: Mihalik, Imre, ed. Theological Soundings: Notre Dame Seminary Jubilee Studies, 1923-1973, p. 11-19. New Orleans, 1973.

0433. (Israel) Rost, Leonhard. Israel bei den Propheten. Stuttgart, 1937. 140 p.

0434. (Israel) Sachsse, Eduard. Die Bedeutung des Namens Israel. Bonn, Gütersloh, 1910-22. 2 vol.

0435. (Israel) Sachsse, Eduard. "Die Etymologie und älteste Aussprache des Namens Israel." Zeitschrift für die alttestamentliche Wissenschaft 34 (1914): 1-15.

0436. (Israel) Sachsse, Eduard. "Der Ursprung des Namens Israel." Zeitschrift für Semitistik und Verwandte Gebiete 4 (1926): 63-69.

0437. (Israel) Walker, Norman. "Israel." Vetus Testamentum 4 (1954): 434.

(Israel, see also 0439, 0442, 0444-0446)

(Issachar, see 0304)

(Ithiel, see 0499)

0438. (Jacob) Caspari, Wilhelm. "Der Name Jaqob in israelitischer Zeit." In: Festschrift Georg Jacob, p. 24-40. Leipzig, 1932.

0439. (Jacob) Cassuto, Umberto. "I nomi Giacobbe e Israel." Studi e Materiale di Storia delle Religioni 9 (1933): 1-16.

0440. (Jacob) Dickerman, Lysander. "The Names of Jacob and Joseph in Egypt." The Old Testament Student 7 (1887-88): 181-185.

0441. (Jacob) Freedman, David Noel. "The Original Name of Jacob." Israel Exploration Journal 13 (1963): 125-126.

0442. (Jacob) Heinisch, Paul. "Der Wechsel der Namen Jakob und Israel in der Genesis." Bonner Zeitschrift für Theologie und Seelsorge 6 (1929): 115-129.

0443. (Jacob) Jacob, Georg. "Der Name Jacob." Litterae Orientalis Heft 54 (1933): 16-19.

0444. (Jacob) Luther, Bernhard. "Die israelitischen Stämme." Zeitschrift für die alttestamentliche Wissenschaft 21 (1901): 1-76. Die Namen Jakob und Israel: p. 60-76.

0445. (Jacob) Naor, Menahem. "Jacob und Israel. Zur ältesten Etymologie und Aussprache." Zeitschrift für die alttestamentliche Wissenschaft 49 (1931): 317-321.

0446. (Jacob) Segal, Moses Hirsch. "The Names Jacob and Israel in the Boo of Genesis." (Hebrew) Tarbiz 9 (1937-38): 243-256.

(Jacob, see also 0251)

(Jehoiachin, see 0308)

(Jehoiakim, see 0308)

0447. (Jehu) Munck, Johannes. "Hat das Judentum den Namen Jehu gebraucht?" Studia Theologica (Lund) 5 (1951): 167-172.

(Jeroboam, see 0506)

0448. (Jesus) Jones, Lewis Bevan. "On the Use of the Name 'Isa." Bible Translator 4 (1953): 83-86.

0449. (Jesus) Krauss, Samuel. "Le Nom de Jésus chez les Juifs." Revue des Études Juives 55 (1908): 148-151.

0450. (Jesus) Poznański, Samuel. "Le Nom de 'Isâ' porté par les Juifs." Revue des Études Juives 54 (1907): 276-279.

(Jesus, see also Elsdon C. Smith, Personal Names; A Bibliography, p. 77-82, for additional material)

0451. (Jethro) Königsberger, Bernhard. "Die Namen Jethro's." Jüdisches Literatur-Blatt 21 (1892): 201-202, 204-206.

(Jezebel, see 0369)

0452. (Joash) Malamat, Abraham. "On the Akkadian Transcription of the Name of King Joash." American Schools of Oriental Research. Bulletin no. 204 (1971): 37-39.

(Job, see 0369)

0453. (Joseph) Allis, Oswald T. "The Name Joseph." Princeton Theological Review 18 (1920): 646-659.

0454.   (Joseph) MacLaurin, E.C.B. "Joseph and Asaph." Vetus Testamentum 25 (1975): 27-45.

(Joseph, see also 0370, 0440)

0455.   (Joshua) Nestle, Eberhard. "The Genealogy and Name of Joshua." Expository Times 20 (1908-1909): 45.

0456.   (Josiah) Hommel, Fritz. "The Hebrew Name Josiah." Expository Times 8 (1896-97): 562-563; 9 (1897-98): 144.

0456A   (Judah) Lipiński, Edward. "L'étymologie de 'Juda.'" Vetus Testamentum 23 (1973): 380-381.

0457.   (Judah) Millard, Alan Ralph. "The Meaning of the Name Judah." Zeitschrift für die alttestamentliche Wissenschaft 86 (1974): 216-218.

0458.   (Judah) Müller, Friedrich Max. "The Supposed Name of Judah in the List of Shoshenq." Society of Biblical Archaeology. Proceedings 10:1 (1887-88): 81-86.

(Judah, see also 0370, 0422)

0459.   (Leah) Haupt, Paul. "Lea und Rahel." Zeitschrift für die alttestamentliche Wissenschaft 29 (1909): 281-286.

0460.   (Levi) Gaster, Theodor Herzl. "The Name Levi." Journal of Theological Studies 38 (1937): 250-251.

0461.   (Maccabeus) Bevan, Anthony Ashley. "The Origin of the Name Maccabee." Journal of Theological Studies 30 (1929): 191-193.

0462.   (Maccabeus) Curtiss, Samuel Ives. The Name Machabee Historically and Philologically Examined. Leipzig, 1876. 41 p. Inaug.-Dissertation, Leipzig.

0463.   (Maccabeus) Feilchenfeld, Wolf. "Die Beinamen der fünf Hasmonäer-Söhne." Magazin für die Wissenschaft des Judenthums 15 (1888): 53-57.

0464.   (Maccabeus) Lehrman, Simon Maurice. "The Name Maccabi." Jewish Chronicle (London), 17 Dec. 1954, p. 29.

0465.   (Maccabeus) Marcus, Ralph. "The Name Makkabaios." In: The Joshua Starr Memorial Volume, p. 59-65. New York, 1953.

0466.   (Maccabeus) Perles, Felix. "The Name Makkabaios." Jewish Quarterly Review (N.S.) 17 (1926-27): 404-405.
See also additional note by H. Hirschfeld, Ibid., 18 (1927-28): 57.

0467.   (Machir) Lewy, Heinrich. "Der Personenname Machir." Monatsschrift für Geschichte und Wissenschaft des Judentums 73 (1929): 325-326.

(Machnadebai, see 0373)

(Maria, see Miriam)

0468.   (Meri-baal) Humbert, Paul. "Der Name Meri-ba'al." Zeitschrift für die alttestamentliche Wissenschaft 38 (1919-20): 86.
See also additional note by W. Spiegelberg, Ibid., p. 172.

(Methuselah, see 0516)

0469.   (Michal) Jirku, Anton. "Das he. n. pr. f. Mikal." Zeitschrift für die alttestamentliche Wissenschaft 48 (1930): 229-230.

0470. (Miriam) Cohen, Naomi G. "The Greek and Latin Transliterations Mariam and Maria: Their Sociological Significance." (Hebrew) Leshonenu 38 (1973-74): 170-180.

0471. (Miriam) Grimme, Hubert. "Der Name Mirjam." Biblische Zeitschrift 7 (1909): 245-251.

0472. (Miriam) Hösl, Ignaz. "Zur orientalischen Namenkunde: Maria - Moses - Aaron." In: Serta Monacensia Franz Babinger ..., p. 80-85. Leiden, 1952.

0473. (Miriam) König, Eduard. "Woher stammt der Name 'Maria'?" Zeitschrift für die neutestamentliche Wissenschaft 17 (1916): 257-263.

0474. (Miriam) Zorell, Franz. "Was bedeutet der Name Maria?" Zeitschrift für Katholische Theologie 30 (1906): 356-360.

0475. (Mordecai) Shmeruk, Chone. "The Name Mordecai - Markus; Literary Metamorphosis of a Social Ideal." (Hebrew) Tarbiz 29 (1959-60): 76-98.

(Mordecai, see also 0334)

0476. (Moses) Abramson, Shraga. "The Name Moses." (Hebrew) Leshonenu 40 (1975-76): 54-56.

0477. (Moses) Buxtorf, Johannes (The Younger). Dissertationes philologico-theologicae ... Basel, 1662. 499 p.
De nomine Mosis: p. 486-490.

0478. (Moses) Černý, Jaroslav. "Greek Etymology of the Name of Moses." Egypt. Service des Antiquités. Annales 41 (1942): 349-354.

0479. (Moses) Döller, Johann. "Zum Namen 'Moses' (Ex. 2,10)" Biblische Zeitschrift 3 (1905): 151-153.

0480. (Moses) Enciso, Jesús. "El nombre de Moisés." Estudios Bíblicos 11 (1952): 221-223.

0481. (Moses) Griffiths, J. Gwyn. "The Egyptian Derivation of the Name Moses." Journal of Near Eastern Studies 12 (1953): 225-231.

0482. (Moses) Johns, Claude Hermann Walter. "The Name Moses." Expository Times 14 (1901-1902): 141-142.

0483. (Moses) Krauss, Samuel. "The Names of Moses." Jewish Quarterly Review (O.S.) 10 (1898): 726.

0484. (Moses) Nestle, Eberhard. "Moses - Moyses." Zeitschrift für die alttestamentliche Wissenschaft 27 (1907): 111-113.

0485. (Moses) Scheurer, Samuel. "Disquisitio de nomine Mosis, ad locum Exodi ii,10." In: Hase, Theodor. Thesaurus novus theologico-philologicus ... Vol. 1, p. 255-259. Leiden, 1732.

0486. (Moses) Smith, John Merlin Powis. "The Name Moses." American Journal of Semitic Languages and Literatures 35 (1918-19): 110-112.

0487. (Moses) Towers, John Robert. "The Name Moses." Journal of Theological Studies 36 (1935): 407-409.

0488. (Moses) Walker, Norman. The Meaning of 'Moses.' West Ewell, Epsom (Surrey), 1948. 16 p.

(Moses, see also 0472, 0870)

(Nabal, see 0371)

(Nahash, see 0370)

0489. (Nahum) Baniel, Ya'akov. "Nahum." (Hebrew) <u>Sinai</u> (Jerusalem) no. 171-172 (1951): 108.

0490. (Naphtali) Montgomery, James Alan. "The Nominal Prefix N in Some Hebrew Names." <u>American Oriental Society</u>. <u>Journal</u> 43 (1923): 50-51.

(Nebo, see 0373)

0491. (Nimrod) Kraeling, Emil Gottlieb Heinrich. "The Origin and Real Name of Nimrod." <u>American Journal of Semitic Languages and Literatures</u> 38 (1921-22): 214-220.

0492. (Nimrod) Prince, John Dyneley. "A Possible Sumerian Original of the Name Nimrod." <u>American Oriental Society</u>. <u>Journal</u> 40 (1920): 201-203.

0493. (Noah) Goldziher, Ignaz. "Zur Geschichte der Etymologie des Namens Noah." <u>Deutsche Morgenländische Gesellschaft</u>. <u>Zeitschrift</u> 24 (1870): 207-211.

0494. (Noah) Kraeling, Emil Gottlieb Heinrich. "The Interpretation of the Name Noah in Gen. 5,29." <u>Journal of Biblical Literature</u> 48 (1929): 138-143.

0495. (Noah) Morgenstern, Julian. "A Note on Genesis 5,29." <u>Journal of Biblical Literature</u> 49 (1930): 306-309.

(Noah, see also 0339)

0496. (Obadiah) Braver, A.J. "The Name Obadiah: Its Punctuation and Explanation." (Hebrew) <u>Bet Mikra</u> no. 54 (1973): 418-419.

0497. (Ophir) Loewe, Herbert. "The Name Ophir." <u>Jewish Quarterly Review</u> (N.S.) 15 (1924-25): 503-506.

0498. (Ophrah) Schunck, Klaus Dietrich. "Ophra, Ephron und Ephraim." <u>Vetus Testamentum</u> 11 (1961): 188-200; 12 (1962): 339-341 (J. Heller).

0499. (Peninnah) Lipiński, Edward. "Peninna, Iti'el et l'Athlète." <u>Vetus Testamentum</u> 17 (1967): 68-75.

0500. (Potiphera) Tomkins, Henry George. "'Potiphera,' and Similiar Names." <u>The Academy</u>, 31 Jan. 1891, p. 113-114.

0501. (Puah) Dvir, Jehuda. "The Study of Biblical Names." (Hebrew) <u>Sinai</u> (Jerusalem) no. 240 (1956): 177-182.
Also deals with the name Shiphrah.

0502. (Rachel) Kraeling, Emil Gottlieb Heinrich. "The Names 'Rachel' and 'Reu.'" <u>American Journal of Semitic Languages and Literatures</u> 41 (1924-25): 193-194.

(Rachel, see also 0459)

0503. (Raphael) Thurén, Jukka. "Raphael." In: <u>Opuscula exegetica Aboensia in honorem Rafael Gyllenberg octogenarii</u>, p. 77-100. Abo, 1973.

0504. (Rebecca) Albright, William Foxwell. "The Name Rebecca." <u>Journal of Biblical Literature</u> 39 (1920): 165-166.

0505. (Rebecca) Nestle, Eberhard. "Zur traditionellen Etymologie des Namens Rebekka." <u>Zeitschrfit für die alttestamentliche Wissenschaft</u>

25 (1905): 221-222.

0506. (Rehoboam) Stamm, Johann Jakob. "Zwei alttestamentliche Königs-
namen." In: Near Eastern Studies in Honor of William Foxwell Albright, p. 443-452. Baltimore, 1971.
Rehoboam and Jeroboam.

(Reu, see 0502)

0507. (Ruth) Bruppacher, Hans. "Die Bedeutung des Namens Ruth." Theologische Zeitschrift 22 (1966): 12-18.

0508. (Samuel) Jastrow, Morris. "The Name of Samuel and the Stem Sha'al."
Journal of Biblical Literature 19 (1900): 82-105.

0509. (Samuel) Zyl, A.H. van. "The Meaning of the Name Samuel." Biblical
Essays (1969): 122-129. (Proceedings of the 12th Meeting of Die Ou-
Testamentiese Werkgemeenskap in Suid-Afrika, 1969).

(Sarah, see 0428)

0510. (Shebaniah) Honeyman, Abraham Mackie. "A Note on the Names Shebaniah, Shebna, etc." Palestine Exploration Quarterly (1944): 168-169.

(Shebna, see 0510)

(Shenazzar, see 0511)

0511. (Sheshbazzar) Berger, Paul-Richard. "Zu den Namen Sheshbazzar und
Shenazzar." Zeitschrift für die alttestamentliche Wissenschaft 83
(1971): 98-100.

(Shiphrah, see 0501)

0512. (Simon) Fitzmyer, Joseph A. "The Name Simon." Harvard Theological
Review 56 (1963): 1-5; 57 (1964): 60-61.
See also 0513.

0513. (Simon) Roth, Cecil. "Simon - Peter." Harvard Theological Review
54 (1961): 91-97; 57 (1964): 60.
See also 0512.

0514. (Sirach) Krauss, Samuel. "The Name Sirach." Jewish Quarterly Review (O.S.) 11 (1899): 150-152.

0515. (Solomon) Stamm, Johann Jakob. "Der Name des Königs Salomo." Theologische Zeitschrift 16 (1960): 285-297.

0516. (Terah) Kraeling, Emil Gottlieb Heinrich. "Terach." "Metušelach."
Zeitschrift für die alttestamentliche Wissenschaft 40 (1922): 153-
155.

(Terah, see also 0304)

0517. (Uriah) Gustavs, Arnold. "Hethitische Parallelen zum Namen Uriah."
Zeitschrift für die alttestamentliche Wissenschaft 33 (1913): 201-
205.

(Yehudah, see Judah)

(Yitshak, see Isaac)

0518. (Zakarbaal) Offord, Joseph. "The Name Zakarbaal." Palestine Exploration Fund. Quarterly Statement (1916): 192.

XI

Ancient Near East

0519. Albright, William Foxwell. "An Ostracon from Calah and the North-Israelite Diaspora." American Schools of Oriental Research. Bulletin no. 149 (1958): 33-36.
See also 0549, 0560.

0520. Cohen, Naomi G. "Historical Conclusions Gleaned from the Names of the Jews of Elephantine." (Hebrew) Leshonenu 31 (1966-67): 97-106, 199-210.

0521. Coogan, Michael David. "Life in the Diaspora; Jews at Nippur in the Fifth Century B.C." Biblical Archaeologist 37 (1974): 6-12.

0522. Coogan, Michael David. "More Yahwistic Names in the Murashu Documents." Journal for the Study of Judaism in the Persian, Hellenistic and Roman Period 7 (1976): 199-200.
See also 0557A.

0523. Coogan, Michael David. "Patterns in Jewish Personal Names in the Babylonian Diaspora." Journal for the Study of Judaism in the Persian, Hellenistic and Roman Period 4 (1973): 183-191.

0524. Coogan, Michael David. West Semitic Personal Names in the Muraŝû Documents. 1971. 187 ℓ.
Unpublished dissertation, Harvard University.

0525. Cowley, Arthur Ernest. "Some Egyptian Aramaic Documents." Society of Biblical Archaeology. Proceedings 25 (1903): 202-208, 259-266, 311-316.
"Notes on the Names in the Papyrus" by G.B. Gray: p. 259-263.

0526. Daiches, Samuel. "Einige nach babylonischem Muster gebildete hebräische Namen." Orientalistische Literaturzeitung 11 (1908): col. 276-280.

0527. Daiches, Samuel. The Jews in Babylonia in the Time of Ezra and Nehemiah According to Babylonian Inscriptions. London, 1910. 36 p.
The Jewish names in the Murashū documents: p. 11-29.

0528. Driver, Godfrey Rolles. "Aramaic Names in Accadian Texts." Rivista degli Studi Orientali 32 (1957): 41-57.

0529. Driver, Godfrey Rolles. "New Aramaeo-Jewish Names in Egypt." Journal of Egyptian Archaeology 25 (1939): 175-176.

0530. Goetze, Albrecht. "The Aramaic Names." In: The Excavations at Dura-Europos Conducted by Yale University and the French Academy of Inscriptions and Letters. Preliminary Report of the Seventh and Eighth Sessions of Work, 1933-1934 and 1934-1935, p. 438-441. New Haven, 1939.

0531. Goldberg, Ariella Deem. Northern-Type-Names in the Post-Exilic Jewish Onomasticon. 1973. 174 ℓ.
Unpublished dissertation, Brandeis University.
cf. Dissertation Abstracts 34-A (1973-74): 229-230-A.

0532. Gray, George Buchanan. "Children Named After Ancestors in the Aramaic Papyri from Elephantine and Assuan." In: Studien zur semitischen Philologie und Religionsgeschichte Julius Wellhausen ... ge-

35

widmet, p. 161-176. Giessen, 1914.

0533.   Grelot, Pierre. "Notes d'onomastique sur les textes araméens
        d'Égypte." Semitica 21 (1971): 95-117.

0534.   Jirku, Anton. "Bemerkungen zu einigen syrisch-palästinischen Namen
        in ägyptischer Schrift." Archiv Orientální 32 (1964): 354-357.

0535.   Jirku, Anton. "Zu einigen Orts- u. Eigennamen Palästina-Syriens."
        Zeitschrift für die alttestamentliche Wissenschaft 75 (1963): 86-88.

0536.   Johns, Claude Hermann Walter. The Religious Significance of Semitic
        Proper Names. Cambridge, Eng., 1912. 156 p.

0537.   Kornfeld, Walter. "Beiträge zur aramäischen Namenforschung." Aka-
        demie der Wissenschaften, Vienna. Philosophisch-Historische Klasse.
        Anzeiger 111 (1974): 374-383.

0538.   Kornfeld, Walter. "Onomastica aramaica und das Alte Testament."
        Zeitschrift für die alttestamentliche Wissenschaft 88 (1976): 105-
        112.

0539.   Lipiński, Edward. Studies in Aramaic Inscriptions and Onomastics.
        Leuven, 1975- . vol.

0540.   Liverani, Mario. "Antecedenti dell'onomastica aramaica antica."
        Rivista degli Studi Orientali 37 (1962): 65-76.

0541.   Loewe, Heinrich. "Aegyptische Namen bei den Hebräern." Sinai (Bucu-
        rest) 5 (1933): 29-36.

0542.   Naveh, Joseph. "Aramaica dubiosa." Journal of Near Eastern Studies
        27 (1968): 317-325.
        See also "Onomastic notes to 'Aramaica dubiosa'" by Michael H. Sil-
        verman, Ibid., 28 (1969): 192-196.

0543.   Nöldeke, Theodor. Beiträge zur semitischen Sprachwissenschaft.
        Strassburg, 1904. 139 p.
        Einige Gruppen semitischer Personennamen: p. 73-106, etc.

0544.   Offord, Joseph. "Babylonian and Hebrew Theophoric Names." Palestine
        Exploration Fund. Quarterly Statement (1916): 85-94.

0545.   Pinches, Theophilus Goldridge. "Hebrew Names in Inscriptions from
        Babylonia." Palestine Exploration Fund. Quarterly Statement (1898):
        137-138.

0546.   Renan, Ernest. "Des noms théophores apocopés dans les anciennes
        langues sémitiques." Revue des Études Juives 5 (1882): 161-177.

0547.   Sayce, Archibald Henry. Aramaic Papyri Discovered at Assuan. Lon-
        don, 1906. 79 p., 27 plates.
        Index of proper names: p. 51-52.

0548.   Schneider, Nikolaus. "Patriarchennamen in zeitgenössischen Keil-
        schrifturkunden." Biblica 33 (1952): 516-522.

0549.   Segal, Judah Benzion. "An Aramaic Ostracon from Nimrud." Iraq 19
        (1957): 139-145.
        See also 0519, 0560.

0550.   Segert, Stanislav. "Aramäische Studien I." Archiv Orientální 24
        (1956): 383-403.
        Zu den Eigennamen: p. 393-394.

0551. Sidersky, David. "L'Onomastique hébräique des tablettes de Nippur." Revue des Études Juives 87 (1929): 177-199.

0552. Silverman, Michael H. "Aramean Name-Types in the Elephantine Documents." American Oriental Society. Journal 89 (1969): 691-709.

0553. Silverman, Michael H. "Hebrew Name-Types in the Elephantine Documents." Orientalia 39 (1970): 465-491.

0554. Silverman, Michael H. Jewish Personal Names in the Elephantine Documents: A Study in Onomastic Development. 1967. 299 ℓ.
Unpublished dissertation, Brandeis University.
cf. Dissertation Abstracts 28-A (1967-68): 2233-2234-A.

0555. Spiegelberg, Wilhelm. "Die ägyptischen Personennamen in der kürzlich veröffentlichten Urkunden von Elephantine." Orientalistische Literaturzeitung 15 (1912): col. 1-10.

0556. Spiegelberg, Wilhelm. "Ein demotisches Ostrakon mit jüdischen Eigennamen (Tell el-Yehudiya)" Orientalistische Literaturzeitung 10 (1907): col. 595-596, 642.

0557. Spiegelberg, Wilhelm. "Zu den ägyptischen Personennamen der Urkunden von Elephantine." Orientalistische Literaturzeitung 16 (1913): col. 346-347.

0557A Stolper, Matthew W. "A Note on Yahwistic Personal Names in the Murašû Texts." American Schools of Oriental Research. Bulletin no. 222 (1976): 25-28.
See also 0522.

0558. Tallqvist, Knut L. Neubabylonisches Namenbuch zu den Geschäftsurkunden aus der Zeit des Šamaššumukîn bis Xerxes. Helsingsfor, 1905. 338 p.
Review:
   Ranke, Hermann. American Journal of Semitic Languages and Literatures 23 (1907): 358-365.

   Sarsowsky, Abraham. ha-Kedem (St. Petersburg) 1 (1907): 37-40 (Non-Hebrew section).

0559. Vincent, Albert Léopold. La Religion des judéo-araméens d'Éléphantine. Paris, 1937. 723 p.
Les noms théophores d'Éléphantine: p. 392-445.

0560. Vogt, Ernst. "Nomina Hebraica-Phoenicia in Assyria exeuntis saec. 7 a. Chr." Biblica 39 (1958): 114-115.
See also 0519, 0549.

See also 0168-0169, 0188, 0226, 0659.

XII

Greco-Roman Period

0561. Ascoli, Graziadio Isaia. Iscrizioni inedito o mal note, greche, latine, ebraiche, di antichi sepolcri giudaici del Napolitano. Torino, 1880. 120 p.
I nomi ebraici o aramaici, che occorrano nelle epigrafi giudaiche o greco-latine: p. 20-25.

0562. Berliner, Adolf. Geschichte der Juden in Rom von der ältesten Zeit bis zur Gegenwart (2050 Jahre). Frankfurt a.M., 1893. 2 vol. in 3. Namen: vol. 1, p. 54-56; Zur Namenkunde: vol. 2:1, p. 114-116.

0563. Cohen, Naomi G. "Jewish Names as Cultural Indicators of Antiquity." Journal for the Study of Judaism in the Persian, Hellenistic and Persian Period 7 (1976): 97-128.

0564. Cohen, Naomi G. Shemot Yehudiyim u-mashma'utam ba-tekufa ha-Helenistit veha-Romit be-Asyah ha-ketana. 1969. 2 vol.
In Hebrew.
Dissertation, Hebrew University, Jerusalem.

0565. Delling, Gerhard. "Biblische Namen im ägyptischen Judentum; Ein Beitrag zur Frage der Hellenisierung der Diaspora." Theologische Literaturzeitung 92 (1967): col. 249-252.

0566. Frey, Jean-Baptiste. Corpus Inscriptionum Iudaicarum. Città del Vaticano, 1936-1952. 2 vol.
Noms propres grecs: vol. 1, p. 605-617; Noms propres latins: vol. 1, p. 618-626.

0567. Hengel, Martin. Judaism and Hellenism; Studies in Their Encounter in Palestine During the Early Hellenistic Period. Philadelphia, 1974. 2 vol.
The advance of Greek names: vol. 1, p. 61-65.

0568. Isserlin, B.S.J. "Ancient Hebrew Pronunciation Types in the Light of Personal and Place Names in Greek and Latin Transcriptions." In: International Congress of Orientalists, 27th, Ann Arbor, Mich., 1967. Proceedings, p. 100-101. Wiesbaden, 1971.

0569. Juster, Jean. Les Juifs dans l'Empire romain: Leur condition juridique, économique et sociale. Paris, 1914. 2 vol.
Nom: vol. 2, p. 221-234.

0570. Lamer, Hans. "Jüdische Namen im griechisch-römischen Altertum. Der Name Jesu." Philologische Wochenschrift 50 (1930): col. 763-765.

0571. Leon, Harry Joshua. The Jews of Ancient Rome. Philadelphia, 1960. 378 p.
The names of the Jews of Rome: p. 93-121.

0572. Leon, Harry Joshua. "The Jews of Venosa." Jewish Quarterly Review (N.S.) 44 (1953-54): 267-284.
Names: p. 278-281.

0573. Leon, Harry Joshua. "The Names of the Jews of Ancient Rome." American Philological Association. Transactions and Proceedings 59 (1928): 205-224.

0574. Leon, Harry Joshua. "New Material About the Jews of Ancient Rome." Jewish Quarterly Review (N.S.) 20 (1929-30): 301-312.
Names: p. 308-310.

0575. Müller, Nikolaus. Die jüdische Katakombe am Monteverde zu Rom, der älteste bisher bekannt gewordene jüdische Friedhof des Abendlandes. Leipzig, 1912. 142 p.
Eigennamen: p. 100-106.

0576. Ruozzi Sala, Susanna Maria. Lexicon nominum Semiticorum quae in papyris Graecis in Aegypto repertis ab anno 323 a. Ch. n. usque ad annum 70 p. Ch. n. laudata reperiuntur. Milano, 1974. 43 p.

0577. Salzmann, Milka (Cassuto). "La corrispondenza tra nomi ebraici e greci nell' onomastica giudaica." Società Asiatica Italiana. Giornale (N.S.) 2 (1932-33): 209-230.

0578. Salzmann, Milka (Cassuto) "Greek Names Among Jews." (Hebrew) Eretz-Israel 3 (1954): 186-190.

0579. Tcherikover, Avigdor. Hellenistic Civilization and the Jews. Philadelphia, 1959. 566 p.
Names: p. 346-347, 523-524.

0580. Tcherikover, Avigdor. ha-Yehudim be-Mitsrayim ba-tekufat ha-Helenistit-ha-Romit le-or ha-papirologiyah. 2d rev. ed. Jerusalem, 1963. 225 p.
In Hebrew.
Jewish names: p. 180-203.

0581. Thylander, Hilding. Étude sur l'épigraphie latine. Lund, 1952. 191 p.
Le gentilice des Juifs: p. 139-140; Les surnoms des Juifs: p. 167-169.

0582. Vogelstein, Hermann. Rome. Philadelphia, 1940. 421 p.
Names of Jews found in the catacombs: p. 40-41; Names of Roman Jewish families: p. 157.

0583. Willrich, Hugo. Das Haus der Herodes; Zwischen Jerusalem und Rom. Heidelberg, 1929. 195 p.
Zu den Wechselnamen der Juden in hellenistisch-römischer Zeit: p. 168-172.

0584. Wuthnow, Heinz. Die semitischen Menschennamen in griechischen Inschriften und Papyri des vorderen Orients. Leipzig, 1930. 175 p.
Review:
Brockelmann, Karl. Orientalistische Literaturzeitung 34 (1931): col. 959-962.

0585. Zorell, Franz. "Spiritus asper und lenis hebräischer Wörter und Eigennamen im Griechischen." Zeitschrift für Katholische Theologie 24 (1900): 734-738.

XIII

Koran

0586. Horovitz, Josef. "Jewish Proper Names and Derivatives in the Koran." Hebrew Union College Annual 2 (1925): 145-227.
See also review under 0587.

0587. Horovitz, Josef. Koranische Untersuchungen. Berlin, 1926. 171 p. Ausserkoranische Namen jüdischer oder christlicher Herkunft aus vorislamischer Zeit: p. 156-165.
Review:
Heller, Bernát. Monatsschrift für Geschichte und Wissenschaft des Judentums 72 (1928): 328-332.

0588. Sycz, Samuel. Ursprung und Wiedergabe der biblischen Eigennamen im Koran. Frankfurt a.M., 1903. 64 p.
Inaug.-Dissertation, Bern.

XIV

Rabbinical Literature

0589. Albeck, Schalom. Mishpeḥot sofrim. Warsaw, 1903. 46, 112 p.
In Hebrew.
No more published.

0590. Bacher, Wilhelm. "Contribution à l'onomatologie talmudique." Revue des Études Juives 42 (1901): 43-47.

0591. Chajes, Hirsch Perez. "Sur quelques noms propres talmudiques." Revue des Études Juives 44 (1902): 126-128.

0592. Duensing, Hugo. Verzeichnis der Personen- und der geographischen Namen in der Mischna. Stuttgart, 1960. 51 p.

0593. Edelmann, Mordecai Isaac. Me'arat 'Adulam. Bialystok, 1912. 106 col.
In Hebrew.

0594. Freehof, Solomon B. "Father's Name Forgotten." Central Conference of American Rabbis. Journal (Autumn 1974): 53-56.
A responsum.
See also 0618.

0595. Goldberger, Israel. "Various Amoraim Bearing the Same Name." (Hebrew) ha-Soker (Budapest) 5 (1937-38): 87-95.
Also published in: Emlékkönyv Dr. Mahler Ede. Budapestini, 1937.

0596. Harduf, David Mendel. The Exegesis of Biblical Proper Names in the Midrashim and Talmudim. 1957 or 58?
Unpublished dissertation, Jews' College, London.
cf. Index of Theses Accepted for Higher Degrees in the Universities of Great Britain and Ireland 8 (1957-58): 4.
See also 0161.

0597. Harduf, David Mendel. Milon u-mafteaḥ le-midrashe ha-shemot ha-TaNaKHiyim be-Agadah. Tel-Aviv, 1960. 182 p.
In Hebrew.
Supplement to 0596.

0598. Horowitz, Jakob. "Ueber einige Namen der Rabbinen im Talmud und Midrasch." Monatsschrift für Geschichte und Wissenschaft des Judentums 32 (1883): 306-317.

0599. Klein, Samuel. "The Study of Names and Nicknames." (Hebrew) Leshonenu 1 (1928-29): 325-350; 2 (1929-30): 260-272.

0600. Klein, Samuel. "The Study of Nicknames and Titles." (Hebrew) ha-Soker (Budapest) 5 (1937-38): 3-15.
Also published in: Emlékkönyv Dr. Mahler Ede. Budapestini, 1937.

0601. Klein, Samuel. "Zur jüdischen Altertumskunde. 5. Zur mischnisch-talmudischen Namenkunde." Monatsschrift für Geschichte und Wissenschaft des Judentums 77 (1933): 356-365.

0602. Kosovsky, Binyamin. Otsar ha-shemot shel Mekhilta de-rabi Yishma'el. Jerusalem, 1965. 96 p.
In Hebrew.

0603. Krauss, Samuel. Talmudische Archäologie. Leipzig, 1910-12. 3 vol. Namengebung: vol. 2, p. 12-18.

0604. Margulies, Reuben. Le-ḥeker shemot ve-kinuyim ba-Talmud. Jerusalem, 1959-60. 72 p.
In Hebrew.

0605. Margulies, Reuben. Shemot ve-kinuyim ba-Talmud. Lwów, [192-?]. 10 ℓ.
In Hebrew.

0606. Margulies, Reuben. "The Study of Names and Nicknames in the Talmud." (Hebrew) Sinai (Jerusalem) no. 57-59 (1941-42): 82-91.

0607. Moses ben Maimon. "Commentary on Sacred Names." (Hebrew) Debir (Berlin) 1 (1923): 191-222.
Edited by Moses Gaster.

0608. Neuda, S. "Namen der Talmudisten." Literaturblatt des Orients 6 (1845): col. 129-133, 242-247.

0609. Oppenheimer, Joseph. Kuntres ve-yikare shemo be-Yisrael. Buenos Aires, 1974-75. 47 p.
In Hebrew.

0610. Peiser, Simon ben Judah Loeb. Naḥalat Shim'oni. Wandsbeck, 1728. 2 vol. in 1.
In Hebrew.

0611. Sarsowsky, Abraham. Die ethisch-religiöse Bedeutung der alttestamentlichen Namen nach Talmud, Targum und Midras. Kirchhain N.-L., 1904. 90 p.
Inaug.-Dissertation, Königsberg.

0612. Schorr, Joshua Heschel. "Personal Names in Rabbinical Literature." (Hebrew) he-Ḥaluts 9:2 (1873): 1-83.

0613. Schuerer, Emil. Verzeichnis der Personennamen in der Mischna. Leipzig, 1913. 23 p.

0614. Shapira, El'azar. Kuntres ve-yikare shemo be-Yisrael. Jerusalem, 1971-72. 70 p.
In Hebrew.

0615. Sidon, A. "Eine Namensformel im Talmud." Jüdisches Litteratur-Blatt 8 (1879): 186, 200.

0616. Steif, Max. "Besondere Namenswortspiele im Talmud und Midrasch." Jeschurun (Berlin) 11 (1924): 501-507; 14 (1927): 610-614.

0617. Tchorsh, Katriel Fishel. "Law Concerning Foreign Names for Jewish Children." (Hebrew) Shanah be-Shanah (1974-75): 136-142.

0618. Trepp, Leo. "The Naming of the Child - The Secular Name." Central Conference of American Rabbis. Journal (Winter 1975): 94-95. See also 0594.

XV

Names in Divorce

0619. Alfandari, Aaron ben Moses. Yad Ahron. Izmir, 1756-66. 2 vol. In Hebrew. Proper names used in bills of divorce: vol. 2, ℓ. 102b-134.

0620. Alfandari, Elijah ben Jacob. Mikhtav me-Eliyahu. Constantinople, 1723. 214, 2, 15 ℓ. In Hebrew.

0621. Arlosoroff, Eliezer. Hagahot Eliezer. Pietrokov, 1902. 129 p. In Hebrew.

0622. Aryeh Loeb ben Asher. Sha'agat Aryeh. Neuwied, 1736. 38 ℓ. In Hebrew. Names in divorce: ℓ. 27-32.

0623. Estrumsa, Ḥayyim Abraham. Yerekh Avraham. Salonika, 1815. 2 vol. In Hebrew. Names in divorce, by Daniel Estrumsa: 4 ℓ. inserted after vol. 1, ℓ. 110.

0624. Frenkel, Chaskel. Divre Avraham. Kolomea, 1885-94 (vol. 1, 1894). In Hebrew. Vol. 2 published in Przemyśl. "Kuntres ha-shemot" at end of vol. 2 (33 ℓ.)

0625. Ganzfried, Solomon. Ohole shem. Lwów, 1907. 124 ℓ. In Hebrew. Reprinted: Jerusalem, 1969-70.

0626. Gordon, Aaron. Even Me'ir. Pietrokov, 1909. 81 p. In Hebrew.

0627. Gordon, Aaron. Minḥat Ahron. New York, 1918-21. 4 vol. In Hebrew. Vol. 2-4 published in Jerusalem.

0628. Gordon, Aaron. Teshuvot milu'ot even. Pietrokov, 1912. 98 p. In Hebrew.

0629. Ḥagiz, Jacob. Halakhot ketanot. Venice, 1704. 71 ℓ. In Hebrew. Names: ℓ. 69-71.

0630. Halberstam, Ḥayyim. _Divre Ḥayyim_. Zolkiew, 1864. 2 vol. in 1.
In Hebrew.
Reprinted: Brooklyn, 1957-58.

0631. Hazan, Solomon. _Ben Shelomo_. Alexandria, 1900. 54, 56 ℓ.
In Hebrew.
Contains "Devar Eliyahu" by Elijah Hazan.

0632. Henkin, Yosef Eliyahu. "Orthography of Proper Names in Bills of Divorce." (Hebrew) _Talpioth_ 1 (1943-44): 537-550.

0633. Horovitz, Markus. _Mateh Levi_. Frankfurt a.M., 1891-1932. 2 vol.
In Hebrew.
'Et barzel: vol. 1, p. 1-15.

0634. Ibn Ḥabib, Moses ben Solomon. _'Ezrat nashim_. Constantinople, 1731.
65, 64 ℓ.
In Hebrew.
Also published: Leipzig, 1859.

0635. Jellinek, Adolf. _Kuntres ha-mazkir_. Wien, 1877. 26 p.
In Hebrew.

0636. Karasik, Dov. _Tiv shemot gitin_. Vilna, 1873. 130 p.
In Hebrew.

0637. Karsonski, Azriel Dov. _Shemen la-ma'or_. Zhitomir, 1871. 47 ℓ.
In Hebrew.

0638. Katz, Joel. _She'elot u-teshuvot Tirat kesef_. Waitzen, 1920-21.
184 p.
In Hebrew.

0639. _Kuntres ha-shemot_. Berdichev, 1894. 18 ℓ.
In Hebrew.

0640. Lawat, Abraham David. _Kav naki_. Pietrokov, 1914. 117, 77 p.
In Hebrew.

0641. Michael ben Joseph, of Krakow. _Berekhath ha-mayim_. Wien, 1862.
69 ℓ.
In Hebrew.

0642. Michael ben Joseph, of Krakow. _Seder gitin va-ḥalitsah_. Vilna,
1873. 92 p.
In Hebrew.

0643. Minz, El'azar. _Get mesudar_. Bilgoria, 1932. 6, 360 p.
In Hebrew.

0644. Moda'i, Ḥayyim. _Tiv gitin_. Jerusalem, 1874-75. 28 ℓ.
In Hebrew.

0645. Nicberg, Eliezer. _Yad Eli'ezer_. Warsaw, 1931. 533 p.
In Hebrew.

0646. Notovich, Isaac. _Shulḥan ha-ma'arekhet_. Warsaw, 1876. 136 p.
In Hebrew.

0647. Pardo, Moses. _Hora'ah de-bet din_. Izmir, 1872. 77 ℓ.
In Hebrew.

0648. Pipano, David. Higur ha-ephod. Sofia, 1925. 138 ℓ.
       In Hebrew.

0649. Rawicz, Isaac. Avne zikhron. Lwów, 1899. 100 ℓ.
       In Hebrew.

0650. Samuel ben Uri Shraga Phoebus. Bet Shemuel. Fürth, 1694. 147 ℓ.
       In Hebrew.
       Names in divorce: ℓ. 95-101.

0651. Samuel ben Uri Shraga Phoebus. Tiv gitin. Zolkiew, 1822. 43, 43,
       10 ℓ.
       In Hebrew.
       Edited by Ephraim Zalman Margolioth.
       Frequently reprinted.

0652. Sancho, Isaac ben Elijah. Be'erot ha-mayim. Salonika, 1755. 216 ℓ.
       In Hebrew.
       Names: ℓ. 210-211.

0653. Silberfarb, Baruch. Minhat Barukh. Zhitomir, 1900. 2 vol. in 1.
       In Hebrew.
       Published with the author's Makor Barukh.

0654. Simhah ben Gershon, ha-Kohen. Sefer shemot. Venice, 1656-57. 119,
       i.e., 126 ℓ.
       In Hebrew.

0655. Taubes, Jehiel Ikhel. Shem 'olam. Czernowitz, 1886-87. 107 ℓ.
       In Hebrew.

0656. Zuenz, Aryeh Loeb. Get mekushar ve-tiv gitin. Warsaw, 1931-32.
       46, 142 p.
       In Hebrew.

XVI

Names of Women

0657. Grunwald, Max. "Die hebräischen Frauennamen." Monatsschrift für
       Geschichte und Wissenschaft des Judentums 41 (1897): 667-671.

0658. Löhr, Max Richard Hermann. Die Stellung des Weibes zu Jahwe-Reli-
       gion und- Kult. Leipzig, 1908. 54 p.
       Names of women: p. 6-32.

0659. Löhr, Max Richard Hermann. "Die weiblichen Eigennamen in Sachaus
       'Aramäischen Papyrus und Ostraka.'" Orientalistische Literaturzei-
       tung 16 (1913): col. 103-106.

0660. Noy, Dov. "Animal Names as the Names of Women." (Hebrew) Mahanayim
       No. 98 (1965): 150-159.

0661. Praetorius, Franz. "Ueber einige weibliche Caritativnamen im He-
       bräischen." Deutsche Morgenländische Gesellschaft. Zeitschrift 57
       (1893): 530-534.

0662. Stamm, Johann Jakob. "Hebräische Frauennamen." In: Hebräische
       Wortforschung. Festschrift zum 80. Geburtstag von Walter Baumgart-
       ner, p. 301-339. Leiden, 1967.

0663. Zipser, Maier. "Die Namen der Mütter biblischer Personen." Ben Chananja 6 (1863): col. 709-713.

0664. Zmora, Israel. Nashim ba-TaNaKH ... Tel-Aviv, 1964. 640 p. In Hebrew.
Names of women in the Bible: p. 5-20.

See also 0243, 0311.

XVII

Jewish Names: Europe

Austria

0665. Alphabetisches Verzeichniss derjenigen Männer und Weibernamen, welche zum Gebrauch der jüdischen Nazion vom ersten Jenner 1788 nur blos nach der deutschen, oder christlichen Aussprache zu führen gestattet sind. Nebst jenen Namen, welche für die Zukunft gänzlich zu unterbleiben haben. Wien, 1787. 56 p.

0666. Flesch, Heinrich. "Das Neu-Raussnitzer Steuerbuch." Jüdisch-literarische Gesellschaft. Jahrbuch 21 (1930): 89-108.

0667. Grunwald, Max. "Zur jüdischen Kulturgeschichte im österreichischen Vormärz." Mitteilungen zur Jüdischen Volkskunde Heft 46 (1913): 18-26; Heft 47 (1913): 19-32.
Die Annahme deutscher Namen (13. Juli 1787): p. 23.

0668. Klampfer, Josef. Das Eisenstädter Ghetto. Eisenstadt, 1965. 289 p. Vornamen: p. 234-238.

0669. Rosenfeld, Julius. Die Matrikelführung der Israeliten in Oesterreich nach den bestehenden staatlichen Vorschriften. Wien, 1912. 222 p.
Namensänderung: p. 51-53.

0670. Tänzer, Aaron. Die Geschichte der Juden in Tirol und Vorarlberg. Meran, 1905. 2 vol.
Familienregister: vol. 2, p. 683-789.

0671. Wolf, Gerson. "Jüdische Namen." Allgemeine Zeitung des Judenthums 51 (1887): 36-37.

Bohemia, see Czechoslovakia

Bulgaria

0672. Avi-Shlomo, Ya'akov. "Family Names Among the Jews in Plovdiv." (Hebrew) Shevet ve-'am 4 (1958): 117-119.

0673. Moskona, Isak M. "About the Origin of the Family Names of the Bulgarian Jews." (Bulgarian) Social Cultural and Educational Association of the Jews in the People's Republic of Bulgaria. Godishnik 2 (1967): 111-137.

Czechoslovakia

0674. Bartušek, Josef. "Novodobá osobní jména u českých židů." Židovská ročenka (1972-73): 28-37.

0675. Bartušek, Josef. "O židovských příjmeních." Židovská ročenka (1971-72): 21-28.

0676. Bartušek, Josef. "K židovským osobním jménům nové doby." In: Onomastické práce. Vol. 2, p. 13-20. Praha, 1968.

0677. Beneš, Josef. "Zu Max Brods Namendeutungen." Beiträge zur Namenforschung (N.F.) 4 (1969): 215-216.

0678. Brilling, Bernhard. "On Jewish Names in Teplice in 1752." (Hebrew) Yeda'-'am vol. 1, no. 1 (1948): 8-9.

0679. Cramer, Anton. Vollständige Gesetz-Sammlung für die Judenschaft in den königl. Staaten. Prag, 1793- . vol.
Männernamen: vol. 1, p. 261-293; Weibernamen: vol. 1, p. 293-308; Fernere Männernamen: vol. 1, p. 308; Fernere Weibernamen: vol. 1, p. 309-310.

0680. Flesch, Heinrich. "Mährische Städtenamen und čechische Vornamen im jüdischen Schrifttums."
Unidentified offprint (5 p.)

0681. Fried, Samuel. "Kehillah kedoscha Kalladey. Kulturskizze aus jüdischer Vergangenheit." Jüdisches Archiv 2 (1928-29): 39-43, 50-51, 61-64.
No more published.
Die Namen der Kalladeyer Juden: p. 62-64.

0682. Kestenberg-Gladstein, Ruth. Neuere Geschichte der Juden in den böhmischen Ländern. Tübingen, 1969- . vol.
Namen: vol. 1, p. 68-69.

0683. Muneles, Otto. "Zur Namengebung der Juden in Böhmen." Bohemia Judaica 2 (1966): 3-13.

0684. Schwenger, Heinrich. "Die Namensbeilegung der Juden in Kostel im Jahre 1787." Zeitschrift für die Geschichte der Juden in der Tschechoslowakei 1 (1930-31): 116-126.

0685. Valiska, Juraj. "Z histórie a výstavby židovských mien na Spiši." In: Slovenská onomastická konferencia, 4th, Bratislava, 1971. Zbornik materálov. p. 89-97. Bratislava, 1973.

0686. Žáček, Wenzel. "Eine Studie zur Entwicklung der jüdischen Personennamen in neuerer Zeit." Gesellschaft für Geschichte der Juden in der Cechoslovakischen Republik. Jahrbuch 8 (1936): 309-397.

England, see Great Britain

France: Books

0687. Anchel, Robert. Napoléon et les Juifs. Paris, 1928. 598 p.
Les Juifs sont astreints par le décret du 20 juillet 1808 à déclarer leurs prénoms et des noms de famille: p. 433-461.

0688. Baugey, Georges. <u>De la condition légale du culte israélite en France et en Algérie</u>. Paris, 1898. 293 p.
Noms et prénoms des Juifs: p. 58.

0689. Berg, Roger. <u>Guide juif de France</u>. Nouv. éd. Paris, 1971. 509 p.
Patronymie des Juifs de France: p. 77-78.

0690. Bloch, Joseph, and Picard, Salomon. <u>Grussenheim; Communauté juive disparue</u>. Grussenheim?, 1960. 52 p.
Les déclarations des Juifs de Grussenheim pour l'adoption de noms et prénoms fixes: p. 30-37.

0691. Catane, Mochè. "Eléments français dans l'anthroponymie juive." (Hebrew) In: <u>World Congress of Jewish Studies, 3d, Jerusalem, 1961</u>. <u>Report</u>, p. 219-220. Jerusalem, 1965.
See also 0715.

0692. Dauzat, Albert. <u>Les Noms de famille de France</u>. Paris, 1945. 454 p.
Les noms israélites: p. 249-253.

0693. Decourcelle, Jacques. <u>La Condition des Juifs de Nice au 17e e 18e siècles</u>. Paris, 1923. 309 p.
L'État civil et le nom des Juifs: p. 147-151.

0694. Drumont, Édouard Adolphe. <u>La France juive</u>. Essai d'histoire contemporaine. 77e éd. Paris, ₁886?₃. 2 vol.
Les noms juifs: vol. 1, p. 317-321.

0695. France. Sovereigns, etc., 1799-1814 (Napoléon I). <u>Décret imperial concernant les Juifs qui n'ont pas de Nom de Famille et de Prénom fixes (A Bayonne, le 20 Juillet 1808)</u>. 1 ℓ.
Reproduced in: <u>Historia Judaica</u> 6 (1944): between p. 156-157.

0696. Gerson, Michel Aron. <u>Essai sur les Juifs de la Bourgogne au Moyen-Age et principalement aux XIIe, XIIIe et XIVe siècles</u>. Dijon, 1893. 68 p.
Liste génerale de tous les noms israélites ...: p. 51-61.

0697. Gygès (pseud.). <u>Les Israélites dans la société française; Documents et témoignages</u>. Paris, 1956. 238 p.
Répertoire onomastique (Les noms juifs): p. 95-231.

0698. Gygès (pseud.). <u>Les Juifs dans la France d'aujourd'hui</u>. Paris, 1965. 268 p.
Onomastique israélite: p. 105-261.

0699. Institut d'étude des questions juives. <u>L'Émancipation des Juifs en France</u>. Paris, ₁940?₃. 61 p.
Signed: Henri-Robert Petit.

0700. Institut d'étude des questions juives. <u>Leurs noms... Petite philosophie des patronymes juifs</u>. Paris, ₁94-?₃. 32 p.

0701. Jerôme (archivist). <u>Dictionnaire des changements de noms de 1803 à 1956</u>. Paris, 1957. 230 p.

0702. Katz, Solomon. <u>The Jews in the Visigothic and Frankish Kingdoms of Spain and Gaul</u>. Cambridge, Mass., 1937. 182 p.
Names: p. 163-165.

0703. Lebel, Paul. <u>Les Noms de personnes en France</u>. 6e éd. Paris, 1968. 127 p.

Noms juifs: p. 114-116.

0704. Lemoine, Albert. Napoléon Ier et les Juifs. Paris, 1900. 388 p.
Le décret sur les noms et prénoms: p. 352-357.

0705. Léon, Henry. Histoire des Juifs de Bayonne. Paris, 1893. 436 p.
Les sobriquets: p. 384-386.

0706. Lévy, Paul. Les Noms des Israélites en France; Histoire et dictionnaire. Paris, 1960. 210 p.

0707. Maslin, Shimon J. An Analysis and Translation of Selected Documents
of Napoleonic Jewry. 1957. 169 ℓ.
Unpublished rabbinic thesis, Hebrew Union College-Jewish Institute of
Religion (Cincinnati).
Names: ℓ. 69-77 (Includes English translation of Napoleon's decree of
July 20, 1808, relative to the names of Jews).

0708. Menninger, August. Das Napoleonische Dekret vom Jahre 1808, wegen
der Vor- und Zunamen der Juden. Mainz, 1928. 14 p.

0709. Obituaire (Un) israélite: Le "Memorbuch" de Metz (vers 1575-1724).
Traduit de l'hébreu, avec une introduction et de notes par Simon
Schwarzfuchs. Metz, 1971. 117 ℓ.
Index des noms individuels: p. 101-114; Index des surnoms d'origine
et des noms de lieux: p. 115-117.

0710. Roblin, Michel. "Noms de lieux de la France romane et noms de famille juifs en France et à l'étranger." In: International Congress
of Toponymy and Anthroponymy, 3d, Brussels, 1949. Actes et mémoires.
Vol. 3, p. 764-773. Louvain, 1951.

0711. Scheid, Élie. Histoire des Juifs de Haguenau, suivie des recense-
ments de 1763, 1784 et 1808. Paris, 1885. 84, lviii p.
Liste officielle des israélites qui demeuraient à Haguenau en 1808,
avec leurs anciens noms et les nouveaux en regard: p. xlii-lvi.

France: Periodical Literature

0712. Archedebe, E. Houth, Julien le Cram, Saint-Helionet et A.J. "Noms
de famille chez les Israélites." L'Intermédiaire des chercheurs et
curieux 96 (1933): 153-154, 251, 393, 591-592, 778-779.
See also Ibid., 95 (1932): 954; 97 (1934): 31.

0713. Berg, Roger. "Onomastique judéo-lorraine." Bulletin de nos communautés (Strasbourg), 22 juil. 1966, p. 10.

0714. Bernardini, Armand. "Die französischen Familiennamen der Juden."
Weltkampf (1942): 142-151.

0715. Catane, Mochè. "Eléments français dans l'anthroponymie juive."
Almanach K.K.L. (Strasbourg) (1962-63): 159-165.
See also 0691.

0716. Ginsburger, Moses. "Les Juifs de Metz sous l'ancien régime." Revue
des Études Juives 50 (1905): 112-128, 238-260.
See also "Namenkunde" by Moritz Steinschneider, Zeitschrift für hebräische Bibliographie 10 (1906): 125-127.

0717. Ginsburger, Moses. "Die Namen der Juden im Elsass." Elsassland 4
(1924): 237-242.

0718. Ginsburger, Moses. "Unsere Namen." Strassburger Israelitische Wochenschrift 6, Nr. 27, 29-30 (1909). cf. Gesamtarchiv der Deutschen Juden. Mitteilungen 2 (1909): 164.

0719. Heitz, Fernand-J. "Attribution des noms aux Juifs en Alsace au moment de la Révolution." Revue Internationale d'Onomastique 6 (1954): 299-300.

0720. Hemerdinger, Gabriel. "Le Dénombrement des Israélites d'Alsace (1784)" Revue des Études Juives 42 (1901): 253-264.

0721. Hemerdinger, Gabriel. "Les Noms des Israélites d'Alsace (1784) et le décret de 1808." Univers Israélite 57:1 (1901-1902): 467-473.

0722. Kassel, [August?]. "Les Noms des Israélites d'Alsace." Univers Israélite 65:1 (1909-10): 14-21, 45-50, 75-77.

0723. Lévy, Paul. "L'Acte de naissance des patronymes juifs de France." Evidences no. 72 (1958): 37-40.

0724. Loeb, Isidore. "Le Rôle des Juifs de Paris en 1296 et 1297." Revue des Études Juives 1 (1880): 61-71.

0725. Mendel, Pierre. "La Langue et les noms des Juifs en France au Moyen Age." Almanach-Calendrier des communautés israélites de la Moselle (1955): 88-92. cf. Bernhard Blumenkranz. Bibliographie des Juifs en France (Toulouse, 1974), p. 249.

0726. Mendel, Pierre. "Les Noms des Juifs d'Alsace et de Lorraine." Almanach-calendrier des communautés israélites de la Moselle (1959): 101-105. cf. Bernhard Blumenkranz. Bibliographie des Juifs en France (Toulouse, 1974), p. 15.

0727. Mendel, Pierre. "Les Noms des Juifs français modernes." Revue des Études Juives 110 (1949-50): 15-65.

0728. Nordmann, Achille. "Glanes onomatologiques." Revue des Études Juives 82 (1926): 483-494.

0729. Oberreiner, Camille. "Changements de noms et de prénoms des Juifs de Cernay en 1808." Revue d'Alsace 75 (1928): 303-305.

0730. Roblin, Michel. "L'Histoire juive par les noms de famille. De Carcassonne à Vallabrègues, les anciennes communautés du midi de la France." L'Arche no. 13 (1958): 23-24, 52.

0731. Roblin, Michel. "L'Histoire juive par les noms de famille. A l'enseigne des douze tribus." L'Arche no. 16 (1958): 20-21, 43.

0732. Roblin, Michel. "L'Histoire juive par les noms de famille. De Spire à Worms, les antiques communautés des pays rhénans." L'Arche no. 23 (1958): 31-32, 57.

0733. Roblin, Michel: "Introduction à l'onomastique judéo-française." L'Arche no. 162-163 (1970): 80-81.

Galicia, see Poland

0734. Adler, Simon. Geschichte der Juden in Mülhausen i.E. Mülhausen i.E. 1914. 90 p.
Inaug.-Dissertation, Basel.
Unter Napoleon I: p. 64-76.

0735. Andree, Richard. Zur Volkskunde der Juden. Bielefeld, 1881. 296 p.
Jüdische Namen: p. 120-128.

0736. Arndt, Wilhelm. Die Personennamen der deutschen Schauspiele des Mittelalters. Breslau, 1904. 113 p.
Namen der Juden: p. 3-16, 31-37.

0737. Aschkewitz, Max. Zur Geschichte der Juden in Westpreussen. Marburg (Lahn), 1967. 276 p.
Familien- und Vornamen: p. 63-64.

0738. Bach, Adolf. Deutsche Namenkunde. 2. stark erweiterte Aufl. Heidelberg, 1952-56. 3 vol. in 5.
Die Namen der Juden in Deutschland: vol. 1:2, p. 221-225.

0739. Bavaria. Laws, statutes, etc. Sammlung der im Gebiete der innern Staats-Verwaltung des Königreichs Bayern bestehenden Verordnungen ...
Bd. 6: Verhältnisse der israelitischen Glaubensgenossen ... München, 1838. vii, 292, xxxii, 31 p.
Judenmatrikel, Vor- und Familien-Namen der Israeliten: p. 28-30.

0740. Bischoff, Erich. Wörterbuch der wichtigsten Geheim- und Berufssprachen: Jüdisch-Deutsch, Rotwelsch, Kundensprache, Soldaten-, Seemanns-, Weidmanns-, Bergmanns- und Komödiantensprache. Leipzig, 1916. 168 p.
"Bürgerliche"jüdische Vornamen: p. 98-100; Deutsche Familien-Namen für Juden: p. 101-103.

0741. Bodemeyer, Hildebrand. Die Juden. Ein Beitrag zur Hannoverschen Rechtsgeschichte. Göttingen, 1855. 108 p.
Familien-Namen: p. 83-84.

0742. Bücher, Johannes. Zur Geschichte der jüdischen Gemeinde in Beuel. Beuel, 1965. 83 p.
Die Beurkundung des Zivilstands der Juden (1808), die Annahme fester (vererblicher) Familiennamen (1846), die zusätzliche Annahme jüdischer Vornamen (1938): p. 14-22.

0743. Cuno, Klaus. Das Aufkommen der jüdischen Familiennamen im deutschen Sprachgebiet. 1969.
Magisterarbeit, Universität Bonn.

0744. Dietz, Alexander. Stammbuch der Frankfurter Juden. Frankfurt a.M., 1907. 481 p.
Vornamen und Familiennamen: p. 1-8.

0745. Dreifuss, Erwin Manuel. Die Familiennamen der Juden unter besonderer Berücksichtigung der Verhältnisse in Baden zu Anfang des 19. Jahrhunderts. Ein Beitrag zur Geschichte der Emanzipation. Frankfurt a.M., 1927. 143 p.
Review:
Bloch, Joseph. Univers Israélite 83:1 (1927-28): 13-15.

0746. Dreifuss, Erwin Manuel. Die Namen der Juden in Baden zu Anfang des 19. Jahrhunderts. 1925. 210 ℓ.
Dissertation, Heidelberg.
cf. Jüdische Familien-Forschung Heft 2 (1925): 42.

0747. Freund, Ismar. Die Emanzipation der Juden in Preussen unter besonderer Berücksichtigung des Gesetzes vom 11. März 1812. Ein Beitrag zur Rechtsgeschichte der Juden in Preussen. Berlin, 1912. 2 vol.

0748. Germania Judaica. Breslau, etc., 1934- . vol.

0749. Gottschald, Max. Deutsche Namenkunde; Unsere Familiennamen nach ihrer Entstehung und Bedeutung. 3., verm. Aufl. Berlin, 1954. 630 p.
Die Judennamen: p. 123-127.

0750. Grohne, Ernst. Die Hausnamen und Hauszeichen; Ihre Geschichte, Verbreitung und Einwirkung auf die Bildung der Familien- und Gassennamen. Göttingen, 1912. 214 p.
Der Einfluss der Hausnamen auf die Bildung der jüdischen Familiennamen: p. 149-156.

0751. Grosser, Dorothy. A Bibliography of German Personal Names. 1934. 81 ℓ.
Unpublished typescript, University of Chicago.

0752. Güdemann, Moritz. Geschichte des Erziehungswesens und der Cultur der abendländischen Juden während des Mittelalters und der neueren Zeit. Wien, 1888. 3 vol.
Jüdische Vornamen: vol. 3, p. 103-110.

0753. Haarbleicher, Moses M. Zwei Epochen aus der Geschichte der Deutsch-Israelitischen Gemeinde in Hamburg. Hamburg, 1867. 511 p.
Consult index under "Familien-Namen".

0754. Heintze, Albert, and Cascorbi, Paul. Die deutschen Familiennamen, geschichtlich, geographisch, sprachlich. 7., sehr verb. und verm. Aufl. Halle, 1933. 536 p.
Jüdische Namen: p. 74-77.

0755. Hertel, Engelbert. Die deutschen Familiennamen. Ihre Herkunft und ihre Erklärung auf Grund der Namenvergleichung. Bremen, 1935. 164 p.
Judennamen: p. 83-89.

0756. Human, Armin. Geschichte der Juden im Herzogtum S.-Meiningen-Hildburghausen. Hildburghausen, 1898. 157 p.
No more published.
Familiennamen: p. 34.

0757. Jeggle, Utz. Judendörfer in Württemberg. Tübingen, 1969. 361 p.
Namengebung: p. 115-118.

0758. Jellinek, Adolf. Worms und Wien. Liturgische Formulare ihrer Todtenfeier aus alter und neuer Zeit und Namensverzeichniss der Wormser Märtyrer aus den Jahren 1096 und 1349. Wien, 1880. 16, 6 p.

0759. Kessler, Gerhard. Die Familiennamen der Juden in Deutschland. Leipzig, 1935. 151 p.
Review:
Elbogen, J. Zeitschrift für die Geschichte der Juden in Deutschland 6 (1935): 57-58.

0760. Klarmann, Johann Ludwig. Zur Geschichte der deutschen Familiennamen. Lichtenfels, 1927. 76 p.
Familiennamen bei den Juden: p. 37-39.

0761. Kleinpaul, Rudolf Alexander Reinhold. Menschen- und Völkernamen. Etymologische Streifzüge auf dem Gebiete der Eigennamen. Leipzig, 1885. 419 p.
Review:
Steinschneider, Moritz. Litterarischer Merkur 5 (1885): 303-307.

0762. Klemperer, Victor. LTI; Notizbuch eines Philologen. Berlin, 1949. 287 p.
Namen: p. 82-91.

0763. Kober, Adolf. Grundbuch des Kölner Judenviertels 1135-1423. Ein Beitrag zur mittelalterlichen Topographie, Rechtsgeschichte und Statistik der Stadt Köln. Bonn, 1920. 232 p.
Zur jüdischen Namenskunde: p. 191-198.

0764. Levy, Max. Der Napoleonische Erlass von 1808, wegen der Vor- und Zunamen der Juden und seine Ausführung in Worms. Worms, 1914. 15 p.

0765. Lowe, William Henry. The Memorbook of Nürnberg, Containing the Names of the Jews Martyred in that City in the Year 5109 - 1349 A.D. ... London, 1881. 29 p.
Names of men: p. 20-22; Names of women: p. 23-27.

0766. Miedel, Julius. Die Juden in Memmingen. Aus Anlass der Einweihung der Memminger Synagoge. Memmingen, 1909. 177 p.
Jüdische Namen aus Schwaben: p. 104-114.

0767. Nebel, Theobald. Die Geschichte der jüdischen Gemeinde in Talheim. Ein Beispiel für das Schicksal des Judentums in Württemberg. Talheim, 1963. 64 p.
Jüdische Familiennamen: p. 22.

0768. Pollack, Herman. Jewish Folkways in Germanic Lands (1648-1808); Studies in Aspects of Daily Life. Cambridge, Mass., 1971. 410 p.
Consult index under "Name, changing of", etc.

0769. Prussia. Laws, statutes, etc. Edikt, betreffend die bürgerlichen Vorhältnisse der Juden in dem Preussischen Staate. Vom 11. März 1812. Berlin, 1812. 14 p.

0770. Rosenthal, Berthold. Heimatsgeschichte der badischen Juden seit ihrem geschichtlichen Auftreten bis zur Gegenwart. Bühl, 1927. 532 p.
Consult index under "Familiennamen".

0771. Salfeld, Siegmund. Das Martyrologium des Nürnberger Memorbuches. Berlin, 1898. 520 p.
Zur Kunde der Eigennamen: p. 386-418.

0772. Schiff, Adelheid. Die Namen der Frankfurter Juden zu Anfang des 19. Jahrhunderts. Freiburg i.B., 1917. 81 p.
Dissertation, Freiburg.

0773. Schilling, Konrad. Monumenta Judaica: 2000 Jahre Geschichte und Kultur der Juden am Rhein; Handbuch. Köln, 1963. 820 p.
Beschneidung und Namengebung: p. 112-114; Die Gesetzgebung der Jahre 1806 bis 1810: p. 438-439.

0774. Schwarz, Ernst. Deutsche Namenforschung. Göttingen, 1949-50. 2 vol.
Die Namen der Juden in Deutschland: vol. 1, p. 206-208.

0775. Silberstein, Siegfried. "Die Familiennamen der Juden unter besonderer Berücksichtigung der gesetzlichen Festlegung in Mecklenburg."
In: Festschrift zum 75-jährigen Bestehen des Jüdisch - theologischen
Seminars Fraenckelscher Stiftung. Vol. 2, p. 303-366. Breslau,
1929.

0776. Socin, Adolf. Mittelhochdeutsches Namenbuch nach oberrheinischen
Quellen des zwölften und dreizehnten Jahrhunderts. Basel, 1903.
787 p.
Juden: p. 561-564.

0777. Stauff, Philipp. Deutsche Judennamen. Zusammengestellt nach Ver-
zeichnissen jüdischer (Religions)-Behörden. Berlin, 1912. 49 p.

0778. Süssmann, Arthur. Das Erfurter Judenbuch (1357-1407). Leipzig,
1915. 126 p.

0779. Tänzer, Aaron. Die Geschichte der Juden in Jebenhausen und Göppin-
gen. Berlin, 1927. 573 p.
Liste der angenommenen deutschen Familiennamen, etc.: p. 36-43.

Germany: Nazi Period

0780. Ball-Kaduri, Kurt Jakob. Vor der Katastrophe; Juden in Deutschland
1934-1939. Tel-Aviv, 1967. 302 p.
"Israel" und "Sarah": p. 138-139.

0781. Deeg, Peter. Die Judengesetze Grossdeutschlands. Nürnberg, 1939.
245 p.
Das Jüdische Namensrecht: p. 87-92.

0782. Koerner, Bernhard. "Änderungen jüdischer Namen." Der Deutsche Ro-
land (1939): 9-12, 29-32, 55-56, 62-63, 69-71.
cf. Salo W. Baron. Bibliography of Jewish Social Studies, 1938-39
(New York, 1941), #4189.

0783. "Law Regarding Jewish Given Names (Second Decree for the Execution
of the Law of August 17, 1938)" Contemporary Jewish Record (Nov.
1938): 17-19.

0784. Massoutié, Louis. Judaïsme et Hitlérisme. Paris, 1935. 214 p.
L'Onomastique juive: p. 116-128.

0785. Rehm, Friedrich. "Jüdische Reste im deutschen Vornamengut." Weltkampf (1939): 211-216.

0786. Rennick, Robert M. "The Nazi Name Decrees of the Nineteen Thirties."
Names 18 (1970): 65-88.

0787. Warburg, Gustav Otto. Six Years of Hitler; The Jews Under the Nazi
Regime. London, 1939. 317 p.
Special names for Jews: p. 195-198.

0788. Weinryb, Bernard Dov. Jewish Emancipation Under Attack. New York,
1942. 95 p.
Jewish names, August 17, 1938 (Text of Second Decree for the Execution of the Law Regarding the Change of Family Names and Given
Names): p. 51-52.

0789. Arnold, Hermann. "Familiennamen der Juden in der Pfalz. Vor und nach dem Napoleonischen Erlass vom 30.5.1808." Pfälzer Heimat 21 (1970): 20-21.

0790. Bär, L. "Die Judennamen im Wandel der Zeiten. Aus einer oberpfälzischen Gemeinde nachgewiesen." Heimat und Volkstum 17 (1939): 33-46.

0791. Berlet, Eduard. "Aus der Geschichte der jüdischen Gemeinde zu Alzey. Ein Beitrag zur Sozialgeschichte jüdischer Familien Alzeys." Alzeyer Geschichtsblätter Heft 8 (1971): 19-34.
Namensänderungen: p. 22-24; Der Wechsel der Namen: p. 24-27.

0792. Brann, Markus. "Die schlesische Judenheit vor und nach dem Edikt vom 11. März 1812." Jüdisch-theologisches Seminar, Breslau. Jahres-Bericht (1912): 3-44.
Nahmen der in Breslau geduldeten Juden-Familien nebst Frau und Kindern: p. 35-44.

0793. Breslauer, Bernhard. "Ueber Namensänderung." Allgemeine Zeitung des Judenthums 59 (1895): 343-345, 356-358, 367-370.

0794. Brilling, Bernhard. "Aus alten Archiven. Unna - die Stadt mit der dreimaligen Namensannahme durch die Juden." Allgemeine Wochenzeitung der Juden in Deutschland, 9. Mai 1958, p. 5.

0795. Brilling, Bernhard. "Aus der Geschichte der Juden in Westfalen. I. Aus der Gemeinde Warburg: Familiennamen 1812." Mitteilungsblatt für die Jüdischen Gemeinden in Westfalen Nr. 2 (Juni-Juli 1959): 3-4.

0796. Brilling, Bernhard. "Die Familiennamen der Juden in Westfalen." Rheinisch-Westfälische Zeitschrift für Volkskunde 5 (1958): 133-162; 6 (1959): 91-99.

0797. Brilling, Bernhard. "Family Names Created Out of Various Initials." (Hebrew) Yeda'-'am vol. 2, no. 2-3 (1954): 127-129.
Silesia.

0798. Brilling, Bernhard. "Schlesische Ortsnamen als jüdische Familiennamen. Ein Beitrag zur Siedlungsgeographie der schlesischen Juden." Zeitschrift für Ostforschung 15 (1966): 60-67.

0799. Brilling, Bernhard. "Zur Geschichte der Juden in Warburg. I. Die Familiennamen der Warburger Juden (1807-1812)" Zeitschrift für die Geschichte der Juden 10 (1973): 49-72.

0800. Cuno, Klaus. "Namen Kölner Juden." Rheinische Heimatpflege (N.F.) 4 (1974): 278-291.

0801. "Curious Names of German Jews." Jewish Progress (San Francisco), 23 June 1882, p. 1.

0802. Dreifuss, Erwin Manuel. "Jüdische Namenforschung." Jüdische Familien-Forschung Heft 2 (1925): 41-42.

0803. Dreifuss, Erwin Manuel. "Die Namensänderungen der Mannheimer Juden zu Anfang 19. Jahrhunderts." Mannheimer Geschichts-blätter 26 (1925): col. 88-89.

0804. Dreifuss, Erwin Manuel. "Die 'schön klingenden' Judennamen." Jüdische Presszentrale Zürich 10, Nr. 457 (12. Aug. 1927): 5.

0805. Dreifuss, Erwin Manuel. "Der Zweck der Namengesetze, die um 1800 allenthalben den Juden auferlegt wurden." Jüdische Familien-Forschung Heft 9 (1927): 214-216.

0806. "Einige Bemerkungen über jüdische Namen." Allgemeine Zeitung des Judenthums 22 (1858): 282-284.

0807. Einstein, Simon, and Stein, Leopold. "Das Fest der Namensgebung zu Ulm." Der Israelitische Volkslehrer 6 (1856): 126-130.

0808. Epstein, Abraham. "Leontin und andere Namen in den 'Te'amim shel Humash' (Cod. Paris 358). Kabbala bei den deutschen Juden in früheren Zeiten." Monatsschrift für Geschichte und Wissenschaft des Judentums 49 (1905): 557-570.

0809. Gansen, Peter. "Die Familiennamen der rechtsrheinischen Juden." Jüdische Familien-Forschung Heft 16 (1928): 93-98.

0810. Gansen, Peter. "Familiennamen und Bürgerrecht der Juden mit besonderer Berücksichtigung des Siegkreises." Heimatblätter des Siegkreises 4 (1928):

0811. Goldschmidt, Max. "Ueber Entstehung und Änderung jüdischer Namen." Jüdisch-liberale Zeitung (Berlin), 2. Sept. 1927 (Beilage), p. 3. Nordhausen.

0812. Goldsmith, Milton. "What's in a Name?" Jewish Exponent (Philadelphia), 18 Sept. 1895, p. 6. Frankfurt a.M.

0813. Grunwald, Max. "Annahme deutscher Familiennamen." Mitteilungen zur Jüdischen Volkskunde Heft 43 (1912): 75-76. Paderborn, 1808.

0814. Güdemann, Moritz. "Christen- und Judennamen." Oesterreichische Wochenschrift 10 (1893): 932-935. Also in: Jüdische Presse 24 (1893): 543-545.

0815. "Häufigkeit einiger jüdischer Namen." Zeitschrift für Demographie und Statistik der Juden 1, Nr. 10 (1905): 14-15. Berlin.

0816. Heilig, O. "Jüdische Namen aus Schwaben." Mitteilungen zur Jüdischen Volkskunde Heft 37 (1911): 25-27.

0817. Horwitz, Ludwig. "Familiennamen aus Westpreussen." Jüdische Familien-Forschung Heft 3 (1925): 58-61.

0818. Horwitz, Ludwig. "Die Familiennamen Kasseler Israeliten." Jüdische Familien-Forschung Heft 12 (1927): 285-287.

0819. Horwitz, Ludwig. "Familiennamen Königsberger Israeliten. Nach einer amtlichen Liste des Polizeipräsidiums von 1812 mitgeteilt." Jüdische Familien-Forschung Heft 9 (1927): 212-214.

0820. Horwitz, Ludwig. "Hessische Familiennamen. Nach archivalischen Quellen." Jüdische Wochenzeitung für Kassel 5, Nr. 30 (1928): 1-2. cf. Zeitschrift für die Geschichte der Juden in Deutschland 1 (1929): 81.

0821. Horwitz, Ludwig. "Jüdische Familiennamen in der Heimat Mendels-
sohns." Anhaltische Geschichtsblätter (Dessau) Heft 6-7 (1931):
cf. Zeitschrift für die Geschichte der Juden in Deutschland 4 (1932):
164.

0822. Jacobson, Jacob. "Von Familiennamen und Staatsbürgerlisten." Jüdische Gemeinde, Berlin. Gemeindeblatt, 21. Apr. 1934, p. 3-4; 12. Mai
1934, p. 6; 19. Mai 1934, p. 4-5.

0823. Jacobson, Jacob. "Zur Annahme fester Familiennamen durch die Juden
in Württemberg." Jüdische Familien-Forschung Heft 2 (1925): 26-31.

0824. "Jüdische (Die) Namen." Allgemeine Zeitung des Judentums 68 (1904):
421-422.

0825. Kisch, Bruno. "Änderung der Judennamen in Grevenbroich und Wick-
rath (Rheinland) im Jahre 1808." Jüdische Familien-Forschung Heft 27
(1931): 392-398.

0826. Kober, Adolf. "Die Namensregister der Kölner Juden von 1808." Gesamtarchiv der Deutschen Juden. Mitteilungen 6 (1926): 41-53.

0827. Kracauer, Isidor. "Die Namen der Frankfurter Juden bis zum Jahre
1400." Monatsschrift für Geschichte und Wissenschaft des Judentums
55 (1911): 447-463, 600-613.
Republished, with additions and corrections, in: Archiv für Frank-
furts Geschichte und Kunst Folge 3, Bd. 3 (1913): 213-237.

0828. Kuby, Alfred Hans. "Die Namenswahl der Juden im Jahre 1808. Darge-
stellt am Beispiel der jüdischen Gemeinde Edenkoben." Pfälzer Heimat
21 (1970): 139.

0829. Kupka, Elisabeth. "Ueber Namensänderungen." Jüdische Familien-Forschung Heft 11 (1927): 280-285.
Breslau.

0830. Lamm, Louis. "Familien- und Ortsnamen." Jüdische Familien-Forschung
Heft 24 (1930): 318-320.
Erdlingen.

0831. Löwe, Heinrich. "Jüdische Namen vor preussischen Standesämtern."
Zeitschrift für Standesamtswesen 11 (1931): 377-378.
cf. Zeitschrift für die Geschichte der Juden in Deutschland 3 (1931):
293.

0832. Löwe, Heinrich. "Namensänderungen." Jüdische Gemeinde, Berlin. Gemeindeblatt, 6. Mai 1927, p. 110-112.

0833. Löwy, Albert. "German-Jewish Names." Jewish Messenger (New York),
8 May 1891, p. 5.
See also: Jewish Chronicle (London), 24 April 1891, p. 9; Jewish
Standard (London), 22 April 1891, p. 3-4; German text in: Jüdisches
Litteratur-Blatt 20 (1891): 92-93, 101.

0834. Markreich, Max. "A Note on Jewish Nicknames." Jewish Social Studies
20 (1958): 232-233.
Mecklenburg.

0835. Maschke, Alfred. "Jüdische Namen in Sachsen um 1870." Genealogie;
Deutsche Zeitschrift für Familienkunde Jahrg. 13, Heft 6 (1964):
344-346.
See also 0863.

0836. Meyer-Erlach, Georg. "Die 60 häufigsten jüdischen Familiennamen." Jüdische Familien-Forschung Heft 32 (1932): 501-503.

0837. Meyer-Erlach, Georg. "Ueber jüdische Familiennamen." Fränkische Monatshefte 8 (1929): 41-45, 87-89.

0838. Meyer-Erlach, Georg. "Zur Entstehung der jüdischen Familiennamen." Jüdische Familien-Forschung Heft 6 (1926): 142-144.

0839. Moses, Julius. "Vornamen-Studien." Allgemeine Zeitung des Judentums 66 (1902): 270-272.

0840. Moses, Leopold. "Jüdische Familiennamen." Jüdische Familien-Forschung Heft 3 (1925): 54-58; Heft 4 (1925): 89-91; Heft 5 (1926): 103-104; Heft 7 (1926): 163-166.

0841. Moses, Leopold. "Jüdische Familiennamen - deutsches Kulturgut." Jüdische Familien-Forschung Heft 32 (1932): 503-506.

0842. Rackwitz, Anna. "Die Familiennamen der Juden." Süddeutsche Israelitische Wochenschrft, 20. Juli 1924, p. 67-69. No more published?

0843. Rothschild, Samson. "Die Familiennamen der Wormser Israeliten im Jahre 1808." Vom Rhein 10 (1911): 2-3.

0844. Rothschild, Samson. "Namen der Juden." Historischer Verein "Alt-Wertheim." Jahrbuch 24 (1928): 65-68.

0845. Samuel, Gustav. "Familiennamen und Wanderung." Jüdische Rundschau, 15. Juli 1938, p. 4.

0846. Samuel, Gustav. "Hauszeichen als Judennamen." Jüdische Familien-Forschung Heft 36 (1934): 612-617.

0847. Samuel, Gustav. "Die Namengebung der westfälischen Landjudenschaft von 1808." Zeitschrift für die Geschichte der Juden in Deutschland 6 (1935): 47-51.

0848. Samuel, Gustav. "Wie entstanden die 'schönen' Namen der Juden?" Jüdisches Gemeindeblatt für Rheinland und Westfalen, 11. Feb. 1938, p. 51-52.

0849. Samuel, Gustav. "Woher stammen die Tiernamen der Juden?" Israelitisches Familienblatt, 14. Mai 1936.

0850. Samuel, Gustav. "Zur Entstehung deutscher Judennamen." Jüdische Familien-Forschung Heft 34 (1933): 542-547.

0851. Samuel, Gustav. "Zur Sippen- und Namenskunde der Priester- und Lewiten-Familien." Jüdische Familien-Forschung Heft 46 (1937): 842-847.

0852. Schmidt, W. "Straubinger Familiennamen in ihrer geschichtlichen Entwicklung bis zur Neuzeit." Straubinger Hefte 3 (1953): Straubinger Judennamen: p. 15-17.

0853. Schragenheim, Willi. "Hannoversche Judennamen." Jüdische Familien-Forschung Heft 37 (1934): 646-649.

0854. Setzepfandt, R. "Beitrag zur Geschichte der Juden in Oschersleben und zur jüdischen Namensforschung." Geschichts-blätter für Stadt und Land Magdeburg 40 (1905): 325-331.

0855. Stern, Moritz. "Die Ephraims in der Berliner Liste der im Jahre 1812 angenommenen Familiennamen." Jüdische Familien-Forschung Heft 1 (1924): 6-10; Heft 4 (1925): 82-86.

0856. Stern, Moritz. "Nürnberger Judenbürger-Listen des Mittelalters. Eine Quelle für Statistik und Namenkunde." Israelitische Religionsschule, Kiel. Bericht (1893-94): 4-24.

0857. Stern, William. "On the Fascination of Jewish Surnames." Leo Baeck Institute of Jews from Germany. Yearbook 19 (1974): 219-235. German text in: Udim 4 (1973): 121-139.

0858. "Ueber die Namen der Israeliten." Sulamith 6:1 (1820-21?): 73-86, 145-152.
Signed: S. von G.

0859. Weissbrodt, Ernst. "Die lippischen Judennamen 1810." Heimat und Scholle; Heimatkundliche Beilage zur Lippischen Staatszeitung (13. und 15. Aug. 1935).

0860. Weissbrodt, Ernst. "Die Namen der lippischen Juden 1810." Lippische Post Jahrg. 88, Nr. 260-265, 268-271, 275-276, 278-282, 285-288 (5. Nov. - 8. Dez. 1934).

0861. Werwach, Friedrich. "Familiennamen der jüdischen Gemeinde in Potsdam." Jüdische Familien-Forschung Heft 6 (1926): 135-136.

0862. Werwach, Friedrich. "Familiennamen in der jüdischen Gemeinde in Frankfurt a. O." Jüdische Familien-Forschung Heft 9 (1927): 210-211.

0863. Wilhelm, Fritz, and Lejeune, Eckart J. "Jüdische Vornamen der Assimilation." Genealogie; Deutsche Zeitschrift für Familienkunde Jahrg. 14, Heft 6 (1965): 576-579.
See also 0835.

See also 0060, 0977, 1102.

Great Britain

0864. Abrahams, Israel. "The Northampton 'Donum' of 1194." Jewish Historical Society of England. Miscellanies 1 (1925): lix-lxxiv. Name index to the Northampton 'Donum': p. lxxxi-lxxxvi.
See also 0871.

0865. Adler, Elkan Nathan. London. Philadelphia, 1930. 255 p. Consult index under "Names".

0866. "Anglo-Jewish Names." American Hebrew, 17 Aug. 1888, p. 21-22.

0867. Ben-Mowshay (pseud.). "New Names for Old - and the Law." Jewish Chronicle (London), Suppl. (Nov. 1929): vi-vii.

0868. "Changing Names." Jewish Chronicle (London), 8 Dec. 1916, p. 14.

0869. Davis, M.D. ["Troyt, an Anglo-Jewish Name"]. Jewish Quarterly Review (O.S.) 9 (1897): 361-362.

0870. Haes, Frank. "Moyse Hall, Bury St. Edmunds. Whence its Name - What it Was - What it Was Not." Jewish Historical Society of England. Transactions 3 (1899): 18-24.
Notes on the name Moyse, Mose, Mosse in use temp. 1560-1620: p. 23-24.

0871. Jacobs, Joseph. The Jews of Angevin England; Documents and Records. New York & London, 1893. 425 p.
Name list of English Jews of the twelfth century: p. 345-371.
See also 0864.

0872. Murchin, M.G. (pseud.). Britain's Jewish Problem. London, 1939. 223 p.
Jewish secrecy and its dangers: p. 24-37 (name-changing).

0873. Roth, Cecil. A History of the Jews in England. 3d ed. Oxford, 1964. 311 p.
Consult index under "Nomenclature, Anglo-Jewish".

0874. Roth, Cecil. The Jews of Medieval Oxford. Oxford, 1951. 194 p.
Nominal rolls of Oxford Jewry: p. 169-172.

0875. Samuel, Wilfred Sampson. "Sources of Anglo-Jewish Genealogy." The Genealogists' Magazine 6 (1932): 146-159.

0876. Snowman, Leonard Victor. "On Naming a Child." Jewish Chronicle (London), 19 Dec. 1958, p. 19.

0877. Stokes, Henry Paine. Studies in Anglo-Jewish History. Edinburgh, 1913. 304 p.
Jewish surnames: p. 63-67; Jewish double names: p. 68-71.

0878. Wasserzug, D. "Some English Jewish Names." Jewish Chronicle (London), 13 April 1906, p. 20.

Greece

0879. Dalven, Rachel. "The Surnames of the Jannina Jews." The Sephardic Scholar (forthcoming, 1977).

0880. Hasson, Aron. "The Sephardic Jews of Rhodes in Los Angeles." Western States Jewish Historical Quarterly 6 (1973-74): 241-254.
Family names: p. 252-254.

0881. Matsa, Ioseph. "The Names of the Yannina Jews." (Greek) In: Aphierōma eis tēn Epeiron ..., p. 95-102. Athinai, 1956.

0882. Moissis, Asher. Hē onomatologia tōn Hebraiōn tēs Hellados. Athinai, 1969.
In Greek.
cf. Steven Bowman. Towards a Bibliography of Greek Jewry (Athens, 1973), p. 21.

0883. Molho, Michael. Histoire des Israélites de Castoria. Thessaloniki, 1938. 135 p.
Origines onomastiques: p. 26-27.

0884. Molho, Michael. Usos y costumbres de los sefardíes de Salónica. Madrid, 1950. 341 p.
Onomástico de los sefardíes: p. 67-70; Origen de los nombres de familia: p. 70-74; Onomástico de los Aškenazíes: p. 74-75.

0885. Nehama, Joseph. Histoire des Israélites de Salonique. Paris, London, 1935-1959. 5 vol.
Onomastique: vol. 5, p. 32-35.

Holland, see Netherlands

Italy

0886. Barduzzi, Carlo Enrico. **Bibliografia ebraica e giudaica in lingua italiana, con aggiunte dei Cognomi portati da giudei residenti nel regno e Dodecaneso.** Roma, 1939. 133 p.

0887. Ben Jeudi (pseud.). "Cognome degli ebrei." **Giornale degli Eruditi e dei Curiosi** 4, N. 53 (1884): 27-30.

0888. Bernheimer, Carlo. **Paleografia ebraica.** Firenze, 1924. 423 p. Nomi di famiglia e nomi proprii degli ebrei: p. 181-190.

0889. Cassuto, Umberto. **Gli ebrei a Firenze nell'età del Rinascimento.** Firenze, 1918. 447 p. Onomastica: p. 231-244.

0890. **Cognomi (I) delle famiglie ebree in Italia.** Varese, 1938. 8 p. cf. Attilio Milano. **Bibliotheca historica italo-judaica** (Firenze, 1954), #426s.

0891. "Ebrei autorizzati ad assumere cognome ariano ai sensi dell'art. 3, legge 13-7-1939 - XVII,N,1055." **Il Problema Ebraico** (Firenze) anno 1, N. 3 (giugno 1942): 17-19; N. 4 (luglio 1942): 17-19; N. 5 (agosto 1942): 17-19; N. 6 (sett. 1942): 17-18; N. 7 (ott. 1942): 18-19.

0892. **Ebrei (Gli) in Italia. Chi sono, quanti sono, come si chiamano. Tutti i cognomi delle famiglie ebraiche.** Roma, 1938. 18 p. cf. Attilio Milano. **Bibliotheca historica italo-judaica** (Firenze, 1954), #424s.

0893. **Elenco dei cognomi ebraici.** Erba, 1938. 11 p. cf. Attilio Milano. **Bibliotheca historica italo-judaica** (Firenze, 1954), #425s.

0894. Falchi, Luigi. **La dominazione ebraica in Sardegna.** Cagliari, 1936. 18 p. Risonanze onomastiche: p. 10-13.

0895. "Famiglie ebree che hanno cambiato cognome prima dell'entrata in vigore delle leggi razziali." **Il Problema Ebraico** (Firenze) anno 1, N. 9 (dic. 1942): 19; anno 2, N. 1 (gennaio 1943): 19.

0896. Foa, Salvatore. "Cognomi ebraici in Piemonte nei secoli scorsi." **Lunario Israelitico** (Torino) (1932): 15-19. cf. Attilio Milano. **Bibliotheca historica italo-judaica** (Firenze, 1954), #760s.

0897. Milano, Attilio. "I cognomi degli ebrei romani nei secoli XVI e XVII." **Studi Romani** 10 (1962): 10-24.

0898. Milano, Attilio. **Il ghetto di Roma; Illustrazioni storiche.** Roma, 1964. 496 p. I cognomi: p. 415-434.

0899. Milano, Attilio. **Storia degli ebrei in Italia.** Torino, 1963. 727 p. Onomastica: p. 576-581.

0900. Milano, Attilio. **Storia degli ebrei italiani nel Levante.** Firenze, 1949. 226 p. Onomastica: p. 156-157.

0901. Pavoncello, Nello. Gli ebrei in Verona (delle origini al secolo XX).
Verona, 1960. 108 p.
Onomastica degli antichi ebrei veronesi: p. 63-72.

0902. Roblin, Michel. "La Démographie historique du judaïsme italien et
l'anthroponymie." Revue Anthropologique (N.S.) 1 (1955): 147-155.

0903. Roblin, Michel. "L'Histoire juive par les noms de famille. De Gua-
stalla à Volterra, le bi-millénaire des communautés italiennes."
L'Arche no. 54 (1961): 52-55, 95.

0904. Roth, Cecil. The Jews in the Renaissance. New York, 1965. 378 p.
Names: p. 19-20, 47.

0905. Schaerf, Samuel. I cognomi degli ebrei d'Italia. Con un'appendice
sulle famiglie nobili ebree d'Italia. Firenze, 1925. 89 p.

0906. Schaerf, Samuel. "Eigennamen der Juden Roms einst und jetzt." Jüdische Familien-Forschung Heft 12 (1927): 287-289.

0907. Schaerf, Samuel. "Die Familiennamen der Juden in Italien." Jüdische
Familien-Forschung Heft 48 (1938): 906-907; Heft 49 (1938): 921-924.

0908. Servi, Flaminio. "Cognomi dubbi." Vessillo Israelitico 31 (1883):
256-257.

0909. Servi, Flaminio. "Sui cognomi degl'israeliti italiani." Educatore
Israelita 14 (1866): 86-87.

0910. Servi, Flaminio. "Sui nomi." Educatore Israelita 29 (1881): 108-110.

0911. Shulvass, Moses Avigdor. "Ashkenazic Jewry in Italy." Yivo Annual of
Jewish Social Science 7 (1952): 110-131.
Names: p. 122-123.

0912. Shulvass, Moses Avigdor. The Jews in the World of the Renaissance.
Leiden, 1973. 367 p.
Names and surnames: p. 32-37.

0913. "Sui cognomi israeliti." Vessillo Israelitico 38 (1890): 341-342.

0914. Toaff, Ariel. Gli ebrei a Perugia. Perugia, 1975. 342 p.
Onomastica: p. 101-104.

0915. Torre, Lelio della. "Die jüdischen Vornamen in Italien." Jüdisches
Volksblatt 1 (1854): 147-148.

0916. Waagenaar, Sam. The Pope's Jews. LaSalle, Ill., 1974. 487 p.
Names of Roman Jews: p. 249-250.

0917. Zolli, Eugenio (formerly Israel Zoller). "Intorno ad alcuni nomi di
famiglie ebraiche di Ancona." Rassegna Mensile di Israel 7 (1932):
278-279.

0918. Zolli, Eugenio (formerly Israel Zoller). "Ueber italienisch-jüdi-
sche Familiennamen." Archiv für Jüdische Familienforschung, Kunstgeschichte und Museumswesen 2 (1917?): 31-34.

See also 0562-0585 passim.

Jugoslavia, see Yugoslavia

Lithuania

0919. Altbauer, Moshe. "On the Hebrew of Lithuanian Karaites and on Hebrew
       Elements in Their Language." (Hebrew) Leshonenu 21 (1956-57): 117-
       126; 22 (1957-58): 258-265.
       Names: vol. 21, p. 123-124.

0920. Ganuz, Yitshak. "The Origin of Jewish Family Names at Lidda (Lithua-
       nia)" (Hebrew) ha-'Avar 16 (1969): 192-204.

0921. Grodner, A. "Nicknames Used in Grodno." (Yiddish) Yidishe Shprakh
       11 (1951): 58-60.
       See also "Supplements to Grodno Nicknames" (Yiddish) by Hyman Shesh-
       kin, Ibid., 19 (1959): 100-101.

0922. Tomback, David. "Nicknames Used in Some Lithuanian Townships."
       (Yiddish) Yidishe Shprakh 12 (1952): 50-58.

       See also 0931.

Moravia, see Czechoslovakia

Netherlands

0923. Beem, H. "Joodse namen en namen van Joden." Studia Rosenthaliana
       3 (1969): 82-95.

0924. Koenen, Hendrik Jacob. Geschiedenis der Joden in Nederland. U-
       trecht, 1843. 519 p.
       Genealogische bescheiden van sommige voorname Geslachten: p. 3-4.

0925. Ornstein, S.L. "Jüdische Vornamen in Holland." Zeitschrift für De-
       mographie und Statistik der Juden 3 (1907): 137-138.

0926. Stichting Nederlands Joods Familiearchief. Nederlands Joods familie-
       archief. Amsterdam, 1967-70. 3 vol. in 1.

0927. Uitman, G.J. Hoe komen wij aan onze namen? Oorsprong en betekenis
       van onze familie- en voornamen. Amsterdam, 1941. 195 p.
       Geslachtsnamen, eigen aan Nederlandse Joden: p. 170-173.

Poland

0928. Altbauer, Moshe. "Dublety imion biblijnych w polszczyźnie." Ono-
       mastica 10 (1965): 196-203.

0929. Altbauer, Moshe. "Jeszcze o rzekomych 'chazarskich' nazwach miejs-
       cowych na ziemiach polskich." Onomastica 13 (1968): 120-128.

0930. Bystroń, Jan Stanisław. Nazwiska polskie. 2., popr. i rozsz.
       Lwów, 1936. 334 p.
       Nazwiska żydów, neofitów, ormian i tatarów polskich: p. 237-264.

0931. Centnerszwerowa, Róza. O języku żydów w Polsce, na Litwie i Rusi.
       Warszawa, 1907. 43 p.
       O języku żydów: p. 9-17.

0932. "Familiennamen (Die) der Juden Galiziens." Oesterreichische Wochen-
       schrift 33 (1916): 341.

0933. Güdemann, Moritz. "Jüdische Vornamen." Oesterreichische Wochen-schrift 29 (1912): 238-239.
See also "Der Wiener Oberrabiner - gegen biblische Vornamen!" Der Welt (Berlin) 16 (1912): 473-474.

0934. "Jüdische Namen in Warschau." Zeitschrift für Demographie und Statistik der Juden 5 (1909): 31.

0935. Opas, Tomasz. "Uwagi o wpływie języka polskiego na tworzenie się nazwisk żydów polskich (od drugiej połowy XVI do XVIII w.)" Żydows-ki Instytut Historyczny, Warsaw. Biuletyn 89 (1974): 47-63.

0936. Rothwand, Jacob. Imiona przez żydów polskich używane. Zebrał i ułozył w dwoch jezykach. Warszawa, 1866. 86 p.

0937. Sider, Fishl. "Borysław, Capital City of Jewish Nicknames." (Yid-dish) Yivo Bleter 44 (1973): 281-282.

0938. Stöger, Michael. Darstellung der gesetzlichen Verfassung der galizi-schen Judenschaft. Lemberg, 1833. 2 vol.
Annahme bestimmter Namen: vol. 1, p. 57-59.

See also 0955.

Portugal, see Spain and Portugal

Prussia, see Germany

Russia

0939. Amster, Moriz. "Zur Namengebung bei Juden." Der Urquell (N.F.) 2 (1898): 265.
Bukovina.

0940. Gessen, Iŭliĭ Isidorovich. "Imena sobstvennyĭà po russkomu zakono-datel'stvu." (Russian) In: Evreĭskaĭà éntsiklopedlĭà. Vol. 8, col. 149-153. S.-Peterburg, 1906? - 191-?

0941. Gessen, Iŭliĭ Isidorovich. "Pravo evreev na imena." (Russian) Novyĭ Voskhod (1910): No. 31, col. 22-24; No. 32, col. 19-21.

0942. Güdemann, Moritz. "Verbot christlicher Namen für Juden in Russland." Oesterreichische Wochenschrift 28 (1911): 397.

0943. Harkavy, Abraham Elijah. "Jüdisch-chazarische Analekten." Jüdische Zeitschrift für Wissenschaft und Leben 3 (1864-65): 204-210, 286-292.
Die persönlichen Eigennamen der Chazaren: p. 204-207.

0944. Harkavy, Abraham Elijah. "Mittheilungen über die Chasaren." Russi-sche Revue 10 (1877): 310-324; 11 (1877): 143-167.
Personennamen bei den Chasaren: vol. 10, p. 318-324.

0945. Ikhilov, M.I. "Bol'shaĭà sem'ĭà i patronimiĭà u gorskikh evreev." (Russian) Sovetskaĭà Étnografiĭà (1950:1): 188-192.

0946. Kruglevich, I. "Familĭi i imena karaimov." (Russian) Evreĭskaĭà Starina 9 (1916): 317-319.

0947. Kulisher, I.I. Sbornik dlĭà soglasovaniĭà raznovidnosteĭ imen ...
Zhitomir, 1911. 138, 180, 144 p.
Review:
Weissenberg, Samuel. Mitteilungen zur Jüdischen Volkskunde Heft

45 (1913): 26-27.

0948. Levanda, Lev Osipovich. Polnyĭ khronologicheskiĭ sbornik zakonov i polozheniĭ, kasaíushchikhsíà evreev ... S.-Peterburg, 1874. 1158 p. See #59, 304, 510, 615, 945, 952, 959.

0949. Meltzer, Milton. World of Our Fathers; The Jews of Eastern Europe. New York, 1974. 274 p. Surnames: p. 38-39.

0950. Munitz, Benzion. "Identifying Jewish Names in Russia." Soviet Jewish Affairs 3 (May 1972): 66-75.

0951. Mysh, Mikhail Ignatevich. Rudkovodstvo k russkim zakonam o evreĭakh. 3d ed. S.-Peterburg, 1904. 550 p. Russkiĭ zakon o evreĭskikh imenakh: p. 30-31.

0952. Pogorel'skiĭ, Mesala V. Evreĭskiíà imena sobstvennyíà. S.-Peterburg, 1893. 134 p.

0953. Prostonarodnyíà evreĭskiíà imena, raspolozhennyíà v poríàdkíè russkago alfavita. S.-Peterburg, 1878. 16 p.

0954. Rabinovich, Osip A. Sochineniíà. S.-Peterburg, 1880-88. 3 vol. Sobstvennyíà imena evreev: vol. 3, p. 64-99.

0955. Rabinovitz, Eliezer Shlomo. "Jewish Family Names, Found Chiefly Among the Jews of Russia and Poland." (Hebrew) Reshumot 5 (1926-27): 295-323; 6 (1927-28): 324-358.

0956. Roblin, Michel. "Quelques remarques sur les noms de famille des Juifs en Europe Orientale." Revue Internationale d'Onomastique 2 (1950): 291-298.

0957. Steinschneider, Moritz. "Zur Namenkunde, mit besonderer Rücksicht auf Karaiten." Monatsschrift für Geschichte und Wissenschaft des Judenthums 31 (1882): 324-332.

0958. Weissenberg, Samuel. "Die Familien der Karäer und der Krimtschaken." Mitteilungen zur Jüdischen Volkskunde Heft 52 (1914): 99-109.

0959. Weissenberg, Samuel. "Familii karaimov i krymchakov." (Russian) Evreĭskaíà Starina 6 (1913): 384-399.

0960. Weissenberg, Samuel. "Imena íùzhno-russkikh evreev." (Russian) Étnograficheskoe Obozríèníe No. 96-97 (1913): 76-109.

0961. Weissenberg, Samuel. "Prozvishcha íùzhno-russkikh evreev." (Russian) Étnograficheskoe Obozríèníe No. 101-102 (1914): 78-105.

0962. Weissenberg, Samuel. "The Surnames of the Jews in the District of Elisabethgrad, Ukraine." (Yiddish) In: Yiddish Scientific Institute (Yivo). Filologishe shriftn. Vol. 1, col. 79-90. Vilno, 1926.

0963. Weissenberg, Samuel. "Yiddish Surnames in the Ukraine." (Yiddish) In: Yiddish Scientific Institute (Yivo). Filologishe shriftn. Vol. 3, col. 312-366. Vilno, 1929.

0964. Zhurakovski, Konstantin Stepanovich, and Rabinowitz, Eliezer Simcha. Polnoe sobranie evreĭskikh imen ... Suvalki, 1874. 79 p.

See also 0931.

Spain and Portugal

0965. Gottheil, Richard James Horatio. "The Jews and the Spanish Inquisition (1622-1721)" Jewish Quarterly Review (O.S.) 15 (1903): 182-250.
Index of names: p. 234-250.

0966. Kayserling, Meyer. "Notes sur les Juifs d'Espagne. Les Juifs de Barcelone." Revue des Études Juives 48 (1904): 142-144.

0967. Leite de Vasconcellos Pereira de Mello, José. Antroponimia portuguêsa. Lisboa, 1928. 659 p.
Nomes de judeus: p. 387-421.

0968. Loeb, Isidore. "Liste nominative des Juifs de Barcelone en 1392." Revue des Études Juives 4 (1882): 57-77.

0969. Miret y Sans, Joaquín, and Schwab, Moïse. "Documents sur les Juifs catalans au XIe, XIIe et XIIIe siècles." Revue des Études Juives 68 (1914): 49-83, 174-197.
Noms: p. 188-197.

0970. Moll y Casanovas, Francisco de B. Els llinatges catalans (Catalunya, País Valencià, Illes Balears); Assaig de divulgació lingüística. Palma de Mallorca, 1959. 445 p.
Noms hebreus: p. 67-69.

0971. Origen genealógico de algunos apellidos existentes en Mallorca e historia de los judíos de España. Origen, genealogía, pruebas de nobleza y blasones de los apellidos: Aguiló, Bonnín, Cortés, Forteza, Fuster, Martí, Miró, Picó, Piña, Pomar, Rey, Segura, Valls y Vives. ¿Tuvieron relación dichos nobles linajes con los hebreos? Valencia, 1965. 345 p.

0972. Quadrado, José María. "La judería de la capital de Mallorca en 1391." Museo Balear (2.a época) 4 (1887): 281-305.
Pobladores hebreos, nombre cristiano que adoptan, sus viviendas, y uso ulterior que respecto de ellas se proponen: p. 293-305.

0973. Roblin, Michel. "L'Histoire juive par les noms de famille; Sefarad, l'âge d'or des communautés espagnoles et portugaises." L'Arche no. 63 (1962): 47-49, 69, 71; 64 (1962): 42-45, 69.

0974. Schwarz, Samuel. Os cristãos-novos em Portugal no século XX. Lisboa, 1925. 110 p.
Nomes luso-hebraicos: p. 13-15.

0975. Velozo, Francisco José. "Alguns nomes de judeus portugueses dos séculos XIII a XV." Revista de Portugal 34 (1969): 126-140.

See also 0702, 0980-0990, 1118-1131, 1149.

Sweden

0976. Olán, Eskil. Judarna pa svensk mark. Historien om israeliternas invandring till Sverige. Stockholm, 1924. 204 p.
De svenska judarnas namn: p. 102-103.

Switzerland

0977.   Tobler-Meyer, Wilhelm. Deutsche Familiennamen nach ihrer Entstehung
        und Bedeutung, mit besonderer Rücksichtnahme auf Zürich und die Ost-
        schweiz. Zürich, 1894. 234 p.
        Juden-Namen: p. 182-198.

Turkey, see 1071-1075.

Ukraine, see Russia

Yugoslavia

0978.   Constantinov, D.H. "The Bulgarian Fascists and the Names of Jews and
        Macedonians." (Macedonian) Prilozi (Bitola) 2 (1961): 83-90.
        cf. Kirjath Sepher 36 (1960-61): 513.

0979.   Eventov, Yakir. Toldot Yehude Yugoslavyah. Tel-Aviv, 1971- .
        vol.
        In Hebrew.
        Names: vol. 1, p. 199.

Sephardic Names

0980.   Broussie de Chelminsky, Goldie. "Los apellidos sefaradíes." Tribuna
        Israelita (México) No. 252 (abril 1966): 7-9.

0981.   Cassuto, Alfonso. "Die Familiennamen der kreolischen Juden." Jüdi-
        sche Familien-Forschung Heft 23 (1930): 289-290; Heft 25 (1931): 326-
        328.

0982.   Emanuel, Yitsḥak Moshe. Mah rotsim u-mi atem ha-Panterim ha-sheḥo-
        rim bi-Medinat Yisrael. Ḥolon, 1971. 31 p.
        In Hebrew.
        Includes transcriptions of three radio broadcasts on Sephardic names.

0983.   Estrugo, José M. "Nombres y apellidos sefaraditas." Tribuna Israe-
        lita (México) No. 138 (junio 1956): 15-17.

0984.   Estrugo, José M. El retorno a Sefard; Un siglo después de la Inqui-
        sición. Madrid, 1933. 131 p.
        Nombres y apellidos sefarditas: p. 105-113.

0985.   Grünwald, Moriz. "Spanisch-jüdische Familiennamen." Jüdisches Lit-
        teratur-Blatt 23 (1894): 25-26, 30-31.

0986.   Henriquez Pimentel, M., and Cassuto, Isaac. "Sephardische familien-
        namen." In: Encyclopaedia Sefardica Neerlandica. Vol. 2, p. 135-
        142. Amsterdam, 1949-50.

0987.   Lévy, Sam. "L'Onomastique sépharadite." Judaïsme Sepharadi No. 25
        (1 jan. 1935): 6-7.

0988.   Millás y Vallicrosa, José María. "Desinencias adjetivales romances
        en la onomástica de nuestros judíos." In: Estudios dedicados a
        Menéndez Pidal. Vol. 1, p. 125-133. Madrid, 1950.

0989.   Roblin, Michel. "Les noms de famille des Juifs d'origine ibérique."
        Revue Internationale d'Onomastique 3 (1951): 65-72.

0990. "What's in a Name?" American Sephardi (Dec. 1966): 18; (June 1967):
67-68; (1968): 83-85; (Sept. 1969): 104-105; (Autumn 1971): 59-62;
(Winter 1973): 91-92; (Autumn 1975): 103-104.

Yiddish Names

0991. Altbauer, Moshe. "Od typu metronimicznego do 'pajdonimicznego'
(Przyczynki do onomastyki jidyszowej i nowohebrajskiej)" Onomastica
4 (1958): 355-364.

0992. Braude, Gershon Zev, and Segal, Berl. "Old Roots of Jewish Names and
of Yiddish Orthography." (Yiddish) Yidishe Shprakh 21 (1961): 21-24.

0993. Feinsilver, Lillian Mermin. The Taste of Yiddish. South Brunswick,
N.J., c1970. 437 p.
Special names: p. 52-54.

0994. Fischer, Jechiel. "Zur Erklärung einiger jüdischer Namen." In:
Festschrift für Leo Baeck, p. 151-160. Berlin, 1938.

0995. Golomb, Zebi Nisan. Shemot ha-anashim veha-nashim shebi-Yehudit mi-
lashon ha-kodesh. Vilna, 1905. 16 p.
In Hebrew.

0996. Hall, R.M.R., and Hall, Beatrice L. "Some Apparent Orthographic In-
consistencies in American Family Names of Yiddish Origin." Names 17
(1969): 250-262.
See also article by David L. Gold, Ibid., 19 (1971): 223-228.

0997. Harkavy, Alexander. Yiddish-English-Hebrew Dictionary. 2d ed., im-
proved and enlarged. New York, 1928. 583 p.
Yiddish names: p. 525-530.

0998. Schiper, Ignacy. "The Beginnings of Old Yiddish in the Light of
Onomastic Sources." (Yiddish) Yidishe Filologye 1 (1924): 101-112,
272-287.

0999. Sheshkin, Hyman. "Names in Various Expressions and Sayings." (Yiddish) Yidishe Shprakh 20 (1960): 94-100.

1000. Shpirn, Tsvi. "Proper Names and Their Importance in Yiddish." (Yid-
dish) In: Yiddish Scientific Institute (Yivo). Filologishe shriftn.
Vol. 2, col. 175-186. Vilno, 1928.
See also supplement by A.A. Roback, Ibid., Vol. 3, col. 375-378.
Vilno, 1929.

1001. Stankiewicz, Edward. "The Derivational Pattern of Yiddish Personal
(Given) Names." In: Conference on Yiddish Dialectology, New York,
1965. The Field of Yiddish; Studies in Language, Folklore, and Literature. Third Collection, p. 267-283. The Hague, 1969.

XVIII

Jewish Names: North Africa

1002. Abbou, Isaac D. "Histoire des noms et des prénoms des Israélites du
Maroc." Judaïsme Sephardi (N.S.) No. 32 (juil. 1966): 23-26.
English text in: The Alliance Review (Spring 1968): 35-36.

1003. Abbou, Isaac D. *Musulmans andalous et judéo-espagnols*. Casablanca, 1953. 432 p.
Réflexions sur les noms et prénoms des judéo-espagnols au Maroc: p. 389-400.

1004. Ben-Simon, Mas'ud Ḥai. *Shem ḥadash*. Cairo, 1917. 310 p. In Hebrew.

1005. Berghem, Paul. "Jewish Names of the Orient." *Reform Advocate* (Chicago), 21 July 1906, p. 722-723.

1006. Corcos, David. "Quelques aspects de la société juive dans le vieux Maroc; Les prénoms des Juifs marocains." *Folklore Research Center Studies* 3 (1972): 143-229.
Reprinted in the author's *Studies in the History of the Jews of Morocco*. Jerusalem, 1976.

1007. Corcos, David. "Réflexions sur l'onomastique judéo-nord-africaine." *Folklore Research Center Studies* 1 (1970): 1-27.
Reprinted in the author's *Studies in the History of the Jews of Morocco*. Jerusalem, 1976.

1008. Eisenbeth, Maurice. *Le Judaïsme nord-africain. Études démographiques sur les Israélites du Département de Constantine*. Constantine, 1931. 285 p.
Essai de classification des noms patronymiques juifs se rencontrant de nos jours dans le Département de Constantine: p. 126-163.

1009. Eisenbeth, Maurice. *Les Juifs de l'Afrique du Nord; Démographie & Onomastique*. Alger, 1936. 189 p.

1010. Goitein, Solomon Dob Fritz. *Jews and Arabs: Their Contacts Through the Ages*. New York, 1955. 257 p.
Names: p. 138-140.

1011. Goldberg, Harvey E. "Patronymic Groups in a Tripolitanian Jewish Village; Reconstruction and Interpretation." *Jewish Journal of Sociology* 9 (1967): 209-225.

1012. Goldberg, Harvey E. "The Social Context of North African Jewish Patronyms." *Folklore Research Center Studies* 3 (1972): 245-257.

1013. Hamet, Ismaël. "Les Juifs du Nord de l'Afrique (Noms et surnoms)" *Académie des Sciences Coloniales. Comptes rendus des séances. Communications* 10 (1927-28): 149-208.

1014. Hirschberg, Haim Zeev. *A History of the Jews in North Africa*. Leiden, 1974- . vol.
Names: vol. 1, p. 155-156.

1015. Laredo, Abraham Isaac. *Bereberes y hebreos en Marruecos. Sus origines, según las leyendas, tradiciones y fuentes hebraicas antiguas*. Madrid, 1954. 244 p.
Apellidos judíos de origen fenicio: p. 144-146; Nuevos aportes históricos de la onomástica: p. 158-162.

1016. Laredo, Abraham Isaac. "Fragments d'onomastique judéo-marocaine." *Tinga* (Tangier) No. 1 (1953): 36-53.
cf. Robert Attal. *Les Juifs d'Afrique du Nord; Bibliographie* (Jerusalem, 1973), #4767.

1017. Marty, Paul. "Folklore tunisien; L'Onomastique des noms propres de personnes." Revue des Études Islamiques 10 (1936): 363-432. L'Onomastique israélite: p. 379.

1018. Perez, Z.S. "Les Noms juifs nord-africains." L'Information (Tel-Aviv), 30 juil. 1957.
cf. Robert Attal. Les Juifs d'Afrique du Nord; Bibliographie (Jerusalem, 1973), #698.

1019. Poznański, Samuel. "Sur quelques noms propres dans des documents de la Gueniza." Revue des Études Juives 65 (1913): 40-46.

1020. Raccah, Gabriele. "L'origine di alcuni cognomi di ebrei tripolini." Israel (Firenze), 24 feb. 1938, p. 6-7.
cf. Robert Attal. Les Juifs d'Afrique du Nord; Bibliographie (Jerusalem, 1973), #1263.

1021. Slousch, Nahum. Hébraeo phéniciens et judéo-berbères: Introduction à l'histoire des Juifs et du judaïsme en Afrique. Paris, 1908. 473 p. Noms judéo-berbères: p. 469-470.

1022. Sutton, T. "Les Israélites tripolitains; Langue, coutume, noms et prénoms." Alliance Israélite Universelle. Revue des Écoles No. 8 (1903): 62-63.

1023. Trenga, Victor. "Essai sur les Juifs berbères; Contribution à l'onomastique judéo-berbère." Association Française pour l'Avancement des Sciences. Comptes rendus 51 (1927): 353-356.

1024. Vroonen, Eugène. Les Noms de personnes en Orient et spécialement en Égypte. Le Caire, 1946. 191 p.
Noms des israélites: p. 157-178.

1025. Zafrani, Haïm. Les Juifs du Maroc. Paris, 1972- . vol.
Études onomastiques: vol. 1, p. 229.

XIX

Jewish Names: Asia

Arabia

1026. Steinschneider, Moritz. "An Introduction to the Arabic Literature of the Jews." Jewish Quarterly Review (O.S.) 9 (1897): 224-239, 604-630; 10 (1898): 119-138, 513-540; 11 (1899): 115-149, 305-343, 480-489, 585-625; 12 (1900): 114-132, 195-212, etc.
On Arabic names of the Jews.

China

1027. Laufer, Berthold. "A Chinese-Hebrew Manuscript; A New Source for the History of the Chinese Jews." American Journal of Semitic Languages and Literatures 46 (1929-30): 189-197.

1028. Loewenthal, Rudolf. "The Nomenclature of Jews in China." Collectanea Commissionis Synodalis 17 (1944): 354-370.
Also published in: Monumenta Serica 12 (1947): 97-126.

India

1029. Bab, Arturo. "Jüdische Familiennamen in Südindien am Ausgange des 17. Jahrhunderts." Jüdische Familien-Forschung Heft 21 (1930): 217-220.

1030. Ezekiel, Moses. History and Culture of the Bene-Israel in India. Nadiad, 1948. 123 p.
Names of Bene-Israel taken after the names of the villages from which they came: p. 102-103.

1031. Lord, James Henry. The Jews in India and the Far East. Kolhapur, 1907. 120, 17 p.
Appendix II: A list of the majority of surnames of the Bene-Israel.

1032. Musleah, Ezekiel N. On the Banks of the Ganga; The Sojourn of Jews in Calcutta. North Quincy, Mass., 1975. 568 p.
Names: p. 81-83.

1033. Strizower, Schifra. The Bene Israel of Bombay; A Study of a Jewish Community. New York, 1971. 176 p.
Names: p. 56-58.

Israel

1034. Adler, Curtis. "Name Changes in Israel." Names 2 (1954): 38-39.

1035. Alpert, Carl. "Name-Changes Common in Israel as Newcomers Drop 'Jewish' Ones." Jewish Post and Opinion, 10 Feb. 1967, p. 7.

1036. Altbauer, Moshe. "Slavic Elements in Israeli Toponyms and Surnames." (Hebrew) Leshonenu la-'am 42 (1953): 13-20.

1037. Arikha, Jacob A. Beḥar lekha shem-mishpaḥah 'ivri. Jerusalem, 1954. 44 p. (Leshonenu la-'am, 51-52).
In Hebrew.

1038. Arikha, Jacob A. Nivḥar shem; Reshimat shemot peratiyim 'ivriyim. 2d ed. Jerusalem, 1959. 24 p. (Leshonenu la-'am, 28).
In Hebrew.
Originally published in 1952.

1039. "Biblical Names in Israel." Dor le Dor 1, No. 1 (Fall 1972): 26-27.

1040. Bič, Miloš. "Zur Theologie der israelitischen Personennamen." (Czech) Křest'anká Revue 21 (1954): 93-100, 125-132.
cf. Zeitschrift für die alttestamentliche Wissenschaft 69 (1957): 256.

1041. Bondy, Ruth. The Israelis: Profile of a People. New York, 1969. 319 p.
By no other name: p. 176-182.

1042. Brilling, Bernhard. "Die Hebraisierung unserer Namen." Mitteillungsblatt (Tel-Aviv), 10. Nov. 1948.

1043. Caine, Ivan. "Names in Agnon." Conservative Judaism 23 (Spring 1969): 25-41.

1044. Catane, Mochè. "Les Changements de noms en Israël." Par Paul Klein. Revue Internationale d'Onomastique 3 (1951): 301-313.

See also article with same title in: <u>Evidences</u> No. 25 (1952): 38-41.

1045. Dotan (Deutscher), Ahron. "On Changing Family Names." (Hebrew) <u>Leshonenu la-'am</u> 50 (1954): 17-21.

1046. Dotan (Deutscher), Ahron. "On Name Changing in Israel." (Hebrew) <u>Leshonenu la-'am</u> 30-31 (1952): 29-33.

1047. Eisenstadt, Sh. <u>Shemot nivḥarim le-yeladot</u>. Jerusalem, 1942. 26 p. In Hebrew.

1048. Eshel, Mosheh Ḥanina. <u>Shemot ha-mishpaḥah be-Yisrael</u>. Haifa, 1967. 177 p. In Hebrew.

1049. Even-Shoshan, Avraham. <u>Yalkut shemot peratiyim 'ivriyim, yashanim ve-ḥadashim</u>. Jerusalem, 1958. 77 p. In Hebrew.

1050. Gouldman, M.D. "The Reputed Wife's Surname. Zemulun v. Minister of the Interior & Rosenheim." <u>Israel Law Review</u> 2 (1967): 278-282.

1051. Gross, Moses David. "Choosing a Hebrew Family Name." (Hebrew) <u>Sinai</u> (Jerusalem) No. 220 (1955): 61-63.

1052. Harduf, David Mendel. <u>Otsar ha-shemot ba-sifrut ha-'ivrit uva-'itonut ha-Yisrae'elit</u>. Tel-Aviv, 1974. 290 p. In Hebrew.

1053. Jewish Agency for Israel. <u>5704, shenat hitazraḥut veha-shem ha-'ivri</u>. Tel-Aviv, 1944. 3 vol. In Hebrew. Vol. 2: <u>ha-Shem ha-'ivri</u>.

1054. Keneset Israel. General Council. <u>Tazkir ... 'al shitat ha-ketiv be-ha'atakat ha-shemot ha-ge'ografiyim veha-peratiyim</u>. Tel-Aviv, 1932. 91 p. In Hebrew. "Memorandum on the Method of Transliteration of Geographical and Personal Names." Second ed. published in 1938.

1055. Kessary, Ouri. "These are the Names of the Children of Israel." <u>Jewish Chronicle</u> (London), 27 Dec. 1957, p. 15, 23.

1056. Kosover, Mordecai. "The Change of Family Names in the State of Israel." (Hebrew) <u>Bitzaron</u> 26 (1952): 1-12, 96-102, 181-191; 27 (1952-53): 42-46, 199-210.

1057. Levensohn, Lotta. "The Name's the Thing. In Palestine They Reverse the Process of Name-Changing." <u>The New Palestine</u>, 26 Apr. - 3 May 1929, p. 369.

1058. Lipkin, Tsevi. "Choose a Hebrew Family Name, But ..." (Hebrew) <u>Leshonenu la-'am</u> 78-79 (1957): 30-33.

1059. Maass, Ernest. "Israel: New Names, Old Memories." <u>New York Times Magazine</u>, 19 June 1949, p. 27.

1060. Mikes, George. <u>Coat of Many Colors: Israel</u>. Boston, 1969. 157 p. Names: p. 75-76.

1061. "Names Law, 5716 - 1956." <u>Laws of the State of Israel</u> 10 (1955-56): 95-98.

1062. Nimtza-vi, Mordechai. <u>Beḥar lekha shem 'ivri!</u> Tel-Aviv, 1948-49. 67 p. In Hebrew. cf. <u>Kirjath Sepher</u> 27 (1950-51): 142.

1063. Palestine (Government). <u>Transliteration from Arabic and Hebrew into English, from Arabic into Hebrew, and from Hebrew into Arabic with Transliterated Lists of Personal and Geographical Names for Use In Palestine.</u> Jerusalem?, ₍1930 or 31?₎. 85 p.

1064. Rubin, Israel. "Changing Names in Ancient and Modern Israel." (Hebrew) <u>Yeda'-'am</u> 1, No. 7-8 (1951): 9-10.

1065. Talpimon, S. <u>Ketsad li-veḥor shem 'ivri?</u> Tel-Aviv, 1949. 78 p. In Hebrew.

1066. Wood, Frances Hariott. <u>Notes on Names in the Holy Land.</u> London, 1906. 208 p.

1067. "You Think It's Easy to Change Your Name in Israel?" <u>Jewish Digest</u> (July 1970): 65-68.

Kurdistan

1068. Sabar, Yona. "First Names, Nicknames, and Family Names Among the Jews of Kurdistan." <u>Jewish Quarterly Review</u> (N.S.) 65 (1974-75): 43-51.

Palestine, see Israel

Persia

1069. Landau, Alfred. "Die Namen der persischen Juden." Von M. Abeshus. <u>Mitteilungen zur Jüdischen Volkskunde</u> Heft 37 (1911): 28-29.

Syria

1070. Macalister, Robert Alexander Stewart. "Occasional Papers on the Modern Inhabitants of Palestine: Personal Names." <u>Palestine Exploration Fund. Quarterly Statement</u> (1904): 150-160; (1905): 48-61. Names of Jews and Jewesses in Damascus: (1905): 56-61.

Turkey

1071. Fahri, Findikoğlu Z. "Essai typologique sur les patronymes à Istanbul." In: <u>International Congress of Toponymy and Anthroponymy, 5th, Salamanca, 1955. Proceedings and Transactions.</u> Vol. 2, p. 325-332. Salamanca, 1958. (<u>Acta Salmanticensia: Filosofía y Letras</u>, Vol. 11, No. 2). Les patronymes des Juifs: p. 330-331.

1072. Franco, Moise. <u>Essai sur l'histoire des Israélites de l'empire ottoman depuis les origines jusqu'à nos jours.</u> Paris, 1897. 296 p. Origine des noms des Israélites de Turquie: p. 284-285.

1073. Franco, Moise. "Origin of Jewish Family Names in Turkey." (Hebrew)
       Luaḥ Erets-Yisrael 9 (1902-1903): 75-80.

1074. Goldman, Israel M. The Life and Times of Rabbi David Ibn Abi Zimra.
       New York, 1970. 256 p.
       Names: p. 144.

1075. Rosanes, Salomon Abraham. Divre yeme Yisrael be-Togarmah. 2d ed.
       Tel-Aviv, 1930. vol.
       In Hebrew.
       Jewish names: vol. 1, p. 203-316 passim.

Yemen

1076. Brauer, Erich. Ethnologie der jemenitischen Juden. Heidelberg,
       1934. 402 p.
       Der Namen der Jemeniten: p. 196-202.

1077. Goitein, Solomon Dob Fritz. "Nicknames as Family Names." American
       Oriental Society. Journal 90 (1970): 517-524.

XX

Jewish Names: United States

1078. Adamic, Louis. What's Your Name? New York, 1942. 248 p.

1079. Argus (pseud.). "Euphonic Nomenclature." American Hebrew, 25 May
       1888, p. 41.

1080. Caplan, Marvin. "The Caplan Theory of Names." Chicago Jewish Forum
       26 (1968): 198-200.

1081. "Changing Names." Jewish Messenger (New York), 3 July 1891, p. 4.

1082. "Changing Names." Jewish Messenger (New York), 10 Aug. 1894, p. 4.

1083. Cohen, Maurice. "Keeping Our First Names Jewish." United Synagogue
       Review (Summer 1969): 10-11.

1084. "Curious Changes in Names." Jewish Messenger (New York), 19 Aug.
       1898, p. 4-5.

1085. Doe, Jane (pseud.). "Concerning Hebrew Names." The Reflex (Brook-
       lyn) 3, No. 4 (Nov. 1928): 27-31.

1086. Duker, Abraham G. "Emerging Cultural Patterns in American Jewish
       Life." American Jewish Historical Society. Publications 39 (1949-
       50): 351-388.
       Names: p. 384-387.

1087. ₍Ford, Henry?₎. Aspects of Jewish Power in the United States. Being
       a Reprint of a Fourth Selection of Articles from The Dearborn Inde-
       pendent (Vol. 4 of The International Jew). Dearborn, Mich., 1922.
       246 p.
       The gentle art of changing Jewish names: p. 109-119 (Issue of 12
       Nov. 1921).

1088. Friedman, Lee M. "American Jewish Names." Historia Judaica 6
       (1944): 147-162.
       Reprinted in the author's Pilgrims in a New Land. New York, 1948.

73

1089. Glanz, Rudolf. "German-Jewish Names in America." Jewish Social Studies 23 (1961): 143-169.
Reprinted in the author's Studies in Judaica Americana. New York, 1970.

1090. Glanz, Rudolf. "Jewish Names in Early American Humour." In: For Max Weinreich on his Seventieth Birthday; Studies in Jewish Languages, Literature, and Society, p. 63-71. The Hague, 1964.
Reprinted in the author's Studies in Judaica Americana. New York, 1970.

1091. Glenn, Menahem G. "Name, Please?" Recall (Los Angeles) 2 (Winter 1961): 15-19.

1092. Glenn, Menahem G. "These are the Names of the Sons of Israel in America." (Hebrew) ha-Doar, 9 Jan. 1953, p. 161-162, 164.

1093. Horowitz, Chaim Morris. "The Estimated Jewish Population of New York, 1958: A Study in Techniques." Jewish Journal of Sociology 3 (1961): 243-253.
The Jewish name method: p. 245.

1094. "How New York Jews Come to Take Irish Names." The Hebrew (San Francisco), 10 Feb. 1905, p. 4.

1095. Hurwitz, Eliahu S. "The Current Fashion in Jewish Names." The Jewish Parent (Jan. 1965): 10-11, 31.

1096. "I Changed My Name." Atlantic Monthly (Feb. 1948): 72-74.
See also reply by David L. Cohn, "I've Kept My Name." Ibid., (Apr. 1948): 42-44; Shlomo Katz, "So You Changed Your Name." Congress Weekly (6 Feb. 1948): 8-9.

1097. Israel ben Maimon (pseud.) "Should We Retain Our Specifically Jewish Names-The Principal Breeders of Anti-Jewish Prejudice?" American Hebrew, 4 July 1919, p. 199-200.

1098. Kaplan, Nathan. "Irving, Seymour Popular Names 30 Years Ago." National Jewish Post and Opinion, 22 Jan. 1965, p. 3; 29 Jan. 1965, p. 10.

1099. Klonsky, Milton. "The Importance of Being Milton (That Talent Which is Death to Hide)" Commentary 14 (Oct. 1952): 362-368.

1100. Kugelmass, J. Alvin. "Name-Changing - And What It Gets You." Commentary 14 (Aug. 1952): 145-150.

1101. Levinson, Samuel J. "What's in a Name?" Jewish Herald (Melbourne), 19 Mar. 1909, p. 121.

1102. Maass, Ernest. "Integration and Name Changing Among Jewish Refugees from Central Europe in the United States." Names 6 (1958): 129-171.

1103. McDavid, Raven I., and Levin, Samuel R. "The Levys of New Orleans: An Old Myth and a New Problem." Names 12 (1964): 82-88.

1104. Marcus, Jacob Rader. The Colonial American Jew, 1492-1776. Detroit, 1970. 3 vol.
Garb and names: vol. 3, p. 1187-1194.

1105. Mencken, Henry Louis. The American Language; An Inquiry into the Development of English in the United States. 4th ed. New York, 1957-60. 3 vol. (Vol. 2-3 are Supplement 1-2).

Jewish surnames: Suppl. 2, p. 415-425; Jewish given names: Suppl. 2, p. 516-519.

1106. Ozick, Cynthia. "Geoffrey, James or Stephen." Midstream 3 (Winter 1957): 70-76.

1107. Parry, Albert. "Name-Changing Among American Jews." Jewish Tribune (New York), 4 July 1930, p. 1-2, 11-12; 1 Aug. 1930, p. 8, 11-13; 5 Sept. 1930, p. 3, 16.

1108. Roback, Abraham Aaron. "Name-Changing Among American Jews." Chicago Jewish Forum 19 (1960-61): 123-128.

1109. Roback, Abraham Aaron. "Sarah to Sylvia to Shirley; A Jew By Any Other Name." Commentary 2 (Sept. 1946): 271-274.

1110. Rosenthal, Erich. "The Jewish Population of Chicago, Ill." In: Rawidowicz, Simon, ed. The Chicago Pinkas, p. 9-112. Chicago, 1952. The name method: p. 33-34; The selection of Jewish names: p. 58-65.

1111. Roskolenko, Harry. "Names." Congress Monthly 42 (May 1975): 17-18.

1112. Shneyer, Pearl. "The Rite of the Hebrew Name." United Synagogue Review (Summer 1963): 14-15.

1113. Smith, Elsdon Coles. American Surnames. Philadelphia, 1969. 370 p. Jewish change of names: p. 30-34; Jewish surnames: p. 261-267.

1114. Smith, Elsdon Coles. New Dictionary of American Family Names. New York, 1973. 570 p. Jewish names: p. xxiv-xxv.

1115. Stern, Malcolm H. "The Function of Genealogy in American Jewish History." In: Essays in American Jewish History ..., p. 69-97. Cincinnati, 1958.

1116. Stungo, Symon. "Jewish Nomenclature." The Menorah (New York) 37 (Dec. 1904): 358-360.

1117. Tenenbaum, Samuel. "What's in a Name?" Jewish Tribune (New York), 17 Feb. 1928, p. 2, 16.

1117A Yaffe, James. The American Jews. New York, 1968. 338 p. Name-changing: p. 70.

See also 0996.

XXI

Jewish Names: South America

1118. Bab, Arturo. "Die Familiennamen der kreolischen Juden." Jüdische Familien-Forschung Heft 22 (1930): 255-261; Heft 24 (1930): 312-315.

1119. Bab, Arturo. "Die Namen der Juden in Argentinien." Jüdische Familien-Forschung Heft 13 (1928): 20-23; Heft 14 (1928): 51-55.

1120. Basadre, Jorge. "Apellidos españoles y portugueses en el Perú, de procedencia judía." Judaica (Buenos Aires) No. 51-53 (1937): 190-193.

1121. Böhm, Günter. Nuevos antecedentes para una historia de los judíos en Chile colonial. Santiago de Chile, 1963. 134 p.

Los apellidos de los marranos: p. 97-98; Apellidos sefardíes: p. 99-102; Apellidos judíos relacionados con "El Libro Verde del Aragón": p. 103-120.
Republished under title: "Los apellidos de los conversos." In: Comunidades judías de Latinoamérica (1966): 196-208.

1122. Böhm, Günter. Los judíos en Chile durante la colonia. Santiago de Chile, 1948. 141 p.
Los apellidos judíos: p. 25-26; Lista de apellidos judíos: p. 131-137.

1123. Emmanuel, Isaac S. "Het oude joodsche kerkhof op Curaçao." Lux (Curaçao) No. 4 (Jan.-Febr. 1944): 1-7.
De familienamen van de Joden op Curaçao: p. 6-7.
Paging determined from offprint.

1124. Emmanuel, Isaac S. Precious Stones of the Jews of Curaçao; Curaçaon Jewry, 1656-1957. New York, 1957. 584 p.
Forenames and surnames of the Jews of Curaçao: p. 97-99; Family names: p. 99-104; Names of the Jews of Curaçao: p. 556-558.

1125. Grandon, Alejandro Fuenzalida. "Apellidos judeo-españoles en América." Judaica (Buenos Aires) No. 97-98 (1941): 21-24.

1126. Grandon, Alejandro Fuenzalida. "Apellidos judíos en la historia de Chile." Judaica (Buenos Aires) No. 133-134 (1944): 37-44.

1127. Link, Pablo. El aporte judío al descubrimiento de América. Buenos Aires, 1974. 39 p.
Los patronímicos hispanos de los judíos: p. 34-37; Los patronímicos portugueses de los judíos: p. 37-38.

1128. Tibón, Gutierre. "Los apellidos judíos." Bené Berith (México) (dic. 1944): 77-79.

1129. Tibón, Gutierre. Onomástica hispanoamericana; Indice de siete mil nombres y apellidos castellanos, vascos, árabes, judíos, italianos, indoamericanos, etc. y un índice toponímico. México, 1961. 360 p.

1130. Wiznitzer, Arnold. "The Members of the Brazilian Jewish Community (1648-1653)" American Jewish Historical Society. Publications 42 (1952-53): 387-395.

1131. Wolff, Egon, and Wolff, Frieda. Judeus no Brasil imperial. São Paulo, 1975. 549 p.
Nomes portugueses: p. 232-236.

XXII

Individual Jewish Names

1132. (Abravanel) Blondheim, David Simon. "Notes étymologiques et lexicographiques." In: Mélanges de linguistique et de littérature offerts à M. Alfred Jeanroy, p. 71-80. Paris, 1928.
Abravanel: p. 71-74.

1133. (Abravanel) "True (The) Orthography of Abravanel's Name." The Menorah (New York) 27 (Nov. 1899): 287-290.
"From ancient publications and original documents in possession of Professor F. Rivas Puigcerver, Mexico."

1134. (Badchan) Löwe, Heinrich. "The Name Badḥan." (Hebrew) Yeda'-'am
No. 31-32 (1967): 66-71.

1135. (Ballin) Ballin, Jakob Moritz. "Der Familienname Ballin." Jüdische
Familien-Forschung Heft 5 (1926): 113-114.

1136. (Baneth) Brilling, Bernhard. "The Name 'Baneth.'" (Hebrew) Yeda'-
'am 1, No. 10 (1953): 99-101.

1137. (Barhun) Poznański, Samuel. "Il nome Barhun." Rivista Israelitica
7 (1910): 66-71.

1138. (Bar Kochba) Zeitlin, Solomon. "Bar Kokba and Bar Kozeba." Jewish
Quarterly Review (N.S.) 43 (1952-53): 77-82.

1139. (Berfet) Bloch, Isaac. "Le Nom patronymique de Ribasch." Revue des
Études Juives 10 (1885): 255.

1140. (Brandes) Simonsen, David. "Name und Abstammung von Georg Brandes."
Jüdische Familien-Forschung Heft 10 (1927): 231-232.

1141. (Breslauer) Brilling, Bernhard. "Breslau(er) als jüdischer Familienname." Breslauer Jüdisches Gemeindeblatt, 1937, Nr. 7, 9.

1142. (Chaim) Crammer, Simon. "The Origin of Chaim." Jewish Digest (June
1974): 58-60.

1143. (Chelbo) Poznański, Samuel. "Der Namen Chelbo." Zeitschrift für
Hebräische Bibliographie 8 (1904): 158-159.

1144. (Cohen) Nurnberg, Maxwell. ["Cohen - Kagan"]. Names 14 (1966): 192.

1145. (Dreyfus) Bréal, Michel. "Que signifie le nom de Dreyfuss?" Revue
Bleue 49:1 (1911): 417-418.

1146. (Dreyfus) "Familienname (Der) Dreifuss." Der Israelit (Frankfurt
a.M) 53, Nr. 22 (1912): 3.

1147. (Falk) Friedländer, Josua. "Der Name Falk bei den Juden in Märk.
Friedland." Jüdische Familien-Forschung Heft 8 (1926): 184-188.

1148. (Farisol) Gaster, Moses. "Faresol, nicht Feritsol." Monatsschrift
für Geschichte und Wissenschaft des Judentums 80 (1936): 489-490.

1149. (Franco) Franco, Arnold C. "An Inquiry into the Origin and Derivation of the Spanish Surname: Franco." Judaïsme Sephardi (N.S.) No.
32 (juil. 1966): 21-22.

1150. (Goetz) Birnbaum, Eduard. ["Der Eigenname 'Goetz'"]. Jüdisches
Litteratur-Blatt 23 (1894): 132.

1151. (Gordon) Gordon, Benjamin L. Between Two Worlds; The Memoirs of a
Physician. New York, 1952. 354 p.
The story of a name: p. 42-62.

1152. (Gordon) "Name (The) of Gordon." Jewish Chronicle (London), 18
Aug. 1905, p. 21.
See also M. Davis, "The Name of Gordon." Ibid., 1 Sept. 1905, p. 15.

1153. (Gordon) Rollin, A. Rapoport. "The Name 'Gordon' Among Jews."
Jewish Chronicle (London), 1 June 1934, p. 21.
See also rejoinder by M. Sanders, Ibid., 22 June 1934, p. 36; M.
Kliman, Ibid., 6 July 1934, p. 37; M.G. Liverman, Ibid., 20 July
1934, p. 30.

1154. (Gutmann) Bab, Arturo. "Gutmann - Guzmán." Jüdische Familien-Forschung Heft 28 (1931): 421.

1155. (Hai Gaon) Morag, Shelomo. "On the Form and Etymology of Hai Gaon's Name." (Hebrew) Tarbiz 31 (1961-62): 188-190.

1156. (Hitler) Rennick, Robert M. "Hitlers and Others Who Changed Their Names and a Few Who Did Not." Names 17 (1969): 199-207.

1157. (Ibn) Gaster, Moses. "Aben oder Ibn in hebräischen Namen?" Monatsschrift für Geschichte und Wissenschaft des Judentums 77 (1933): 210-211.
       See also rejoinder by David Herzog, Ibid., p. 386-387; Bruno Finkelscherer, Ibid., p. 467.

1158. (Ibn) Leshem, Haim. "Aben - Ibn." (Hebrew) Sinai (Jerusalem) No. 423-424 (1971): 57-78.

1159. (Ibn Baron) Stern, Samuel Miklos. "The Explanation of a Difficult Verse of Yehuda Halevi and the Spanish Etymology of the Name Ibn Baron." Jewish Quarterly Review (N.S.) 40 (1949-50): 189-191.

1160. (Isidore) Bacher, Wilhelm. "Le Nom d'Isidore porté par un ancien Juif." Revue des Études Juives 57 (1909): 102-104.

1161. (Isidore) Corley, Douglas Hilary. "Isidore in Jewry." American Journal of Semitic Languages and Literatures 37 (1920-21): 240.

1162. (Isidore) "Jüdische Vornamen." Allgemeine Zeitung des Judenthums 67 (1903): 29-30.
       Signed: J.C.

1163. (Isidore) Lamer, Hans. Wörterbuch der Antike. 3. Aufl. Stuttgart, 1950. 883 p.
       Isidore: p. 353.

1164. (Kanzi) Poznański, Samuel. "Il cognome Kanzi." Rivista Israelitica 9 (1912): 115-120, 212-213.

1165. (Kimhi) Aptowitzer, Vigdor. "Sur la pronunciation du nom Kimḥi." Revue des Études Juives 54 (1907): 63.

1166. (Lachmann) Brilling, Bernhard. "The Names Lachmann, Bettsack, Sanwil." (Hebrew) Yeda'-'am 2, No. 1 (1953): 13-15.

1167. (Loewengart) Loewengart, Stephan. "Der Familienname 'Loewengart.'" Israelitische Religionsgemeinschaft Württembergs. ⌐Halbjahresschrift⌐ (Sept. 1971): 29-30.

1168. (London) Chelminsky-Lajmer, Enrique. "London, Berlin and Other Jewish Surnames." Names 23 (1975): 59-60.

1169. (London) Czellitzer, Arthur. "Die Namen Landé und London." Jüdische Familien-Forschung Heft 46 (1937): 862.

1170. (Maram) Brilling, Bernhard. "Der Name Maram, Marum. Zur Geschichte der Familien Guggenheim, Weil und anderer Nachkommen des Meir von Rothenburg." In: Forschung am Judentum. Festschrift zum 60. Geburtstag von Lothar Rothschild, p. 99-125. Bern, 1970.

1171. (Maram) Brilling, Bernhard. "On the History of the Name 'Marum.'" (Hebrew) Yeda'-'am 2, No. 4-5 (1954): 232-233.

1172. (Meborak) Poznański, Samuel. "Il nome Meborak." _Rivista Israeli-tica_ 7 (1910): 171-179, 214-224; 8 (1911): 33.

1173. (Meisterlein) Herzog, David. "Die Träger des Namens 'Meisterlein' in der Steiermark. Eine Untersuchung zur jüdischen Gelehrtenge-schichte." _Monatsschrift für Geschichte und Wissenschaft des Juden-tums_ 79 (1935): 31-49.

1174. (Melchior) Scheil, Jean Vincent. "Melchior, Gaspar, Balthasar." In: _Florilegium ou recueil de travaux d'érudition dédiés à Monsieur le marquis Melchior de Vogüé_ ..., p. 551-554. Paris, 1909.

1175. (Mendelssohn) Schneider, Max Ferdinand. _Mendelssohn oder Bartholdy? Zur Geschichte eines Familiennamens._ Basel, 1962. 28 p.

1176. (Nadler) Cohen, L., and Kroner, Dr. "Der Ursprung des Namens 'Nad-ler.' Episode aus der Zeit der Judenverfolgung in Polen gegen Ende des XV. Jahrhunderts." _Jüdisches Litteratur-Blatt_ 14 (1885): 150-151, 165-166.

1177. (Oppenheim) Rapp, Eugen, and Böcher, Otto. "Bedeutende Träger der jüdischen Namen Oppenheim und Oppenheimer." In: _1200 Jahre Oppen-heim am Rhein; Festschrift_, p. 106-116. Oppenheim, 1965.

1178. (Peretz) Pribluda, A.S. "Imia i familiia Perez ... Avigdor." (Rus-sian) _Onomastica_ 18 (1973): 261-265.

1179. (Perwer) Boehmer, Julius. "Was bedeutet der Name Perwer?" _Jahres-bericht des Altmärkischen Vereins für Vaterländische Geschichte zu Salzwedel_ 45 (1927): 4-17.
cf. _Zeitschrift für die Geschichte der Juden in Deutschland_ 2 (1930): 323.

1180. (Pevzner) Pribluda, A.S. "O proiskhozhdenii familii Pevzner ... Shapiro." (Russian) _Onomastica_ 16 (1971): 225-232.

1181. (Remak) Kronthal, Arthur. "Der Name Remak." _Jüdische Familien-Forschung_ Heft 47 (1937): 872-876.

1182. (Spinoza) Gebhardt, Karl. "Der Name Spinoza." _Chronicon Spinozanum_ 1 (1921): 272-276.

1183. (Spinoza) Roth, Leon. "The Name Spinoza." _Chronicon Spinozanum_ 3 (1923): 348.

1184. (Spinoza) Waryński, T.; Myślicki, Ignace; and Gebhardt, Karl. "Le Nom de Spinoza." _Chronicon Spinozanum_ 2 (1922): 251-254.

1185. (Surinam) Dentz, Fredrik Oudschans. "The Name of the Country Suri-nam as a Family Name." _American Jewish Historical Society. Publica-tions_ 48 (1958-59): 19-27, 262-264.

1186. (Wahl) Wettstein, Feivel Hirsch. "Ursprung des Familiennamens Wahl." _Monatsschrift für Geschichte und Wissenschaft des Judentums_ 45 (1901): 92-94.

1187. (Wallach) Back, M. "Zur Herkunft des Namens 'Wallach.'" _Jüdische Familien-Forschung_ Heft 33 (1933): 530
See also additional material, _Ibid._, Heft 34 (1933): 551-557.

1188. (Zangwill) Kohut, George Alexander. "The Name Zangwill; A Study in Lexicography." _American Hebrew_, 16 Mar. 1900, p. 577.
Satirical.

Supplement

1189. Ben Sheviya, Eytan. "Your Hebrew Name." <u>Davka</u> (Los Angeles)
       (Spring 1974): 52-53.

1190. Greenfield, Eugene. "What's in a Name?" <u>Jewish Life</u> (New York)
       (Feb. 1962): 48-53.

1191. Levy, Solomon. "The Duplication of Names." <u>The Jewish Annual</u> (Lon-
       don) 9 (1946-47): 89-93.
       On names repeated in the same biblical verse.

1192. Minkoff, Harvey. "Surnames: A Key to Where Jews Lived and What They
       Did." <u>Di Yidishe Heym</u> 17, No. 4 (Winter 1975-76): 14-16 (English
       section.

1193. Sekles, Simon. "Jewish Names." <u>Jewish Messenger</u> (New York), 12 Feb.
       1875, p. 5.

1194. Winokur, Harvey Jay. <u>A Psychological Analysis of Jewish Life Cycle</u>
       <u>Liturgy</u>. 1976. 149 ℓ.
       Unpublished rabbinic thesis, Hebrew Union College-Jewish Institute of
       Religion (Cincinnati).
       Naming: ℓ. 98-111.

1195. Zimmels, Hirsch Jakob. <u>Magicians, Theologians and Doctors. Studies</u>
       <u>in Folk-Medicine and Folk-Lore as Reflected in the Rabbinical Respon-</u>
       <u>sa (12th - 19th Centuries)</u>. London, 1952. 293 p.
       Change of name: p. 143-144.

Appendix

Index of Norbert Pearlroth's
"Your Name" column, <u>Jewish
Post and Opinion</u>, Sept. 7,
1945 to Sept. 24, 1976.

Abady (7 Dec. 1951)
Abbady (7 Dec. 1951)
Abenyacar (27 July 1962)
Aberman (19 Dec. 1958)
Abidan (8 Aug. 1975)
Abidon (8 Aug. 1975)
Abkin (9 Mar. 1951)
Abrahamson (19 Dec. 1958)
Abramczyk (12 Oct. 1973)
Abrams (19 Dec. 1958)
Abrashkin (29 May 1953)
Abremel (12 Aug. 1966)
Achtentuch (14 Sept. 1956)
Ackerman (4 May 1956)
Ader (31 Jan. 1969)
Adress (13 Oct. 1967)
Afromel (17 Apr. 1964)
Agata (15 Nov. 1968)
Agron (26 Aug. 1960)
     (6 Apr. 1973)
Aguado (15 July 1955)
Ahl (6 Nov. 1959)
Akerman (4 May 1956)
Alembik (7 July 1972)
Aleph (19 Nov. 1965)
Alexander (8 Feb. 1946)
     (23 Mar. 1973)
     (23 May 1975)
Algus (20 Aug. 1954)
Allweiss (24 Aug. 1956)
Aloe (11 Nov. 1966)
Alper (20 Nov. 1959)
     (14 July 1967)
Alpern (5 Mar. 1954)
Alperovich (14 July 1967)
Alter (19 July 1957)
Altfield (31 July 1959)
Altneu (12 Mar. 1954)
Altney (12 Mar. 1954)
Altschul (15 Dec. 1961)
Altschuld (15 Dec. 1961)
Altschuler (23 Nov. 1945)
     (15 Dec. 1961)
Aluph (19 Nov. 1965)
Alyea (23 Jan. 1970)
Amarant (6 Apr. 1956)
Amdurski (5 Apr. 1968)
Amsel (14 Oct. 1949)
Amster (8 Mar. 1974)
Amter (5 Apr. 1968)
Ancier (31 Dec. 1971)
Andrussier (15 Apr. 1955)
Anger (25 Oct. 1963)
Anker (27 Feb. 1976)

Annenberg (2 Mar. 1973)
Annenburg (2 Mar. 1973)
Anolik (24 June 1955)
Anzicher (31 Dec. 1971)
Apatoff (6 Jan. 1961)
Apfelberg (28 Jan. 1949)
Apnopolin (4 Apr. 1958)
Appelbaum (14 Dec. 1945)
Appenfelder (30 Nov. 1951)
Apter (12 Jan. 1968)
Aranoff (10 Aug. 1951)
Aranoffsky (10 Aug. 1951)
Arbesfeld (9 Dec. 1955)
Arem (26 Jan. 1973)
Aren (26 Jan. 1973)
Arfa (6 Nov. 1959)
Arfiany (25 Jan. 1974)
Arfin (25 Jan. 1974)
Arian (31 Dec. 1954)
Arick (31 Oct. 1969)
Arkin (6 Apr. 1973)
Arkules (9 Oct. 1953)
Arkus (1 Feb. 1957)
Arkush (26 Aug. 1960)
Arnopol (3 Aug. 1956)
Arnsfelde (3 Aug. 1956)
Arnstein (7 Oct. 1966)
Aron (7 Aug. 1964)
Aronowitz (10 Aug. 1951)
Aronson (10 Aug. 1951)
Arotsker (20 Feb. 1959)
Asarch (5 June 1970)
Asch (9 June 1950)
Asguth (28 Jan. 1972)
Ashkenazi (2 Nov. 1951)
Ashkevich (23 June 1972)
Askevitch (23 June 1972)
Asner (9 June 1950)
     (11 Oct. 1963)
Aspis (15 May 1970)
Astruc (14 Dec. 1951)
Atlas (27 July 1973)
Atlin (28 Apr. 1967)
Auerbach (2 Jan. 1959)
     (2 Mar. 1962)
Austern (6 Apr. 1951)
Averbach (2 Jan. 1959)
Avigdor (14 June 1960)
Avkin (9 Mar. 1951)
Avromel (17 Apr. 1964)
Avrum (24 June 1966)
Avruskin (1 Aug. 1952)
Axelrad (25 Feb. 1972)
Axelrod (25 Feb. 1972)

Azarche (5 June 1970)
Azarow (31 Mar. 1972)

Bachur (7 Dec. 1956)
Backenroth (25 Mar. 1966)
Badanes (21 Apr. 1972)
Bader (27 Apr. 1962)
Baecker (4 Aug. 1972)
Baer (31 Mar. 1961)
Baerenstecher (9 Sept. 1966)
Bailen (18 May 1951)
Bajer (26 July 1957)
Bajor (26 July 1957)
Bajorek (26 July 1957)
Balaban (4 May 1962)
Balamut (4 Dec. 1959)
Balbus (26 Dec. 1969)
Baldinger (9 July 1971)
Baldkind (29 Aug. 1952)
Balitov (29 Feb. 1952)
Balsam (19 Sept. 1952)
Balsky (27 Jan. 1950)
Balter (22 Apr. 1966)
Balutow (29 Feb. 1952)
Banilower (24 June 1966)
Bank (27 Jan. 1961)
Banner (17 Apr. 1970)
Bar (30 June 1972)
Barak (13 June 1958)
Baram (21 Feb. 1958)
    (30 Aug. 1968)
Baratz (3 Apr. 1970)
Barber (27 Apr. 1951)
Barch (19 Apr. 1957)
Barcus (3 Nov. 1972)
Barell (14 Jan. 1972)
Barkoffsky (17 Sept. 1976)
Barkos (3 Nov. 1972)
Barkowski (17 Sept. 1976)
Barlaz (6 May 1966)
Barmad (16 Oct. 1964)
Barmak (28 June 1968)
Barmash (2 May 1969)
Barmat (16 Oct. 1964)
Baron (30 July 1954)
Barondes (15 Mar. 1946)
Barr (30 June 1972)
Barrash (7 June 1946)
Barrish (7 June 1946)
Barshay (19 Apr. 1957)
Barsky (22 May 1953)
Baru (17 Nov. 1967)
Barza (2 Nov. 1956)
Barzo (2 Nov. 1956)

Bash (3 Feb. 1950)
Bashein (10 Sept. 1954)
Baskin (27 Mar. 1964)
Baskind (22 Dec. 1950)
Bass (31 Aug. 1956)
Bassan (5 Jan. 1962)
Bassewitz (24 May 1946)
Bassin (10 Sept. 1971)
Bassini (5 Jan. 1962)
Baum (28 Dec. 1945)
Bayer (26 July 1957)
Baynish (14 Oct. 1949)
Bear (17 Aug. 1973)
Becher (7 Dec. 1956)
Bechor (29 Aug. 1952)
    (7 Dec. 1956)
Beck (1 Sept. 1950)
Becker (4 Aug. 1972)
Beduinek (11 May 1951)
Bedwinek (11 May 1951)
Beer (31 Jan. 1958)
Beerman (11 Sept. 1953)
Begelman (24 July 1964)
Behar (18 Mar. 1955)
Behrman (11 Sept. 1953)
Beifuss (20 Jan. 1950)
Beigelman (24 July 1964)
Beilin (18 May 1951)
Beilowitz (14 Nov. 1969)
Beiser (28 Dec. 1951)
Bekoff (16 Dec. 1949)
Belas (1 Feb. 1952)
Belenker (21 Oct. 1955)
Belinsky (19 June 1959)
Belmont (20 July 1962)
Belofsky (9 Aug. 1957)
Belostotzky (1 Feb. 1952)
Bemporad (4 Jan. 1974)
Bendel (28 Apr. 1972)
Benejam (30 Oct. 1959)
Benesch (14 Oct. 1949)
Benoudiz (23 Nov. 1973)
Benowitz (3 Feb. 1956)
Bensinger (16 Jan. 1959)
Bentwich (24 Oct. 1975)
Benudiz (23 Nov. 1973)
Benveniste (28 Oct. 1955)
Bereston (8 Jan. 1960)
Berger (6 Feb. 1970)
Berish (24 June 1949)
    (17 Aug. 1973)
Berkal (20 Dec. 1968)
Berkman (15 Jan. 1960)

Berkofski (17 July 1970)
Berkowicz (24 June 1949)
        (8 June 1951)
Berkowitz (24 Nov. 1950)
        (8 June 1951)
        (9 Dec. 1955)
        (15 Jan. 1960)
        (23 Feb. 1962)
Berl (14 Jan. 1972)
    (17 Aug. 1973)
Berlin (28 Dec. 1945)
Berlow (28 Dec. 1956)
Bermak (28 June 1968)
Berman (17 Aug. 1951)
        (4 Jan. 1952)
Bermish (2 May 1969)
Bernanke (17 June 1949)
Bernard (15 Mar. 1963)
Bernhard (31 Mar. 1961)
Bernick (12 Jan. 1973)
        (6 June 1975)
Bernik (12 Jan. 1973)
        (6 June 1975)
Berniker (12 Jan. 1973)
        (6 June 1975)
Bernstecker (9 Sept. 1966)
Bernstein (24 June 1949)
        (9 Dec. 1955)
        (23 Feb. 1962)
Berris (17 Aug. 1973)
Bertisch (9 Oct. 1959)
Beshar (29 Aug. 1952)
        (18 Mar. 1955)
Beskin (12 Oct. 1951)
Besneschuk (17 July 1970)
Bessel (4 Apr. 1952)
Besser (12 Mar. 1971)
Besserer (12 Mar. 1971)
Besunder (16 Dec. 1966)
Bezborodko (3 Mar. 1972)
Bezer (28 Dec. 1951)
Beznezchuk (17 July 1970)
Bialik (21 Dec. 1956)
Biback (27 Oct. 1950)
Bibick (27 Oct. 1950)
Biederman (24 Apr. 1953)
        (24 Jan. 1958)
Bienenstock (9 Jan. 1970)
Bienstock (9 Jan. 1970)
Bildhauer (23 May 1952)
Bililowsky (23 Dec. 1966)
Bilmes (16 Nov. 1973)
Bindler (22 May 1964)
Bing (1 July 1966)

Birenbaum (16 Nov. 1945)
Birkowski (17 July 1970)
Birnbaum (16 Nov. 1945)
Bisem (20 Nov. 1953)
Bisen (20 Nov. 1953)
Bitterman (24 Jan. 1958)
Bixhorn (19 Sept. 1958)
Blach (26 Feb. 1954)
Blacher (22 May 1970)
Blafer (20 Mar. 1970)
Blaffer (20 Mar. 1970)
Blank (21 Dec. 1956)
Blaser (11 Jan. 1946)
Blaugrund (14 Feb. 1958)
Bleich (13 Jan. 1961)
Bleicher (24 Nov. 1967)
Bleiweiss (30 Oct. 1964)
Bliden (25 Nov. 1955)
Blieden (25 Nov. 1955)
Bliedon (25 Nov. 1955)
Blitfeld (2 June 1972)
Blitstein (15 May 1953)
Bloch (26 Feb. 1954)
Bloomenkranz (4 Aug. 1967)
Blum (15 Feb. 1963)
Blumberg (18 Mar. 1949)
Blumenkranz (4 Aug. 1967)
Blumert (17 Dec. 1948)
Bluschein (4 May 1951)
Blustein (4 May 1951)
Bluval (31 Dec. 1948)
Bluwal (31 Dec. 1948)
Boaster (14 Sept. 1973)
Bobis (15 May 1959)
Bobroff (4 Feb. 1949)
Bockshorn (19 Sept. 1958)
Bodek (11 Oct. 1968)
Bodenger (13 Aug. 1971)
Bodenstein (14 Mar. 1952)
Bodner (23 Apr. 1971)
Boerne (15 Mar. 1963)
Bogolub (16 Mar. 1956)
Bogomilski (22 Dec. 1961)
Bogorad (18 Sept. 1959)
Bogumilski (22 Dec. 1961)
Bohrer (23 Apr. 1971)
Bokser (16 Oct. 1959)
Bolotin (13 Jan. 1950)
Bondi (23 Aug. 1963)
Bondy (23 Aug. 1963)
Bonem (12 Nov. 1954)
Borer (23 Apr. 1971)
Borg (9 June 1967)
Borgenicht (2 Nov. 1956)

Bork (3 Nov. 1950)
Borkowitz (18 Mar. 1955)
Bornkin (15 Mar. 1963)
Bornkind (15 Mar. 1963)
Borock (13 June 1958)
    (23 Jan. 1959)
Borodaty (18 Nov. 1949)
Borok (13 June 1958)
    (23 Jan. 1959)
Bortnik (8 Apr. 1966)
Bortschefsky (28 Sept. 1951)
Boses (23 Nov. 1956)
Boshesh (23 Nov. 1956)
Boster (14 Sept. 1973)
Bothshansky (19 Jan. 1951)
Botnick (17 Nov. 1950)
Bottinger (13 Aug. 1971)
Botwinnik (11 May 1951)
Boxer (19 Sept. 1958)
Boxerman (23 Sept. 1949)
Boyarsky (27 Dec. 1963)
Brady (24 Oct. 1958)
Brafman (17 Sept. 1971)
Bragarnik (17 Sept. 1954)
Brahinski (4 Sept. 1970)
Bram (6 Oct. 1972)
Bramson (1 Aug. 1975)
Brandeis (15 Mar. 1946)
    (15 Nov. 1963)
Brander (20 Oct. 1967)
Brandes (15 Mar. 1946)
Brandler (15 Aug. 1975)
Brandt (23 Sept. 1960)
Brateman (17 Mar. 1972)
Bratman (17 Mar. 1972)
Braude (6 Apr. 1951)
    (24 Oct. 1958)
    (3 Oct. 1975)
Braunscher (10 July 1964)
Braunstein (17 Nov. 1950)
Braus (24 Jan. 1969)
Brazina (2 June 1961)
Breger (17 Apr. 1964)
Breindel (10 Aug. 1973)
Breitrose (23 Aug. 1963)
Bremel (12 Aug. 1966)
Bremler (12 Aug. 1966)
Brender (20 Oct. 1967)
Brenner (3 Feb. 1950)
Breslauer (24 Jan. 1958)
    (19 May 1967)
Bresler (24 Jan. 1958)
Brettschneider (7 May 1954)
Breuer (17 Apr. 1964)

Brewda (6 Apr. 1951)
Brickenstein (14 Aug. 1970)
Bril (17 Feb. 1961)
Brill (17 Feb. 1961)
    (20 July 1973)
Brimm (14 Sept. 1956)
Brin (15 Mar. 1963)
Brinberg (15 Mar. 1963)
Brisamt (21 Apr. 1967)
Brock (26 Sept. 1969)
Brodsky (24 Oct. 1958)
    (15 Feb. 1963)
Brodt (24 Oct. 1958)
Brody (19 June 1953)
    (24 Oct. 1958)
    (15 Feb. 1963)
    (3 Oct. 1975)
Broitman (3 Dec. 1971)
Brok (26 Sept. 1969)
Brostoff (6 Mar. 1970)
Brownsher (10 July 1964)
Broza (24 Nov. 1967)
Bruckenstein (14 Aug. 1970)
Bruckstein (14 Aug. 1970)
Bruel (20 July 1973)
Brukstein (14 Aug. 1970)
Brummer (21 Oct. 1960)
Brunner (17 Apr. 1959)
Brusel (13 Apr. 1973)
Brussel (13 Apr. 1973)
Brust (21 Sept. 1973)
Brylawski (3 Oct. 1969)
Brylewski (3 Oct. 1969)
Brylowski (3 Oct. 1969)
Brzoza (24 Nov. 1967)
Buchbinder (22 May 1964)
Buchsbaum (20 May 1966)
Budgar (30 May 1969)
Budkarz (30 May 1969)
Budkowski (2 Apr. 1976)
Bufman (12 July 1957)
Bukatman (7 Feb. 1964)
Buksbazen (27 July 1951)
Bulmash (24 Apr. 1953)
Bulmus (24 Apr. 1953)
    (16 Nov. 1973)
Bunis (18 Jan. 1974)
Burdai (28 Sept. 1962)
Burman (4 Jan. 1952)
Bushman (13 Oct. 1950)
Busis (23 Nov. 1956)
Buxbaum (20 May 1966)
Byck (11 Mar. 1955)
Bykov (16 Dec. 1949)

Bzoza (24 Nov. 1967)

Calisch (29 Nov. 1963)
Candich (25 Apr. 1969)
Cardash (4 Nov. 1955)
Carmona (29 Aug. 1969)
Cartun (28 Dec. 1973)
Casato (21 Aug. 1953)
Cassuto (21 Aug. 1953)
Casuto (21 Aug. 1953)
Celnik (19 Nov. 1971)
Centurja (30 Jan. 1953)
Ceranko (13 Nov. 1964)
Chaber (14 Feb. 1964)
Chabinski (20 Aug. 1971)
Chahonoff (3 May 1968)
Chaiken (19 Dec. 1952)
Chaikin (19 Dec. 1952)
Chaim (2 Oct. 1959)
      (24 Oct. 1975)
Chait (10 June 1966)
Chaiyat (20 Oct. 1972)
Chajes (10 Sept. 1954)
Chak (31 Aug. 1962)
Chakin (31 Aug. 1962)
Chamelis (30 May 1969)
Chanen (7 Jan. 1955)
Chanin (24 Mar. 1950)
      (7 Jan. 1955)
      (22 Aug. 1975)
Chankin (24 Mar. 1950)
Chanoff (3 May 1968)
Chanovitch (22 Aug. 1975)
Chanovitz (4 July 1975)
Chanski (17 Dec. 1971)
Chansky (17 Dec. 1971)
Chaplik (9 Aug. 1968)
Charap (10 Dec. 1965)
Chardash (4 Nov. 1955)
Charmatz (16 Nov. 1956)
            (28 June 1957)
Charnes (30 Nov. 1951)
Charney (11 Dec. 1953)
Chasanoff (13 Oct. 1972)
Chaskin (22 Dec. 1972)
Chavis (6 Oct. 1950)
Chavkin (18 Aug. 1967)
Chayes (10 Sept. 1954)
Chazanov (13 Oct. 1972)
Chazen (24 Feb. 1956)
Chelemsky (19 Aug. 1966)
Chenchenski (31 Jan. 1958)
Chenskovitz (28 Sept. 1973)
Cherkaski (22 Jan. 1971)

Cherniack (7 Jan. 1972)
Chernik (7 Jan. 1972)
Chernin (17 Apr. 1968)
Chernoble (29 Jan. 1971)
Chernobyl (29 Jan. 1971)
Cherulnik (24 Feb. 1950)
Chinitz (15 May 1953)
Chmelnitzky (30 Jan. 1976)
Choffnes (22 July 1966)
Cholet (21 Aug. 1970)
Chomat (15 May 1970)
Choment (15 May 1970)
Chomont (15 May 1970)
Chonewitz (4 July 1975)
Chose (12 July 1957)
Choze (12 July 1957)
Chranovitch (22 Aug. 1975)
Christian (14 Mar. 1952)
Chroniek (13 Feb. 1953)
Chubinsky (20 Aug. 1971)
Chwediuk (11 Feb. 1966)
Chysosky (21 Sept. 1956)
Ciechanow (3 May 1968)
Ciechanowski (6 Jan. 1967)
Cik (5 Jan. 1973)
      (9 May 1975)
Civjan (11 Nov. 1966)
Clare (3 Jan. 1969)
Climans (24 Dec. 1948)
Clolek (5 Sept. 1958)
Cohen (24 Feb. 1950)
Copans (13 Jan. 1956)
Cosneck (24 May 1968)
Courshon (31 May 1957)
Cunix (23 Apr. 1954)
Cunzman (10 Jan. 1969)
Cutler (14 Feb. 1958)
Cwi (7 May 1971)
Cymring (28 Feb. 1964)
Cynaderka (12 Sept. 1958)
Cynkus (19 June 1970)
Cyranka (13 Nov. 1964)
Czerpowiecki (3 Oct. 1969)
Czifer (7 July 1950)
Cziporvetzky (3 Oct. 1969)
Czosnek (24 May 1968)

Daiches (18 Apr. 1958)
Daitch (25 June 1954)
      (30 Dec. 1960)
Dalkoff (23 Nov. 1973)
Danowitz (7 Nov. 1958)
Danto (27 Feb. 1959)
Darrish (29 Dec. 1967)

Datnoff (25 Apr. 1969)
Datnov (25 Apr. 1969)
Daub (5 May 1972)
Dauerman (19 Jan. 1973)
Davidson (3 Mar. 1961)
Dayan (29 Oct. 1948)
Dayenov (2 Sept. 1960)
Deener (10 Dec. 1971)
Deifik (29 Mar. 1946)
Dekovnick (10 Feb. 1956)
Deluganuga (2 Jan. 1970)
Del Vecchio (5 Oct. 1945)
Demb (14 Mar. 1969)
Dembitz (3 Sept. 1971)
Demblinger (3 June 1949)
Demchick (22 Feb. 1957)
Demian (22 Nov. 1968)
Demoratsky (4 June 1976)
Derechinsky (7 Apr. 1961)
Dereczynski (7 Apr. 1961)
Derey (7 Apr. 1972)
Deri (7 Apr. 1972)
Dermaszewski (24 Nov. 1972)
Desberg (23 Feb. 1968)
Desenberg (23 Feb. 1968)
Dess (19 June 1964)
Deutsch (25 June 1954)
        (30 Dec. 1960)
Deutscher (30 Dec. 1960)
Dewoskin (28 Sept. 1956)
Diament (24 Feb. 1956)
        (9 Nov. 1956)
Dick (10 May 1957)
Dicker (16 Dec. 1960)
Dickstein (10 Apr. 1970)
Diener (10 Dec. 1971)
Dienoff (2 Sept. 1960)
Dilean (28 Nov. 1952)
Dinov (2 Sept. 1960)
Dinzes (20 Apr. 1962)
        (17 Aug. 1962)
Disen (3 July 1970)
Dissen (15 June 1951)
Dizon (3 July 1970)
Djament (9 Nov. 1956)
Dlin (28 Nov. 1952)
Dlott (13 Feb. 1976)
Dluginoga (2 Jan. 1970)
Dockterman (12 Dec. 1969)
Docter (16 Apr. 1976)
Doctor (16 Apr. 1976)
Dodek (26 Jan. 1968)
Doginsky (8 Sept. 1967)
Dolgapiata (14 Aug. 1964)

Dolinsky (12 Sept. 1952)
Domoradzki (4 June 1976)
Donat (14 Apr. 1967)
Donath (27 Feb. 1959)
        (14 Apr. 1967)
Doncher (26 Dec. 1952)
Donder (22 Apr. 1955)
Dondis (28 Jan. 1972)
Donner (13 May 1949)
Dorner (28 Nov. 1969)
Dortig (3 June 1966)
Dortort (16 Oct. 1970)
Dortuar (16 Oct. 1970)
Dosianski (25 Feb. 1972)
Drach (19 Mar. 1971)
Drachman (23 Nov. 1951)
Dratwa (19 Dec. 1969)
Draznin (4 May 1956)
Drechsler (15 Mar. 1968)
Dreebin (18 Sept. 1964)
Dreher (15 July 1949)
Dreiblatt (25 Mar. 1966)
Dreier (15 July 1949)
Dreifuss (16 June 1972)
Dreizenstock (20 Apr. 1962)
Dresner (4 May 1956)
Dressler (15 Mar. 1968)
Dreyblatt (25 Mar. 1966)
Dreyer (15 July 1949)
Dreyfuss (16 June 1972)
Driks (9 May 1958)
Drobnes (25 June 1971)
Druckaroff (7 July 1967)
Drucker (27 May 1949)
Druckman (5 Apr. 1946)
Drucks (30 Sept. 1960)
Drukarov (7 July 1967)
Druks (30 Sept. 1960)
Druss (10 Nov. 1972)
Dryer (15 July 1949)
Dubin (15 Apr. 1966)
Duboisky (4 Nov. 1955)
Duchen (10 Dec. 1965)
Duchin (10 Dec. 1965)
Duchoviner (2 May 1958)
Duckstein (10 Apr. 1970)
Dudkevich (21 Jan. 1966)
Dudki (27 Feb. 1959)
Dudkiewicz (21 Jan. 1966)
Duga (13 Apr. 1951)
Duginski (8 Sept. 1967)
Dukat (1 Apr. 1966)
Duna (20 Mar. 1953)
Dunda (27 Feb. 1959)

Dundas (28 Jan. 1972)
Dunie (20 Mar. 1953)
Dunkelman (14 Sept. 1951)
Durchschlag (12 Apr. 1946)
Durmaschiv (24 Nov. 1972)
Duscansky (25 Feb. 1972)
Dutkiewicz (15 July 1960)
Dvorin (27 Oct. 1961)
Dvorkin (18 Sept. 1953)
Dvoshes (18 Apr. 1958)
Dvoshin (28 Sept. 1956)
Dvoshkin (28 Sept. 1956)
Dworaliski (26 Feb. 1971)
Dwoshkin (18 Apr. 1958)
Dyck (10 May 1957)
Dym (29 Oct. 1948)
Dzialowski (20 Mar. 1964)

Eber (1 Aug. 1969)
Eberman (19 Dec. 1958)
Eckstein (24 Sept. 1954)
Edelman (3 Mar. 1950)
Edels (17 Mar. 1967)
      (27 July 1973)
Edles (17 Mar. 1967)
Edlin (21 Apr. 1950)
Edry (7 Apr. 1972)
Efrom (29 Sept. 1950)
Eger (6 Sept. 1968)
Eggert (6 Sept. 1968)
Egoz (4 Feb. 1972)
Ehemann (1 Dec. 1967)
Ehrenfreund (19 Nov. 1954)
Ehrenfrucht (27 Sept. 1968)
Ehrenkrantz (8 Feb. 1952)
Ehrenkranz (25 Jan. 1957)
Ehrlich (3 Mar. 1967)
Ehrman (3 Mar. 1967)
Ehrmann (14 Nov. 1952)
Eichler (24 Apr. 1964)
Eidel (5 Aug. 1949)
Eigen (21 Oct. 1966)
Eiges (4 Oct. 1963)
Ein (28 Dec. 1951)
Einhorn (12 June 1970)
Einleger (20 Mar. 1964)
Einspruch (22 June 1973)
         (27 July 1975)
Einziger (9 July 1976)
Eisbart (9 Jan. 1976)
Eisenberg (1 Dec. 1950)
Eisenman (20 June 1952)
         (1 Dec. 1972)
Eisenmann (5 Nov. 1948)

Eisenstein (20 June 1952)
Eisic (22 Nov. 1963)
Eisman (1 Dec. 1972)
Eisner (11 Oct. 1963)
Eitel (5 Aug. 1949)
      (13 Feb. 1970)
Ejman (1 Dec. 1967)
Elchanan (31 Dec. 1954)
Elconin (31 Dec. 1954)
Elfman (12 Sept. 1975)
Elfus (21 Oct. 1949)
Elgart (9 Oct. 1970)
Elias (28 Feb. 1964)
Eliaszow (28 Feb. 1964)
Elkan (7 June 1946)
      (2 Jan. 1959)
Elkin (2 Jan. 1959)
Elkind (7 June 1946)
Elkins (2 Jan. 1959)
Ellenhorn (19 Feb. 1971)
Elman (31 Aug. 1951)
Elmen (31 Aug. 1951)
Elsner (2 Feb. 1968)
Emale (20 Apr. 1956)
Emmerich (25 May 1951)
Emrock (25 May 1951)
Ende (16 Sept. 1966)
Engelberg (7 Aug. 1953)
Engelhard (31 Mar. 1950)
Engelsberg (7 Aug. 1953)
Englander (3 Nov. 1950)
Engler (3 Dec. 1948)
Enker (27 Feb. 1976)
Epstein (28 Oct. 1955)
Erbsfeld (9 Dec. 1955)
Ergart (3 Mar. 1967)
       (9 Oct. 1970)
Erhardt (9 Oct. 1970)
Erhart (3 Mar. 1967)
Erler (12 July 1968)
Erlich (7 Aug. 1964)
Erteschik (5 Nov. 1971)
Estorick (14 Dec. 1951)
Estrin (6 May 1966)
Etra (8 May 1953)
Ettensohn (11 Dec. 1970)
Ezrochi (5 June 1970)

Faber (28 Nov. 1958)
Factor (14 Nov. 1958)
Faden (19 Apr. 1946)
Faktorov (14 Nov. 1958)
Falik (8 July 1966)
Falk (8 July 1966)

Falkenstein (27 Dec. 1968)
Falkowitz (7 Aug. 1953)
Familier (22 Mar. 1963)
Farber (24 Mar. 1950)
    (28 Nov. 1958)
Farkas (7 Apr. 1972)
Fassbender (22 May 1964)
Fast (16 Sept. 1960)
Favish (4 Dec. 1970)
Feder (7 Sept. 1951)
Federbusch (9 May 1958)
Federman (28 Mar. 1969)
Fediuk (11 Feb. 1966)
Fefer (16 Nov. 1973)
Feffer (21 Jan. 1949)
Feier (6 Nov. 1953)
Feifer (16 Apr. 1976)
Feig (21 May 1954)
Feige (4 Oct. 1963)
Feigel (5 Sept. 1969)
Feigenbaum (6 Nov. 1953)
Feigin (25 Apr. 1958)
Fein (30 July 1971)
Feinberg (22 Mar. 1946)
Feiner (26 Nov. 1954)
Feingold (20 Nov. 1970)
Feinstein (1 Mar. 1957)
Feintuch (9 Jan. 1959)
    (10 Apr. 1959)
Feist (16 Sept. 1960)
Feit (25 Jan. 1946)
    (26 May 1950)
    (17 Feb. 1956)
Feitel (26 May 1950)
    (17 Feb. 1956)
    (2 Oct. 1959)
    (14 June 1968)
Feitelberg (21 June 1946)
Feitelson (13 Nov. 1970)
Fekete (8 Aug. 1975)
Felberg (7 June 1957)
Feld (17 Oct. 1975)
Feldman (17 Oct. 1975)
Fell (25 June 1954)
Fellhandler (25 June 1954)
Fellman (25 June 1954)
Fellner (4 Nov. 1949)
Felltraeger (25 Jan. 1963)
Fellus (2 Jan. 1970)
Feltreger (25 Jan. 1963)
Fenchel (29 Dec. 1961)
Fenichel (29 Dec. 1961)
Fenster (23 Apr. 1976)
Ferdinand (20 May 1966)

Ferman (5 Aug. 1960)
Fern (4 Jan. 1952)
Fertel (23 Mar. 1956)
Fertig (10 Sept. 1976)
Fetterer (28 Mar. 1969)
Feuer (9 Nov. 1951)
Feuerstein (7 Sept. 1945)
    (25 Mar. 1949)
Feuerwerker (1 June 1973)
Fichtenzweig (5 Aug. 1966)
Fiedler (14 Dec. 1945)
Field (17 Oct. 1975)
Fieldman (17 Oct. 1975)
Fier (6 Nov. 1953)
Fierverker (1 June 1973)
Figarsky (15 Mar. 1968)
Figatner (12 Sept. 1958)
Fiks (16 Apr. 1954)
Fin (21 Aug. 1970)
Finander (28 Sept. 1962)
Finder (28 Sept. 1962)
Fine (30 July 1971)
Finger (21 Jan. 1972)
Fingerer (21 Jan. 1972)
Fingerhut (19 May 1950)
    (19 Aug. 1955)
Fingeroth (19 May 1950)
Fink (10 Oct. 1969)
Finka (26 Aug. 1966)
Finkel (30 Dec. 1955)
Finkelstein (16 May 1952)
    (30 Dec. 1955)
    (21 Dec. 1956)
Finkin (31 Mar. 1967)
Finko (26 Aug. 1966)
Finn (21 Aug. 1970)
Firda (23 Aug. 1957)
Firestone (7 Sept. 1945)
Firtha (23 Aug. 1957)
Fischbein (11 Apr. 1969)
Fischel (14 July 1950)
Fish (14 Feb. 1958)
    (4 Apr. 1958)
    (23 Mar. 1962)
Fishbein (11 Apr. 1969)
Fishel (12 Oct. 1956)
    (14 Feb. 1958)
    (4 Apr. 1958)
    (23 Mar. 1962)
    (29 Sept. 1972)
Fisheles (29 Sept. 1972)
Fishkin (19 Feb. 1954)
Fishkind (30 Dec. 1949)
Fishzohn (23 Mar. 1962)

Fitzig (5 Aug. 1966)
Fivozinsky (2 Dec. 1966)
Fogel (5 Sept. 1969)
Fontek (13 July 1951)
Forell (14 Feb. 1958)
Forman (26 Apr. 1946)
Forshberg (3 Aug. 1962)
Fortel (23 Mar. 1956)
Fortgang (29 Dec. 1950)
Flaedle (27 Nov. 1970)
Flatau (9 Sept. 1949)
Flax (5 Apr. 1968)
Flaxman (9 Dec. 1949)
Flaydl (27 Nov. 1970)
Fleischer (19 Apr. 1946)
          (7 July 1961)
          (18 Mar. 1966)
Fleischman (7 July 1961)
          (18 Mar. 1966)
Flieg (2 Feb. 1968)
Fliegel (6 Jan. 1950)
Fradkin (23 Mar. 1951)
Fram (24 June 1966)
Francik (19 Aug. 1966)
Frankel (15 Feb. 1946)
          (8 Dec. 1950)
          (7 Feb. 1958)
Fransig (19 Aug. 1966)
Frantzman (25 Jan. 1957)
          (28 June 1968)
Franzman (28 June 1968)
Frauwirth (23 Jan. 1959)
Freed (17 Aug. 1956)
Freides (28 June 1946)
Freilach (16 Mar. 1956)
Freiman (14 Mar. 1958)
Frey (31 Jan. 1964)
Friduss (28 June 1946)
Fried (17 Aug. 1956)
Friedberg (17 June 1955)
          (20 Dec. 1968)
Friedenberg (20 Dec. 1968)
Friedland (19 May 1950)
Friedman (1 Mar. 1946)
          (1 Aug. 1952)
          (12 June 1953)
          (17 Aug. 1956)
Frohwirth (23 Jan. 1959)
From (24 June 1966)
Fromberg (4 Nov. 1949)
Fromel (17 Apr. 1964)
Fromer (25 July 1969)
Fromm (11 Aug. 1950)
Frommer (25 July 1969)

Fromowitz (18 Dec. 1959)
Frosh (8 Feb. 1963)
Fuchs (7 Apr. 1950)
          (17 Apr. 1959)
Fuchsbrunner (17 Apr. 1959)
Fudym (19 Apr. 1946)
Fuerst (30 Sept. 1960)
Fuld (21 Oct. 1955)
Fulda (21 Oct. 1955)
Fuldauer (21 Oct. 1955)
Fulde (21 Oct. 1955)
Fulman (18 Aug. 1950)
Funkelstein (21 Dec. 1956)
Furman (26 Apr. 1946)
          (24 Dec. 1954)
Furst (30 Sept. 1960)
Futorian (27 May 1966)
          (24 Mar. 1967)
Futterman (8 Mar. 1957)
          (24 Mar. 1967)
Futterweid (1 May 1953)
Futterweit (1 May 1953)

Gabler (30 Jan. 1953)
Gabovitch (16 June 1967)
Gabowicz (16 June 1967)
Gai (7 Sept. 1956)
Gajewski (30 June 1967)
Galaif (10 Jan. 1969)
Galante (14 Jan. 1949)
Galantiere (17 Feb. 1961)
Galanty (14 Jan. 1949)
Gallay (17 June 1966)
Galunsky (8 June 1973)
Galwak (9 Mar. 1973)
Gam (9 Oct. 1964)
Gamzu (25 Aug. 1972)
Gannopolski (2 Apr. 1971)
Ganopolsky (2 Apr. 1971)
Gans (26 Nov. 1954)
          (17 Feb. 1961)
Ganz (17 Feb. 1961)
Garavoy (3 Nov. 1972)
Garbowski (3 Mar. 1972)
Garelick (29 Jan. 1954)
Garfinkel (11 Aug. 1950)
Garmaize (5 June 1964)
Gartenhaus (19 Dec. 1958)
Gawronski (28 Sept. 1948)
Gazen (24 Feb. 1956)
Gdalikovsky (31 Aug. 1962)
Geduld (3 June 1955)
Geffner (3 Feb. 1967)
Geifman (16 May 1969)

Geilfuchs (22 Dec. 1967)
Geilfuss (22 Dec. 1967)
Geist (28 Apr. 1964)
Gelb (21 Aug. 1964)
Gelfand (16 Mar. 1951)
Gelfant (17 Dec. 1971)
Gelfman (2 Nov. 1973)
Gelinchiski (24 Feb. 1961)
Geller (6 June 1952)
Gellerman (25 May 1951)
Gellman (18 Jan. 1946)
Gelman (27 May 1949)
        (31 Aug. 1951)
Gendel (17 Sept. 1954)
Gendelman (29 July 1966)
Gendin (8 May 1964)
Gennis (9 Oct. 1970)
Geratewohl (14 Sept. 1951)
Gerber (23 Apr. 1954)
Gerberg (30 Oct. 1959)
Gerchik (11 June 1976)
Gerka (17 Feb. 1961)
Germaize (5 June 1964)
Gerstein (8 Mar. 1974)
Gerstner (9 Nov. 1945)
Gerwitz (11 Nov. 1960)
Gesner (8 Feb. 1946)
Getmansky (30 Jan. 1976)
Gettleson (15 Feb. 1974)
Giblichman (19 Aug. 1955)
Gidwitzer (9 July 1971)
Giesser (22 Aug. 1975)
Gilalai (17 June 1966)
Gilfix (22 Dec. 1967)
Gilvarg (9 Mar. 1973)
Gimbel (9 Dec. 1966)
Gimmel (7 Oct. 1955)
Gimpel (9 Dec. 1966)
Gimpelson (9 Dec. 1966)
Ginsburg (12 May 1967)
Ginter (19 Dec. 1969)
Gisnir (24 May 1968)
Gisser (22 Aug. 1975)
Gitelson (15 Feb. 1974)
Gitlin (4 Jan. 1957)
        (3 Apr. 1959)
Gitt (23 June 1961)
Gittel (3 Apr. 1959)
Gittelman (14 June 1957)
Gittlemacher (21 May 1954)
Gittleman (21 May 1954)
Givelber (13 Feb. 1953)
Giziner (24 May 1968)
Gladke (5 Oct. 1973)

Glantz (2 Dec. 1949)
Glaser (28 Aug. 1970)
Glasman (22 July 1955)
Glass (30 Mar. 1951)
Glatt (18 Jan. 1957)
Glauber (12 Oct. 1973)
Glauberson (12 Oct. 1973)
Glazer (28 Aug. 1970)
Gleit (24 Mar. 1967)
Glick (2 July 1954)
        (7 Apr. 1967)
Glickman (2 July 1954)
        (7 Apr. 1967)
        (5 Nov. 1971)
Gloeckel (2 July 1954)
Gloger (27 Feb. 1970)
Gluck (2 July 1954)
Glueck (2 July 1954)
Glueckman (5 Nov. 1971)
Gluskoff (2 May 1952)
Glustoff (2 May 1952)
Gnippe (15 Feb. 1952)
Gochfeld (16 Dec. 1955)
Godlin (15 Jan. 1971)
Goitein (10 June 1966)
Goldberg (9 Mar. 1951)
Goldes (1 Aug. 1958)
Goldfeld (1 July 1960)
Goldfinger (18 Dec. 1953)
Goldich (1 Aug. 1958)
Goldin (1 Aug. 1958)
Goldman (28 Aug. 1953)
Goldmann (24 Dec. 1971)
Goldowitz (9 Sept. 1966)
Goldrosen (16 Oct. 1964)
Goldscheider (1 Feb. 1963)
Goldschmidt (20 Jan. 1961)
Goldsmid (20 Jan. 1961)
Goldsmith (20 Jan. 1961)
Goldstein (26 Aug. 1949)
        (19 Nov. 1954)
Goldsticker (30 July 1954)
Goldstock (30 July 1954)
        (15 Jan. 1960)
Goldwasser (30 Sept. 1966)
Goldwater (30 Sept. 1966)
Golinkin (31 Aug. 1973)
Golland (14 Aug. 1964)
Gollomb (16 Apr. 1976)
Gollstein (19 Nov. 1954)
Golonski (8 June 1973)
Golper (20 Oct. 1967)
Golub (3 Aug. 1973)
Golubchin (16 Mar. 1973)

Golubchin (2 May 1975)
Golubtsin (16 Mar. 1973)
Goodman (22 Mar. 1946)
      (9 Sept. 1949)
      (12 Nov. 1954)
      (14 Oct. 1955)
      (30 Dec. 1955)
Gorbach (2 Mar. 1962)
Gorbaty (31 Aug. 1951)
Gorchov (26 Dec. 1958)
Gordon (1 Oct. 1954)
Gorelick (8 Feb. 1952)
Gorelik (29 Jan. 1954)
Goren (21 Jan. 1966)
Gorenstein (2 Dec. 1955)
Gorfine (9 Aug. 1968)
Gorlik (8 Feb. 1952)
Gornitzky (19 Oct. 1973)
Gorowitz (11 Nov. 1960)
Gostryi (31 Aug. 1973)
Gottesman (29 Dec. 1961)
Gottlieb (16 Mar. 1956)
      (18 Sept. 1959)
Grab (7 Sept. 1973)
Gradwohl (14 Sept. 1951)
Graeber (10 Mar. 1961)
Grafpen (17 Nov. 1967)
Gralla (15 Nov. 1968)
Granat (26 Apr. 1968)
Granet (26 Apr. 1968)
Granovsky (21 Sept. 1951)
Granowsky (21 Sept. 1951)
Grau (9 Mar. 1973)
Graubart (18 Nov. 1949)
Graupen (17 Nov. 1967)
Grebelsky (22 June 1973)
      (27 July 1975)
Greenberg (12 May 1950)
Greenhut (26 Dec. 1952)
Greenwald (28 Apr. 1950)
Greif (28 Nov. 1952)
Greifenhagen (2 Jan. 1976)
Greisores (31 May 1968)
Greissler (17 May 1968)
Gribischock (31 Dec. 1971)
Gribochik (31 Dec. 1971)
Griefer (23 June 1972)
Grifenhagen (2 Jan. 1976)
Grinker (22 July 1966)
Griver (23 June 1972)
Grivois (7 Nov. 1969)
Grobiuch (9 Jan. 1959)
Grobtuch (10 Apr. 1959)

Gross (30 June 1950)
      (21 Dec. 1956)
      (1 Apr. 1966)
Grossberg (6 July 1951)
Grossinger (22 May 1970)
Grossky (19 July 1968)
Grosswirt (24 Aug. 1962)
Groszki (19 July 1968)
Gruber (17 Feb. 1950)
Gruendlich (21 Aug. 1959)
Gruenkern (22 July 1966)
Grumet (26 Oct. 1973)
Grummet (26 Oct. 1973)
Grunberg (12 May 1950)
Grundlich (21 Aug. 1959)
Grunis (22 Sept. 1967)
Grunwald (28 Apr. 1950)
Grushkin (14 Apr. 1961)
Grusin (18 Dec. 1970)
Gruska (9 May 1969)
Gruszka (9 May 1969)
Gubkin (4 Mar. 1949)
Gudger (11 Aug. 1967)
Gudis (17 Jan. 1969)
Guedger (11 Aug. 1967)
Guedser (11 Aug. 1967)
Gulko (24 Sept. 1954)
Gumprecht (9 Dec. 1966)
Gundersheimer (10 Dec. 1948)
Gunter (19 Dec. 1969)
Gunzburg (12 May 1967)
Gur-Arya (9 Mar. 1956)
Gurewicz (12 Mar. 1954)
Gurfein (9 Aug. 1968)
Gurievsky (18 Sept. 1959)
Gurland (24 Feb. 1967)
Gurvich (1 Mar. 1946)
      (11 Nov. 1960)
Gurwitch (12 Mar. 1954)
Guss (13 Dec. 1968)
Gute (3 Apr. 1959)
Gutherz (8 July 1966)
Gutkin (30 Nov. 1973)
Gutkind (8 Oct. 1954)
      (30 Nov. 1973)
Gutman (22 Mar. 1946)
      (12 Nov. 1954)
      (14 Oct. 1955)
      (14 May 1976)
Guttman (14 May 1976)
Guyes (10 Sept. 1954)
      (7 Sept. 1956)
Guysenir (22 Jan. 1960)

Guz (13 Dec. 1968)
Guze (27 May 1960)
Gwin (7 June 1968)

Haan (7 June 1946)
Haar (5 Mar. 1971)
Haas (11 Aug. 1972)
Haber (14 Feb. 1964)
Hack (14 Feb. 1964)
Hacken (18 Sept. 1953)
     (5 Sept. 1958)
Hadass (26 Dec. 1958)
Haeck (14 Feb. 1964)
Haffkine (18 Aug. 1967)
Hafkin (18 Aug. 1967)
Haft (27 June 1958)
Haimowitz (2 Oct. 1959)
     (2 Sept. 1966)
Halbreich (3 Dec. 1948)
Halfron (20 Nov. 1959)
Halpern (5 Jan. 1951)
     (5 Mar. 1954)
     (20 Nov. 1959)
     (14 July 1967)
     (20 Oct. 1967)
Hamada (3 Dec. 1965)
Hambro (24 Mar. 1961)
Hament (15 May 1970)
Hanau (7 July 1967)
Hancman (14 Dec. 1956)
Handmacher (24 Oct. 1969)
Handmaker (24 Oct. 1969)
Handsman (14 Dec. 1956)
Handswerker (19 July 1968)
Hankin (24 Mar. 1950)
Hannah (31 Dec. 1948)
Harber (13 Jan. 1961)
Harcak (3 Apr. 1970)
Harchik (3 Apr. 1970)
Harcik (3 Apr. 1970)
Harmatz (28 June 1957)
Harris (27 Jan. 1950)
Hartman (21 July 1967)
Hase (11 Aug. 1972)
Haspel (30 Mar. 1973)
Hatowski (30 Jan. 1959)
Hauben (7 Aug. 1959)
Haupt (11 Sept. 1953)
Hauptman (11 Sept. 1953)
Hauptmann (29 July 1949)
Hausner (23 Mar. 1962)
Havkin (9 Mar. 1951)
Hazen (24 Feb. 1956)
Hecht (6 Mar. 1953)

Hecht (12 Oct. 1956)
     (14 Feb. 1958)
     (4 Apr. 1958)
Hefferman (30 Dec. 1949)
Hefter (28 Aug. 1959)
Heiber (16 Jan. 1959)
Heiferman (30 Dec. 1949)
Heifetz (17 Dec. 1954)
Heilbronn (20 Nov. 1959)
Heilman (2 Oct. 1959)
Heilprin (20 Nov. 1959)
Heimerdinger (12 Mar. 1971)
Heimlich (21 May 1971)
Helbing (4 Jan. 1957)
Held (20 Mar. 1953)
Helfand (16 Mar. 1951)
Helfant (15 May 1959)
     (17 Dec. 1971)
Helfgott (21 Mar. 1958)
Helfman (2 Nov. 1973)
     (12 Sept. 1975)
Heller (6 June 1952)
     (22 Oct. 1971)
Hellman (18 Jan. 1946)
     (31 Aug. 1951)
Helphant (26 Nov. 1954)
Hendel (17 Sept. 1954)
     (8 May 1964)
     (29 July 1966)
Hendelman (29 July 1966)
Hendin (8 May 1964)
Henkin (29 Sept. 1950)
Hennenberg (10 Aug. 1956)
Hepner (22 Mar. 1957)
Heppner (22 Mar. 1957)
Hermele (27 Apr. 1973)
Hermelin (11 Aug. 1967)
Hermle (27 Apr. 1973)
Herrmann (7 Dec. 1951)
Herrschaft (17 Oct. 1969)
Herschlag (27 Mar. 1959)
Hersh (4 Oct. 1963)
     (10 Apr. 1964)
     (1 Nov. 1968)
     (13 Mar. 1970)
Hershaft (17 Oct. 1969)
Hershdorfer (24 June 1949)
Hershenshorn (4 Oct. 1963)
Hershenson (13 Mar. 1970)
Hershkowitz (6 June 1952)
Herstein (10 Apr. 1964)
Herz (1 Nov. 1968)
Herzman (21 July 1967)
Herzschlag (27 Mar. 1959)

Hessberg (30 Jan. 1970)
Heuer (9 May 1952)
Hidalgo (9 Jan. 1976)
Hildebrand (22 Mar. 1968)
Hillman (18 Jan. 1946)
        (31 Aug. 1951)
Hirsch (26 Apr. 1946)
        (9 Mar. 1956)
        (28 Feb. 1958)
        (8 July 1966)
        (7 Nov. 1975)
Hirschberg (7 Nov. 1975)
Hirschhorn (4 Oct. 1963)
Hirschl (27 Feb. 1953)
Hirschman (21 July 1967)
Hirschowitz (27 Nov. 1953)
Hirschson (13 Mar. 1970)
Hirsh (1 Nov. 1968)
Hittleman (14 June 1957)
Hochfeld (16 Dec. 1955)
Hochman (21 Aug. 1953)
Hochzeit (10 Dec. 1954)
Hofele (8 Feb. 1974)
Hofeller (8 Feb. 1974)
Hoffman (17 Mar. 1950)
Hofman (16 May 1969)
Hollender (6 Feb. 1976)
Hoos (11 Aug. 1972)
Horen (7 Dec. 1945)
Horenstein (2 Dec. 1955)
Horodner (4 June 1971)
Horovitz (10 June 1949)
Horowitz (1 Mar. 1946)
        (10 June 1949)
        (12 Mar. 1954)
        (11 Nov. 1960)
Horwitz (1 Mar. 1946)
Houpt (11 Sept. 1953)
Hrab (7 Sept. 1973)
Huberman (16 May 1952)
Hudes (17 Jan. 1969)
Huettner (27 Feb. 1970)
Hurowitz (12 Mar. 1954)
Hurschman (18 Dec. 1953)
Hurtig (1 Sept. 1967)
Hurwitz (10 June 1949)
Hutkin (8 Oct. 1954)
Hutschmuecker (30 Oct. 1970)
Hutschnecker (30 Oct. 1970)
Huttner (27 Feb. 1970)
Hyman (2 Oct. 1959)

Ifshin (7 Apr. 1967)
Ignatowski (1 Sept. 1972)

Ignotowsky (1 Sept. 1972)
Imber (26 June 1970)
Ingber (26 June 1970)
Intrator (7 Aug. 1964)
Introligator (19 May 1972)
Irom (11 Aug. 1972)
Isaacson (31 Aug. 1962)
Isacki (9 Dec. 1960)
Isdaner (23 Oct. 1959)
Isgur (23 July 1971)
Israelovitch (3 May 1968)
Isserles (22 Feb. 1946)
Italiaander (17 Oct. 1969)
Itkin (22 Sept. 1950)
        (11 Apr. 1958)
Itzhaki (9 Dec. 1960)
Itzkow (1 May 1953)
Ivker (7 Sept. 1962)
Ivler (5 Feb. 1971)
Iwker (7 Sept. 1962)
Iwler (5 Feb. 1971)
Iwshin (7 Apr. 1967)
Izraelowicz (3 May 1968)

Jablonski (26 Oct. 1973)
Jackel (8 July 1955)
        (29 Jan. 1960)
Jacobson (8 Sept. 1950)
Jacoby (16 June 1961)
Jaeckel (8 July 1955)
        (29 Jan. 1960)
Jaffe (3 June 1955)
        (18 Sept. 1964)
Jaffess (30 May 1958)
Jagielnicer (31 Jan. 1964)
Jagoda (12 July 1968)
Jagolinzer (31 Jan. 1964)
Jakobovitz (16 June 1961)
Jankel (29 Jan. 1960)
Janowicz (14 Sept. 1945)
Janowitz (14 Sept. 1945)
        (28 May 1976)
Jarnicki (20 Feb. 1970)
Jast (25 July 1969)
Jeffis (30 May 1958)
Jeruchemson (28 Oct. 1949)
Jeske (14 Sept. 1962)
Jessel (14 Sept. 1962)
Jezer (11 June 1954)
Joffis (30 May 1958)
Jolles (7 Mar. 1958)
        (11 Sept. 1959)
Jolofsky (20 Mar. 1964)
Joske (14 Sept. 1962)

Josman (7 Dec. 1973)
Josowicz (15 Sept. 1967)
Jospin (6 Mar. 1964)
Judash (31 Jan. 1969)
Judenfreund (10 May 1968)
Julish (6 Sept. 1963)
Jurinsky (2 Oct. 1959)
Jurjinsky (23 Dec. 1955)
Juster (3 Dec. 1971)
Justus (15 Feb. 1974)

Kabak (31 Mar. 1961)
      (18 July 1975)
Kabaker (10 May 1957)
Kabakoff (31 Mar. 1961)
Kabatchnik (18 July 1975)
Kablotsky (24 May 1957)
Kachinsky (8 Sept. 1967)
Kaczorowicz (24 Apr. 1970)
Kaczynski (8 Sept. 1967)
Kadish (16 June 1961)
Kadishevitz (16 June 1961)
Kagan (3 Feb. 1967)
Kahan (3 Feb. 1967)
Kahlenberg (8 Dec. 1961)
Kaiman (27 Jan. 1956)
Kaimen (27 Jan. 1956)
Kaiss (21 June 1968)
Kalait (10 Jan. 1969)
Kalb (18 Mar. 1966)
Kalich (29 Nov. 1963)
Kalisch (29 Nov. 1963)
Kallus (21 Sept. 1956)
Kalman (12 Apr. 1968)
Kalmanowitz (5 Feb. 1954)
Kalmes (29 June 1973)
Kaltena (18 Mar. 1966)
Kalwaryjski (11 Mar. 1955)
           (25 Feb. 1966)
Kamber (30 July 1971)
Kambjer (30 July 1971)
Kamel (27 Aug. 1971)
Kamiel (27 Aug. 1971)
Kaminsky (3 Feb. 1956)
Kamlet (9 Jan. 1959)
Kan (16 Apr. 1954)
    (19 Jan. 1962)
Kanagur (9 Jan. 1959)
Kananack (15 Sept. 1972)
Kanarek (19 Jan. 1962)
Kann (16 Apr. 1954)
Kannengiesser (16 Apr. 1954)
Kanner (16 Apr. 1954)
       (19 Jan. 1962)
       (6 July 1973)

Kantorowicz (16 Feb. 1951)
            (3 Nov. 1967)
Kanun (8 Feb. 1963)
Kaphan (8 May 1959)
Kapilian (17 Aug. 1962)
Kaplan (9 Nov. 1945)
       (15 Aug. 1952)
       (3 Oct. 1958)
       (17 Aug. 1962)
Kaplinsky (15 Aug. 1952)
Kaplitz (3 Apr. 1964)
Karaban (19 Jan. 1968)
Karabon (19 Jan. 1968)
Karachunski (13 Feb. 1976)
Karash (28 Aug. 1964)
Karashinski (2 Nov. 1973)
Karassick (28 July 1950)
Karaszynski (2 Nov. 1973)
Karawan (20 Jan. 1961)
Karelitz (3 Aug. 1973)
Karfiol (1 Dec. 1961)
Karfiul (1 Dec. 1961)
Karmona (29 Aug. 1969)
Karp (14 Feb. 1958)
     (4 Apr. 1958)
Karpel (12 Oct. 1956)
Karpoff (18 Sept. 1970)
Karpovetzky (5 Feb. 1960)
            (21 Feb. 1964)
Karpow (18 Sept. 1970)
Karr (30 June 1972)
Karrakis (10 Nov. 1950)
Karrer (30 June 1972)
Karsh (21 Apr. 1961)
Kartagener (14 Dec. 1956)
Kartenman (10 Mar. 1967)
Kartman (10 Mar. 1967)
Kartuis (28 Dec. 1973)
Kartupis (28 Dec. 1973)
Karzanevich (7 July 1950)
Karzenevitch (26 June 1964)
Kasdan (24 Apr. 1959)
Kashdan (18 Jan. 1952)
        (24 Aug. 1956)
        (24 Apr. 1959)
        (24 Sept. 1976)
Kaslowsky (7 July 1972)
Kaszinetz (2 Mar. 1951)
Katkin (8 Jan. 1960)
Katz (18 Nov. 1966)
Katzenelson (11 Sept. 1970)
Katziff (18 Mar. 1966)
Katzin (8 Sept. 1967)
Katzinsky (8 Sept. 1967)

Kaufman (5 Oct. 1956)
    (8 May 1959)
Kawaler (26 July 1957)
Kawarsky (8 Dec. 1967)
Kawenoki (9 Feb. 1968)
Kawin (16 Aug. 1968)
Kazdan (24 Aug. 1956)
Keim (10 Mar. 1950)
Keis (21 June 1968)
Kelman (12 Apr. 1968)
Kembler (20 Nov. 1953)
Kemelman (23 Apr. 1954)
Kemeny (14 Feb. 1969)
Kempler (20 Nov. 1953)
Kempner (18 Nov. 1955)
Kerbel (6 Apr. 1973)
Kesselhaut (27 Nov. 1959)
Kesselhauz (27 Nov. 1959)
Kessler (14 Feb. 1958)
    (29 Aug. 1975)
Kesten (18 Oct. 1963)
Kestenbaum (14 June 1957)
Kestlinger (17 Jan. 1964)
Ketcherovitz (24 Apr. 1970)
Keyfetz (17 Dec. 1954)
Keytigerutski (7 Nov. 1958)
Kiaz (27 Dec. 1963)
Kibel (21 Jan. 1972)
Kieval (28 Mar. 1958)
Kieve (14 Dec. 1973)
Kiewe (14 Dec. 1973)
Kijak (29 Mar. 1957)
Kilsheimer (9 Oct. 1959)
Kimchi (2 Oct. 1964)
Kimelman (22 Sept. 1972)
Kimmel (7 Oct. 1955)
Kimmelman (23 Apr. 1954)
Kimmelsderfer (7 Oct. 1955)
Kirchmayer (5 May 1961)
Kirchstein (13 Sept. 1968)
Kirmayer (5 May 1961)
Kirschen (13 Sept. 1968)
Kirstein (13 Sept. 1968)
Kirsten (13 Sept. 1968)
Kirzner (27 May 1966)
Kisselevich (17 Dec. 1965)
Kitain (14 Nov. 1969)
Kitan (14 Nov. 1969)
Kitay (15 Aug. 1975)
Kivel (28 Mar. 1958)
Klagsbrun (6 May 1949)
Klapholz (17 June 1966)
Klaristenfeld (19 June 1959)
Klashman (1 June 1951)

Klatzki (15 Dec. 1967)
Klausner (3 July 1959)
Kleban (18 Apr. 1969)
Klecki (15 Dec. 1967)
Klein (4 July 1952)
    (21 Dec. 1956)
    (1 Apr. 1966)
Kleinfeld (8 Apr. 1955)
Kleinmintz (24 Dec. 1948)
Klementynowski (25 Sept. 1970)
Kletzki (15 Dec. 1967)
Klewansky (3 Dec. 1954)
Klibansky (14 Aug. 1953)
Kligerman (5 Feb. 1960)
Klimenko (5 Feb. 1954)
Klinger (12 Feb. 1954)
    (26 Sept. 1958)
Klingher (26 Sept. 1958)
Klinghoffer (25 Feb. 1955)
Klinkner (18 Sept. 1970)
Klionsky (3 Dec. 1954)
Kliorytis (3 Jan. 1969)
Klitzman (25 Sept. 1959)
Klopman (2 Feb. 1951)
Klotzkin (15 Dec. 1967)
Knauer (17 Oct. 1958)
    (21 Aug. 1959)
Knisbacher (16 Feb. 1951)
Knollen (18 June 1971)
Knoller (18 June 1971)
Knur (17 Oct. 1958)
Kobrofsky (20 May 1960)
Kochnovar (27 Oct. 1972)
Kociol (29 Mar. 1957)
Kodner (12 Feb. 1971)
Koffler (11 July 1975)
Koffman (8 May 1959)
Koiler (15 Oct. 1954)
Kolodkin (4 Sept. 1953)
Kolodney (28 Jan. 1949)
Kolowski (23 June 1967)
Kolpienicki (4 Feb. 1972)
Kolponitzki (4 Feb. 1972)
Koltona (18 Mar. 1966)
Kominy (8 Dec. 1967)
Komisar (18 Dec. 1959)
Koner (6 July 1973)
Konowalow (22 Nov. 1968)
Kopeloff (8 Sept. 1950)
Kopelovich (25 Nov. 1949)
Kophans (13 Jan. 1956)
Kopkind (26 Oct. 1956)
Kopp (13 Jan. 1956)
Koppel (14 Aug. 1953)

Koppel (21 Feb. 1969)
Koreff (11 June 1954)
Korenbaum (20 Nov. 1970)
Korentayer (22 Feb. 1963)
Korf (11 June 1954)
Korff (11 June 1954)
Korkes (3 Sept. 1954)
Korklan (5 Jan. 1962)
Kornbaum (20 Nov. 1970)
Kornfeld (29 Apr. 1949)
Kort (16 Sept. 1966)
Kosch (30 Nov. 1956)
Kosches (15 Aug. 1952)
Kosherkevicz (11 Feb. 1972)
Kosowsky (26 Sept. 1958)
Kostman (11 Apr. 1969)
Koszarkiewicz (11 Feb. 1972)
Kotek (18 Nov. 1966)
Kotelshchik (17 Aug. 1956)
Kotik (18 Nov. 1966)
Kotler (8 Jan. 1971)
Kotlus (14 Feb. 1958)
Kotok (18 Nov. 1966)
Kotzin (8 Sept. 1967)
Kovensky (19 Oct. 1973)
Kovnator (11 Feb. 1972)
Kowarski (8 Dec. 1967)
Kozlowski (7 July 1972)
Kramarski (15 Jan. 1971)
Kramerofsky (7 July 1961)
Krantman (31 May 1968)
Krasnapeerkie (3 Apr. 1964)
Krasnopolin (14 June 1960)
Krasny (6 Mar. 1953)
Kratchman (27 Jan. 1967)
Kraus (27 July 1956)
Kraushaar (27 June 1952)
Krautman (31 May 1968)
Kravitz (10 June 1966)
        (20 Oct. 1972)
Kravtzoff (30 Nov. 1956)
Kravzov (30 Nov. 1956)
Krawczunski (11 June 1976)
Krawczynski (11 June 1976)
Krawitzky (18 June 1976)
Kredenzer (14 May 1971)
Kreindel (3 Aug. 1962)
Kreindler (3 Aug. 1962)
Kreine (3 Aug. 1962)
Kreisler (17 May 1968)
Kreiss (26 Aug. 1949)
Krelof (1 Mar. 1968)
Kremski (23 Oct. 1970)
Krensky (23 Oct. 1970)

Kretske (8 May 1953)
Kreutzenauer (26 Feb. 1971)
Krevorshayov (22 Feb. 1963)
Krieger (5 Apr. 1946)
        (11 May 1956)
        (12 Sept. 1969)
Krigman (12 Sept. 1969)
Kripke (18 June 1971)
Krischer (27 Nov. 1953)
        (3 Apr. 1959)
Krisher (27 Nov. 1953)
Krisofsky (12 Apr. 1968)
Krochmal (18 Mar. 1949)
Kronik (13 Feb. 1953)
Kronish (15 Sept. 1950)
Krosny (6 Mar. 1953)
Kruch (18 Oct. 1968)
Krueger (5 Apr. 1946)
        (11 May 1956)
Krugliak (16 Mar. 1973)
        (2 May 1975)
Kruh (18 Oct. 1968)
Krupa (19 May 1972)
Krupnick (12 Dec. 1952)
Krupnik (12 Dec. 1952)
Krupp (19 May 1972)
Krupsaw (8 Aug. 1952)
Krylov (1 Mar. 1968)
Krystyan (14 Mar. 1952)
Krzyzowski (12 Apr. 1968)
Kubrak (10 Apr. 1959)
Kubrik (10 Apr. 1959)
Kudick (3 July 1964)
Kudish (16 June 1961)
        (1 Jan. 1971)
Kudlick (3 July 1964)
Kuebel (21 Jan. 1972)
Kuflik (11 Dec. 1970)
Kugel (16 Dec. 1955)
Kula (10 July 1959)
Kulefsky (23 June 1967)
Kulp (30 Nov. 1973)
Kumin (8 Dec. 1967)
Kunik (1 May 1959)
Kuniks (23 Apr. 1954)
Kunz (10 Jan. 1969)
Kunzman (10 Jan. 1969)
Kupchin (17 Jan. 1964)
Kurin (10 Oct. 1969)
Kurland (24 Feb. 1967)
Kurtzberg (15 Oct. 1954)
Kurtzig (22 Sept. 1972)
Kuryn (10 Oct. 1969)
Kushner (10 Dec. 1948)

Kushner (27 May 1966)
    (24 Mar. 1967)
Kushnir (22 Jan. 1960)
Kutelchuk (17 Aug. 1956)
Kutner (4 Sept. 1959)
Kuttner (13 June 1952)
Kutz (4 Dec. 1953)
Kutzin (4 Dec. 1953)
Kutzinok (4 Dec. 1953)
Kux (23 Jan. 1970)
Kwilecki (11 Apr. 1958)

Labiner (12 May 1967)
Laborant (16 Mar. 1951)
Lachman (14 June 1946)
Lachs (14 June 1946)
Lack (30 May 1958)
Ladar (30 Dec. 1960)
Laemmel (13 Sept. 1963)
Laffer (2 Sept. 1966)
Lagerman (29 Mar. 1946)
Lagnado (18 Jan. 1974)
Lagnato (18 Jan. 1974)
Laites (4 Sept. 1959)
Lamm (13 Sept. 1963)
Lampel (13 Sept. 1963)
Lamport (12 Apr. 1957)
Landa (5 Apr. 1957)
Landau (11 Nov. 1949)
    (2 June 1950)
    (5 Apr. 1957)
Lande (24 May 1946)
Landfield (3 Nov. 1961)
Landman (9 June 1972)
Lando (2 June 1950)
Langsam (17 Oct. 1958)
Lanzner (23 Feb. 1962)
La Payover (17 May 1957)
Lapides (5 June 1964)
Lapidus (5 June 1964)
Lapine (3 June 1949)
Largeman (29 Mar. 1946)
Lasin (25 Aug. 1968)
Laski (11 July 1958)
Laskowitz (21 Sept. 1945)
    (29 May 1970)
Lasky (11 July 1958)
Laszlo (11 Dec. 1959).
Laufer (2 Sept. 1966)
Lawentman (7 Jan. 1972)
Lazebnik (8 Feb. 1974)
Laziebnik (8 Feb. 1974)
Lebenbaum (3 Sept. 1971)
Lebensbaum (3 Sept. 1971)

Lebenson (27 Mar. 1953)
Leberfarb (13 Dec. 1963)
Lebersfeld (7 May 1954)
Lebwohl (25 Oct. 1968)
Lebzelter (13 July 1973)
Lechner (6 Apr. 1956)
Lederer (15 July 1949)
Leff (26 Nov. 1948)
Lefkowitz (22 Sept. 1950)
    (28 May 1954)
Lehner (6 Apr. 1956)
Lehnhoff (16 Jan. 1970)
Lehrer (26 July 1968)
Leibowitz (12 May 1950)
Leiffer (2 Sept. 1966)
Leiman (14 Aug. 1953)
Leitner (5 Feb. 1971)
Leitson (6 July 1956)
Lekach (17 Jan. 1958)
Lekumovich (12 Feb. 1960)
Leman (14 Aug. 1953)
Lemberski (26 July 1968)
Lencz (10 Oct. 1975)
Lending (10 July 1970)
Lendyk (10 July 1970)
Lenefsky (30 Sept. 1955)
Lengyel (6 Aug. 1971)
Lenhardt (20 Jan. 1956)
Lennhoff (16 Jan. 1970)
Lenoff (18 July 1975)
Lentschitz (7 Sept. 1951)
Lenz (10 Oct. 1975)
Leon (3 Oct. 1958)
Lepavsky (20 Jan. 1967)
Lepcofker (26 May 1967)
Leppok (21 Feb. 1969)
Lepzelter (13 July 1973)
Lerner (14 Apr. 1950)
Leschin (25 Aug. 1968)
Leshanski (21 Nov. 1969)
Leshem (23 Mar. 1973)
    (23 May 1975)
Lessem (23 Mar. 1973)
Letteris (5 June 1970)
Levendula (24 Apr. 1970)
Levenson (27 Mar. 1953)
Leveru (19 Jan. 1973)
Levi (28 June 1946)
Levinbock (15 Dec. 1950)
Levitt (28 June 1946)
Levitz (30 Sept. 1949)
Levtov (24 July 1964)
Levy (28 June 1946)

Lew (26 Nov. 1948)
     (3 Oct. 1958)
Lewent (7 Oct. 1966)
Lewkowitz (22 Sept. 1950)
          (28 May 1954)
Lewton (24 July 1964)
Lewtow (24 July 1964)
Lezman (31 July 1953)
Liberman (15 July 1955)
Licht (22 Apr. 1955)
Lichtenstein (29 Apr. 1966)
Lichtenzweig (5 Aug. 1966)
Lichterman (1 June 1951)
Lichtzer (19 June 1964)
Liebenetsky (30 Dec. 1966)
Lieberfarb (13 Dec. 1963)
Lieberman (15 July 1955)
Liebermann (18 July 1958)
Liebesman (9 Apr. 1971)
Liebgold (29 Apr. 1955)
Liebmann (18 July 1958)
Lief (24 July 1970)
Liff (3 Oct. 1958)
Lifschitz (6 Jan. 1956)
Lifshitz (6 Jan. 1956)
Ligorner (4 July 1958)
Lin (4 Feb. 1949)
     (17 July 1964)
Linefsky (30 Sept. 1955)
Lingel (6 Aug. 1971)
Linker (9 Aug. 1957)
Lipa (23 Nov. 1956)
Lipkin (22 Apr. 1949)
       (13 Nov. 1959)
Lipman (23 Feb. 1951)
       (23 Nov. 1956)
       (26 Apr. 1968)
Lipnak (7 Feb. 1969)
Lipniak (7 Feb. 1969)
Lippel (23 Nov. 1956)
Lippmann (18 July 1958)
Lipscher (10 May 1946)
         (12 Nov. 1948)
Lipschitz (6 Jan. 1956)
Lipsman (26 Apr. 1968)
Lis (1 Apr. 1955)
Liss (1 Apr. 1955)
List (27 Jan. 1961)
Litant (14 Oct. 1955)
Litman (26 Apr. 1968)
Littauer (10 May 1946)
         (14 Oct. 1955)
Littman (10 May 1946)
         (14 Oct. 1955)

Littman (18 July 1958)
Litvin (23 Oct. 1964)
Litwak (10 May 1946)
Litwin (10 May 1946)
Loberant (16 Mar. 1951)
Lockshin (22 Jan. 1960)
Loeb (1 Apr. 1955)
Loetstein (6 Aug. 1971)
Loew (1 Apr. 1955)
     (3 Oct. 1958)
Loewe (1 Apr. 1955)
Loewenheim (8 Dec. 1972)
Loewenstein (26 Aug. 1955)
Loitesh (4 Sept. 1959)
Lokshin (22 Jan. 1960)
Lome (22 Mar. 1957)
Londinski (3 July 1970)
London (24 May 1946)
Londynski (3 July 1970)
Lonschein (25 Aug. 1968)
Lopatnikov (24 Oct. 1969)
Lorman (24 Jan. 1969)
Losos (14 June 1946)
Lossos (14 June 1946)
Lotstein (6 Aug. 1971)
Lubarow (4 Sept. 1970)
Luberoff (4 Sept. 1970)
Lubick (8 June 1973)
Lubitsch (29 Mar. 1968)
Lubner (21 July 1972)
Lubowitz (10 Dec. 1954)
Luchfeld (2 Feb. 1973)
Luchsner (15 Nov. 1963)
Lukacher (27 June 1952)
Lunteschutz (7 Sept. 1951)
Luntschutz (7 Sept. 1951)
Luntz (29 Oct. 1954)
Lunz (29 Oct. 1954)
Luria (28 Oct. 1949)
Lurie (28 Oct. 1949)
Luxner (15 Nov. 1963)
Lynchiz (7 Sept. 1951)

Maccoby (2 Feb. 1951)
Machiz (27 Mar. 1970)
Machlis (1 Feb. 1974)
Macht (18 Nov. 1949)
Machtez (26 Nov. 1965)
Madanick (7 Jan. 1955)
Madel (1 Aug. 1975)
Madfes (5 June 1970)
Magarshak (30 Oct. 1959)
Magenheim (10 Dec. 1971)
Magid (18 Feb. 1949)

Magid (8 Dec. 1950)
Magida (18 Feb. 1949)
Magidson (18 Feb. 1949)
Magiet (18 Feb. 1949)
Magirus (29 Sept. 1972)
Magit (8 Dec. 1950)
Magrish (29 Sept. 1972)
Maharshak (30 Oct. 1959)
Mahit (8 Dec. 1950)
Maibuch (11 Dec. 1959)
Maiman (4 Sept. 1964)
Maimun (4 Sept. 1964)
          (21 Dec. 1973)
Maitin (21 June 1968)
Maizel (21 Jan. 1955)
Maizlish (21 Jan. 1955)
Majdannik (7 Jan. 1955)
Malbin (16 Nov. 1951)
Malev (16 Nov. 1951)
Malik (21 Apr. 1972)
Malioveny (21 Apr. 1961)
Malkes (20 Mar. 1970)
Malkus (20 Mar. 1970)
Mallinger (8 Mar. 1968)
Malman (4 Apr. 1969)
Malovany (25 Jan. 1952)
Malowany (25 Jan. 1952)
          (21 Apr. 1961)
Mammon (21 Dec. 1973)
Mamroth (5 June 1953)
Manba (10 Aug. 1956)
Mandel (23 Oct. 1959)
Mandzuch (5 Aug. 1955)
Manes (1 Feb. 1963)
Maneson (1 Feb. 1963)
Manewitz (2 Sept. 1960)
Manishen (21 Nov. 1952)
Mankofsky (1 July 1966)
Mankovsky (1 July 1966)
Mankuta (1 Feb. 1946)
Manson (28 Oct. 1966)
Marans (12 Jan. 1951)
Marantz (12 Jan. 1951)
Marder (4 Jan. 1946)
Maremont (23 Jan. 1953)
Marenus (29 July 1960)
Margaliot (15 Apr. 1966)
Margolin (15 Apr. 1966)
Margoliot (15 Apr. 1966)
Margolis (15 Apr. 1966)
Margulis (15 Apr. 1966)
Marienbach (13 July 1962)
Marinbach (13 July 1962)
Marinsky (29 Dec. 1972)

Marjampolski (11 Nov. 1955)
Markscheid (28 Mar. 1969)
Marmelstein (29 May 1964)
Marmor (17 May 1946)
Marmurek (29 May 1964)
Marymont (23 Jan. 1953)
Marynski (29 Dec. 1972)
Mase (26 May 1950)
Mash (14 Aug. 1959)
Mashak (9 Nov. 1951)
Mashbir (29 Feb. 1952)
Mashbitz (28 Jan. 1966)
Mashik (9 Nov. 1951)
Masinter (12 Nov. 1971)
Maslin (1 Sept. 1972)
Maslow (18 Dec. 1953)
Matanka (28 Nov. 1975)
Matanky (28 Nov. 1975)
Matel (1 Aug. 1975)
Matis (10 Jan. 1958)
Matises (10 Jan. 1958)
Matlawski (21 May 1971)
Matlin (1 Aug. 1975)
Matlovsky (21 May 1971)
Matoren (7 Mar. 1952)
Matwes (5 June 1970)
Maxwell (20 Mar. 1959)
Maybruch (11 Dec. 1959)
Mayer (26 Nov. 1948)
Mazelsky (10 Apr. 1964)
Mazo (26 May 1950)
          (19 Mar. 1954)
Mazrier (7 June 1968)
Mazur (23 Dec. 1949)
          (7 June 1968)
Medjuck (29 Apr. 1966)
Meer (24 Aug. 1973)
Meersand (8 Nov. 1968)
Mehler (27 June 1958)
Mehlman (4 Apr. 1969)
Meier (24 Aug. 1973)
Meilach (20 May 1960)
Meisels (21 Jan. 1955)
Meketonski (19 Feb. 1971)
Mekitianski (19 Feb. 1971)
Melamed (3 July 1964)
          (26 July 1968)
Melaten (30 Apr. 1971)
Melatyn (30 Apr. 1971)
Melber (14 Aug. 1970)
Melezin (23 May 1952)
Melnick (19 June 1970)
Meltsner (22 Oct. 1954)
Meltz (15 Oct. 1971)

Meltzer (5 Feb. 1954)
Melzner (22 Oct. 1954)
Menachem (3 Oct. 1975)
Menbe (10 Aug. 1956)
Mendel (1 Feb. 1963)
        (22 Mar. 1963)
Mendelsberg (3 Oct. 1975)
Mendelsson (1 Feb. 1963)
Menkes (30 Oct. 1964)
Menkin (22 Mar. 1963)
        (8 May 1964)
Menkus (30 Oct. 1964)
Menschel (13 Nov. 1953)
Mensh (17 Aug. 1951)
Menz (11 Sept. 1970)
Menzel (13 Nov. 1953)
Merman (6 July 1973)
Merr (24 Aug. 1973)
Mersand (8 Nov. 1968)
Mertik (30 Oct. 1970)
Mertz (13 Aug. 1976)
Mesch (20 July 1951)
Meshulam (31 July 1964)
Meslin (1 Sept. 1972)
Messinger (12 Sept. 1969)
Met (2 Oct. 1970)
Metchik (12 Feb. 1954)
Meth (2 Oct. 1970)
Metzger (18 Mar. 1966)
Meyeroff (23 July 1954)
Meyers (26 Nov. 1948)
Michalofsky (7 Nov. 1952)
Michalowski (7 Nov. 1952)
Michthaim (12 Jan. 1951)
Miedzuch (29 Apr. 1966)
Mielnik (19 June 1970)
Migdal (27 July 1956)
Migdalowitz (21 Mar. 1969)
Migdol (21 Mar. 1969)
Mikochinski (27 Feb. 1976)
Mikoshinski (27 Feb. 1976)
Milgrom (1 Nov. 1963)
Miller (25 May 1973)
Millionthaler (6 Feb. 1970)
Minc (11 Sept. 1970)
Minkovsky (19 Oct. 1951)
Minkowski (19 Oct. 1951)
Minowitz (7 Mar. 1969)
Minski (14 Jan. 1972)
Minsky (14 Jan. 1972)
Mintz (11 Sept. 1970)
Mirampolsky (11 Nov. 1955)
Mirel (1 May 1964)

Mirels (1 May 1964)
Mirkes (31 July 1970)
Mirkus (31 July 1970)
Mirman (6 July 1973)
Mirower (14 July 1961)
Mirsky (7 Jan. 1966)
Mirus (2 Sept. 1949)
Mishkin (1 Aug. 1969)
Misunder (12 Nov. 1971)
Mlotok (31 July 1953)
Mochsen (13 Sept. 1968)
Mollen (4 Apr. 1952)
Mollick (21 Apr. 1972)
Mollika (21 Apr. 1972)
Molotok (31 July 1953)
Monastersky (27 May 1955)
Mondrzyk (25 Sept. 1964)
Monin (22 Dec. 1967)
Monjack (25 Sept. 1964)
Monosson (1 Feb. 1963)
Monsky (20 July 1951)
Moraff (18 July 1958)
Mordfin (9 Apr. 1976)
Morgenstern (15 Mar. 1957)
Morin (12 May 1972)
Moritz (29 Oct. 1971)
Morovin (24 Mar. 1972)
Morowin (24 Mar. 1972)
Morozhnik (14 Oct. 1966)
Morushnick (14 Oct. 1966)
Mosak (3 Sept. 1976)
Mosbacher (30 Mar. 1956)
Moschko (5 Dec. 1975)
Mosenkis (16 Jan. 1953)
Mosiefsky (27 Oct. 1972)
Mosiewski (27 Oct. 1972)
Moszko (5 Dec. 1975)
Moteff (2 Sept. 1949)
        (13 Oct. 1950)
Motew (13 Oct. 1950)
Mottus (25 June 1971)
Motzkin (12 Jan. 1973)
        (6 June 1975)
Mrosovitz (16 June 1950)
Muchnik (1 Nov. 1963)
Muehltaler (6 Feb. 1970)
Mugdan (1 May 1959)
Mukdon (1 May 1959)
Mundery (5 Jan. 1968)
Munvez (4 Mar. 1949)
Munz (11 Sept. 1970)
Muravnik (16 July 1971)
Murawczyk (16 July 1971)

Murovannaya (15 July 1960)
Musicus (12 Jan. 1968)
Muskat (15 Dec. 1961)
Mutchnik (23 July 1954)
Mytosky (4 July 1975)

Nachamofski (14 Aug. 1959)
Nachamus (12 Aug. 1955)
Nachman (27 Jan. 1956)
Nachowitch (24 Oct. 1958)
Nadel (6 Nov. 1959)
Naftulin (26 Apr. 1946)
          (14 June 1960)
Nager (21 Dec. 1951)
Nahmias (25 Nov. 1966)
Naiman (29 Jan. 1960)
Najdamast (3 Mar. 1950)
Najmark (16 June 1967)
Najowitz (6 Dec. 1950)
Naparstek (20 July 1973)
Narotsky (10 July 1959)
Nasatir (9 Oct. 1953)
Nathan (23 Jan. 1976)
Nathanson (17 Dec. 1965)
Naymark (16 June 1967)
Nechamkin (13 Nov. 1953)
Nechamus (13 Nov. 1953)
Nechemias (5 Dec. 1952)
Neeman (29 Jan. 1960)
Neier (18 Feb. 1966)
Neiger (21 Dec. 1951)
Neistadt (25 July 1958)
Neleber (14 Nov. 1958)
Nelken (14 Apr. 1972)
Nemeroff (13 Nov. 1953)
Nerenberg (8 Dec. 1961)
Nestel (5 July 1968)
Neugeboren (17 Apr. 1968)
Neuman (29 Jan. 1960)
Neumark (16 June 1967)
Neuwirth (21 Jan. 1949)
Nevelov (7 May 1971)
Nevelson (14 Jan. 1955)
Neviaser (22 Apr. 1955)
Nevler (17 Oct. 1975)
Newmark (4 Jan. 1946)
Nida (8 Dec. 1972)
Nieir (18 Feb. 1966)
Niemirow (13 Nov. 1953)
Nieteckmann (29 Dec. 1972)
Nifka (17 Feb. 1967)
Nisenbaum (6 Mar. 1964)
Nisgoretsky (1 May 1970)
Nistel (5 July 1968)

Nitchie (30 July 1976)
Nitkin (17 Sept. 1976)
Nivelson (14 Jan. 1955)
Niwka (17 Feb. 1967)
Nizgorecki (1 May 1970)
Noel (5 Aug. 1955)
Nogg (17 Mar. 1950)
Nol (5 Aug. 1955)
Noppe (17 Apr. 1970)
Norr (12 Sept. 1975)
Noschkes (18 Feb. 1949)
Nossig (20 Feb. 1976)
Notas (11 Feb. 1966)
Note (23 Jan. 1976)
Noteman (23 Jan. 1976)
Nothman (23 Jan. 1976)
Nottenburg (2 Mar. 1956)
Novack (30 Sept. 1966)
Novak (30 Sept. 1966)
Novemesky (24 Aug. 1973)
Novomieyski (24 Aug. 1973)
Nozick (20 Feb. 1976)
Nudel (8 May 1970)
Nudler (4 Dec. 1970)
Nuger (21 Dec. 1951)
Nurnberg (8 Dec. 1961)
Nussbaum (6 Mar. 1964)
Nusynowicz (18 Nov. 1966)
Nutes (3 May 1946)

Oberlander (13 Aug. 1976)
Oboler (10 Apr. 1970)
Ochacher (7 Sept. 1973)
Ochevsky (9 June 1972)
Ochman (19 Mar. 1976)
Ochowski (9 June 1972)
Ochsenburg (25 Aug. 1967)
Ocman (19 Mar. 1976)
Oczaczer (7 Sept. 1973)
Oder (31 Jan. 1969)
Oelsner (2 Feb. 1968)
Ofen (29 Nov. 1963)
Offen (29 Nov. 1963)
Ofsaniker (20 Sept. 1963)
Ogman (19 Mar. 1976)
Ogorek (8 Nov. 1963)
Ogurek (8 Nov. 1963)
Ogus (4 Feb. 1972)
Ohrbach (2 Jan. 1959)
Ohrenstein (7 Oct. 1966)
Ohringer (17 July 1964)
Okner (11 May 1956)
Okun (27 Sept. 1968)
Olbum (30 June 1961)

Oler (8 Mar. 1968)
Olifant (15 May 1959)
Olim (12 Dec. 1952)
Olimsher (12 Dec. 1952)
Oliphant (15 May 1959)
Olitzki (22 Aug. 1969)
Olmo (10 July 1970)
Olshevitz (2 Feb. 1973)
Olshewitz (2 Feb. 1973)
Onixt (19 Jan. 1968)
Opachinsky (10 Aug. 1962)
Opaczynski (10 Aug. 1962)
Opengart (31 July 1970)
Oppenheim (23 Dec. 1960)
Oppenheimer (23 Dec. 1960)
Optner (12 June 1953)
Ordman (13 Aug. 1971)
Ordner (29 Aug. 1969)
Oren (7 Dec. 1945)
     (21 Jan. 1966)
Orenstein (2 Dec. 1955)
Orkin (19 Aug. 1949)
Orlanski (6 Oct. 1972)
Orlansky (10 Feb. 1956)
Orlik (26 Aug. 1960)
Orlinsky (6 Oct. 1972)
Orner (29 Aug. 1969)
Ornstein (13 Mar. 1964)
        (7 Oct. 1966)
Ortman (13 Aug. 1971)
Orun (26 Aug. 1960)
Orzechowski (27 Aug. 1971)
Osdoby (28 Apr. 1950)
Oselka (23 Feb. 1968)
Osgood (28 Jan. 1972)
Oshinsky (13 Nov. 1964)
Osipany (24 Feb. 1961)
Osipina (24 Feb. 1961)
Oskard (3 Jan. 1969)
Osterweil (26 Mar. 1971)
Ostroff (28 Mar. 1952)
Ostrower (21 Dec. 1945)
Ostroy (31 Aug. 1973)
Ostryi (31 Aug. 1973)
Oswianiker (20 Sept. 1963)
Ottenheimer (14 Apr. 1950)
Oxenburg (25 Aug. 1967)

Pachter (7 Aug. 1959)
Packer (12 Aug. 1966)
Packtraeger (12 Aug. 1966)
Padgug (10 June 1949)
Padibok (1 Jan. 1971)
Padzensky (16 May 1973)

Padziunski (16 May 1973)
Paget (22 Feb. 1952)
Pailet (8 Mar. 1946)
Palant (22 Dec. 1950)
Panet (1 Nov. 1968)
Paneth (1 Nov. 1968)
Panish (24 Nov. 1950)
Panurski (25 Jan. 1974)
Panus (17 Nov. 1972)
Panush (17 Nov. 1972)
Panusz (17 Nov. 1972)
Papernick (11 Oct. 1968)
Papirnik (11 Oct. 1968)
Pares (1 Apr. 1949)
Paris (11 Nov. 1955)
Parnes (24 Apr. 1964)
Parzybok (1 Jan. 1971)
Pascaner (22 July 1960)
Paskind (28 June 1957)
Pasternak (27 Jan. 1967)
Patinka (11 Feb. 1949)
Pauzisky (30 Apr. 1971)
Pauzyszki (30 Apr. 1971)
Paymer (26 Dec. 1975)
Pazumchik (23 May 1958)
Pearlman (14 June 1946)
Pech (7 Mar. 1952)
Pedziasz (28 Feb. 1958)
Pegler (13 Sept. 1963)
Peichik (9 July 1954)
Peilen (22 Oct. 1954)
Peim (26 Dec. 1975)
Peimann (26 Mar. 1971)
Peiper (16 Apr. 1976)
Peiser (17 May 1946)
Peixotto (1 Apr. 1949)
Pekarsky (29 May 1953)
Pelavin (6 May 1949)
Pella (25 Sept. 1964)
Pelofsky (26 Mar. 1954)
Pelzner (9 July 1954)
Penchansky (6 Feb. 1976)
Penczynski (6 Feb. 1976)
Pensak (30 July 1976)
Penzias (28 Feb. 1958)
Penzuch (23 June 1967)
Pepp (24 Mar. 1972)
Pepper (21 Jan. 1949)
       (24 Mar. 1972)
       (16 Nov. 1973)
Perczyk (11 Sept. 1959)
Perepetchai (25 Aug. 1968)
Pergament (30 Nov. 1945)
Perlman (14 June 1946)

Perlmutter (25 Jan. 1946)
Persky (2 June 1950)
Pervin (21 June 1946)
Pesata (28 Mar. 1952)
Pesaty (28 Mar. 1952)
Peseles (5 May 1961)
Peskowsky (14 Apr. 1972)
Pessel (5 May 1961)
Pestcoe (5 Dec. 1975)
Pestka (5 Dec. 1975)
Pestyner (4 Nov. 1966)
Pfau (15 May 1964)
Piade (17 Aug. 1973)
Pianko (27 Mar. 1953)
Piaskowsky (27 Oct. 1961)
Piatelsky (18 Nov. 1960)
Pick (11 Mar. 1955)
Piegel (5 Sept. 1969)
Pierczyk (11 Sept. 1959)
Pieskowski (14 Apr. 1972)
Pigula (22 Oct. 1971)
Pikus (26 Dec. 1975)
Pilawski (26 Mar. 1954)
Pinchas (21 Dec. 1973)
Pinchassoff (21 Dec. 1973)
Pinchefsky (15 Oct. 1971)
Pinchuk (28 May 1971)
Pinczowski (15 Oct. 1971)
Pinczuk (28 May 1971)
Pine (1 Feb. 1946)
Pines (1 Feb. 1946)
Pinkin (31 Mar. 1967)
Pinkus (4 Mar. 1966)
Pinsky (8 Mar. 1946)
Pion (30 Apr. 1954)
Pischonski (4 Jan. 1974)
Piser (10 Feb. 1950)
Pistyanski (4 Jan. 1974)
Pitem (2 Apr. 1971)
Pittel (17 Feb. 1967)
Piwko (26 Nov. 1965)
Piwoszunski (2 Dec. 1966)
Pizer (17 May 1946)
Platke (25 Mar. 1949)
Plaut (18 May 1956)
Plotkin (31 May 1946)
Pochis (3 Jan. 1958)
Podaretzki (24 Jan. 1964)
Podberesky (1 Sept. 1950)
Podgaetsky (11 Jan. 1974)
Podgajecki (11 Jan. 1974)
Podhorecki (24 Jan. 1964)
Podoloff (28 Feb. 1969)
Podolov (28 Feb. 1969)

Podolski (28 Feb. 1969)
Podritzki (24 Jan. 1964)
Poizner (12 May 1961)
Pokempner (18 Nov. 1955)
Pokrzywnicki (15 Aug. 1969)
Polak (10 Aug. 1962)
Polatsek (10 Aug. 1962)
Polay (22 Mar. 1968)
Polier (28 July 1967)
Polisner (10 Mar. 1972)
Politziner (16 July 1971)
Pollock (25 Feb. 1949)
Polster (1 Feb. 1952)
       (20 Feb. 1970)
Pomerantz (27 July 1951)
Pompiansky (6 Sept. 1963)
Ponemonsky (10 Mar. 1972)
Poniemonski (10 Mar. 1972)
Ponnusky (25 Jan. 1974)
Pookman (19 Mar. 1971)
Portnoy (10 June 1966)
       (20 Oct. 1972)
Portugal (19 May 1961)
Posner (12 May 1961)
Possick (17 Dec. 1948)
Poster (14 Sept. 1973)
Postolov (10 Aug. 1951)
       (6 June 1958)
Potashnick (12 Dec. 1958)
Poticha (1 May 1964)
Povodator (28 Dec. 1973)
Powesky (19 Sept. 1975)
Poziomczyk (23 May 1958)
Pravatiner (5 June 1953)
Prawda (21 July 1950)
Preefer (11 Oct. 1968)
Pregozen (14 Mar. 1958)
Pregulnyi (7 Nov. 1975)
Preiss (21 Nov. 1958)
Preissman (21 Nov. 1958)
Prelutzky (11 Sept. 1964)
Press (3 Nov. 1961)
Presser (3 Nov. 1961)
Prifer (11 Oct. 1968)
Prilucki (11 Sept. 1964)
Primack (16 Feb. 1968)
Primak (16 Feb. 1968)
Prince (31 Oct. 1969)
Printz (31 Oct. 1969)
Prinz (31 Oct. 1969)
Prisamt (21 Apr. 1967)
Probstein (6 Dec. 1963)
Proser (4 Mar. 1955)
Proskauer (15 Feb. 1957)

Provda (21 July 1950)
Pruefer (11 Oct. 1968)
Pruskauer (15 Feb. 1957)
Pruslin (28 Jan. 1966)
Prustig (19 Sept. 1975)
Pruzansky (4 Aug. 1950)
Prywitch (25 Aug. 1967)
Przywidz (25 Aug. 1967)
Pugatch (2 Oct. 1953)
Pushkanzer (6 Oct. 1950)
Pustelnik (20 Jan. 1967)
Pustilnik (20 Jan. 1967)
Pytel (17 Feb. 1967)

Quensler (25 Dec. 1970)
Quentzel (25 Dec. 1970)

Rabin (5 May 1950)
Rabinovich (21 Mar. 1951)
Rabinowitz (9 Dec. 1955)
Rachlin (19 Sept. 1969)
Rachlis (17 Sept. 1971)
Radchick (25 Nov. 1960)
Radosiner (4 June 1971)
Radovsky (4 Nov. 1966)
Radusky (21 May 1976)
Raduziner (4 June 1971)
Radzik (12 Mar. 1976)
Raefman (16 Sept. 1960)
Rafer (14 May 1976)
Raginsky (28 Apr. 1972)
Ragunski (28 Apr. 1972)
Rajgrod (30 June 1967)
Rajgrodsky (19 July 1957)
Rakowski (30 Aug. 1968)
Rakusin (23 Mar. 1951)
Ramze (1 Dec. 1950)
Rapaport (23 Nov. 1951)
Raphan (5 Aug. 1960)
Rashall (26 May 1967)
Rashba (25 Jan. 1963)
Rashkovitz (24 July 1970)
Rashkovski (25 Aug. 1972)
Ratafia (9 June 1967)
Ratchkowsky (25 Aug. 1972)
Rathsprecher (9 Feb. 1962)
Ratner (19 Aug. 1949)
Rauch (29 July 1966)
Rauchwerker (27 May 1966)
Rawel (29 Mar. 1968)
Rawicz (3 Jan. 1964)
Rawitsch (25 Aug. 1950)
        (3 Jan. 1964)
Rayach (29 July 1966)
Razumny (13 Jan. 1967)

Rebhuhn (5 Aug. 1960)
Redler (8 Apr. 1966)
Reem (31 May 1957)
Reggel (20 Aug. 1971)
Regiel (20 Aug. 1971)
Rehfisch (3 Jan. 1964)
Rehfish (25 Aug. 1950)
Reibstein (14 June 1968)
Reich (16 Dec. 1949)
Reichelson (11 May 1951)
Reif (25 Apr. 1958)
Reifman (16 Sept. 1960)
Reinisch (29 June 1973)
Reis (18 Feb. 1972)
Reiss (18 Feb. 1972)
Reiter (20 Apr. 1951)
        (21 Aug. 1964)
Reitzes (6 Jan. 1967)
Reivitch (25 Aug. 1950)
Reiwitsch (3 Jan. 1964)
Reles (12 Dec. 1969)
Relovitch (10 Apr. 1959)
Resnick (6 July 1951)
Ressler (4 May 1951)
        (23 July 1954)
Retchin (2 Jan. 1976)
Reznik (7 July 1961)
Ribnick (21 Sept. 1962)
Richter (29 Oct. 1971)
Rickel (8 Mar. 1963)
Riczker (27 Oct. 1950)
Ridel (12 June 1970)
Ridker (15 July 1966)
Rieger (6 Nov. 1970)
Ries (18 Feb. 1972)
Rifkin (18 Apr. 1969)
Rifkind (10 Mar. 1950)
Rigrod (30 June 1967)
Rimell (18 Dec. 1970)
Rimland (5 May 1967)
Ringel (6 Nov. 1970)
Ringle (6 Nov. 1970)
Rinzler (21 Dec. 1945)
Ritz (29 Oct. 1971)
Rivin (18 Jan. 1952)
Rivkin (10 Mar. 1950)
        (18 Apr. 1969)
Rivkind (10 Mar. 1950)
Robak (5 Jan. 1973)
        (9 May 1975)
Roberg (31 Oct. 1952)
Rochkind (11 Nov. 1960)
Rochoff (30 Aug. 1968)
Rochow (23 Apr. 1976)

Rockoff (28 Aug. 1964)
    (14 Oct. 1966)
Roesing (22 Sept. 1967)
Roessing (22 Sept. 1967)
Roffwarg (11 Mar. 1949)
Rogovein (19 Sept. 1958)
Rogovin (19 Sept. 1958)
Rohde (23 Sept. 1960)
Rohrberg (31 Oct. 1952)
Roifeman (16 Sept. 1960)
Rom (19 Jan. 1962)
Roman (4 Aug. 1972)
Romaner (30 Mar. 1956)
Rombro (30 Mar. 1956)
Romm (19 Jan. 1962)
Ronder (28 Aug. 1970)
Rondo (1 Dec. 1967)
Roos (2 July 1971)
Rosenbaum (15 Mar. 1957)
Rosenblatt (25 Aug. 1950)
    (6 Jan. 1956)
Rosenjansky (2 Oct. 1964)
Rosenkwit (25 May 1973)
Rosenman (27 Nov. 1953)
    (11 Jan. 1957)
Rosenmann (27 Nov. 1953)
Rosenofsky (15 Feb. 1957)
Rosenquit (25 May 1973)
Rosenstrauch (3 Nov. 1967)
Rosenthal (23 June 1961)
Rosenwasser (3 Aug. 1951)
    (11 Sept. 1959)
Rosenzweig (15 Mar. 1957)
    (16 Dec. 1960)
Rosichan (17 Apr. 1959)
Roskin (13 July 1973)
Roskoff (17 Mar. 1972)
Rosmarin (2 Mar. 1951)
Rosshaelter (23 Sept. 1966)
Rossi (4 Feb. 1966)
Rossman (11 Jan. 1957)
Rossoff (23 Dec. 1949)
Rostholder (23 Sept. 1966)
Rote Rosen (2 Dec. 1955)
Rothberg (12 Sept. 1952)
Rothenberg (22 July 1949)
Rothenburg (22 July 1949)
Rothfarb (4 Nov. 1960)
Rothman (16 Dec. 1960)
Rothschild (28 July 1967)
Rotter (12 Apr. 1957)
Rovish (25 Aug. 1950)
Rovner (16 Feb. 1968)
Rowner (16 Feb. 1968)

Ruach (29 July 1966)
Rubacha (2 Mar. 1962)
Rubel (27 Feb. 1953)
Rubenchik (13 Apr. 1973)
Rubenstein (12 Nov. 1948)
    (4 Sept. 1953)
Rubin (12 Mar. 1976)
Rubinstein (4 Sept. 1953)
Ruch (14 Apr. 1967)
Ruchansky (3 Mar. 1961)
Rudashevski (20 July 1962)
Rudawski (4 Nov. 1966)
Ruder (7 Dec. 1956)
Ruderfer (29 July 1949)
Rudman (20 Nov. 1959)
Rudow (2 June 1967)
Rueger (6 Nov. 1970)
Rumack (18 Feb. 1955)
Rumak (18 Feb. 1955)
Rundo (1 Dec. 1967)
Ruske (5 Oct. 1962)
Ruskin (5 Oct. 1962)
Rusnak (23 June 1950)
Rusznak (23 June 1950)
Rutner (20 May 1949)
Rydel (12 June 1970)
Rykiel (8 Mar. 1963)
Rymer (5 July 1968)
Ryter (20 Apr. 1951)
Rzodkiewicz (2 Nov. 1951)
Rzotkiewicz (2 Nov. 1951)

Sacarob (1 Dec. 1972)
Sacharov (1 Dec. 1972)
Sacharow (26 Dec. 1969)
Sachs (26 Oct. 1945)
    (7 Oct. 1949)
Sackheim (5 Mar. 1976)
Sacki (9 Dec. 1960)
Sackin (14 May 1954)
Sacks (13 July 1962)
Sadowski (16 Oct. 1970)
Sahn (15 Apr. 1955)
Saichek (5 Oct. 1956)
Sak (13 July 1962)
Sakkin (14 May 1954)
Salander (5 Mar. 1971)
Salant (21 May 1954)
Salasin (15 Dec. 1972)
Salin (26 Jan. 1973)
Salinger (8 Sept. 1972)
Salis (15 Dec. 1967)
Salkin (18 Feb. 1972)
Salpeter (2 May 1952)

Salpeter (10 Feb. 1961)
Saltzman (17 Dec. 1965)
Salzman (14 June 1946)
        (16 Feb. 1973)
Sambol (6 Jan. 1961)
Sameth (8 May 1970)
Sametnik (16 Aug. 1968)
Samogitianski (7 Nov. 1958)
Samotnik (16 Aug. 1968)
Samwil (3 Mar. 1967)
San (15 Apr. 1955)
Sandak (11 Jan. 1946)
Sanditen (11 Apr. 1952)
Sanes (14 Jan. 1966)
Saperda (9 Dec. 1966)
Saperia (9 Dec. 1966)
Saphian (18 Feb. 1966)
Sapir (13 Mar. 1970)
Sapirstein (13 Mar. 1970)
Sapoczinski (17 Feb. 1956)
Sapoczynski (17 Feb. 1956)
Sapovitz (27 Mar. 1970)
Sarachan (30 Aug. 1963)
Sarna (9 Mar. 1956)
Sasregin (5 May 1972)
Sastre (10 June 1966)
Satosky (26 June 1964)
Satovitz (20 June 1958)
Satz (8 July 1955)
Savitzky (22 Apr. 1949)
        (5 Apr. 1957)
Sawicki (5 Apr. 1957)
Sayetta (20 Oct. 1950)
Schachne (24 Aug. 1962)
Schachner (24 Aug. 1962)
Schachter (13 Jan. 1950)
Schaffer (3 Dec. 1965)
Schalit (19 Sept. 1969)
Schandler (12 June 1964)
Scharff (10 Sept. 1971)
Schatz (10 Nov. 1967)
Scheibel (18 Feb. 1955)
Schein (31 Oct. 1952)
Scheinberg (10 Jan. 1958)
Schenberg (20 July 1962)
Schenkel (7 Feb. 1969)
Schenker (5 Dec. 1952)
        (18 July 1975)
Scherer (4 Oct. 1968)
Schertzer (17 May 1957)
Scherzer (17 May 1957)
Schibel (18 Feb. 1955)
Schick (24 Jan. 1964)
Schiffer (21 Feb. 1969)

Schimmel (22 Dec. 1961)
Schindeler (16 Oct. 1959)
Schindler (16 Oct. 1959)
Schinkel (7 Feb. 1969)
Schlachet (11 Apr. 1952)
Schlanger (13 Aug. 1954)
Schlatiner (13 Mar. 1964)
Schleifer (10 Oct. 1952)
Schlenger (23 Dec. 1955)
Schlenker (23 Dec. 1955)
Schlossberg (2 Mar. 1973)
Schlossman (1 July 1955)
Schlusefeld (4 Dec. 1959)
Schmelkin (2 Dec. 1949)
Schmuck (14 May 1971)
Schmukler (30 June 1961)
Schnapik (26 Sept. 1969)
Schneebalg (11 Nov. 1953)
Schneeweiss (16 May 1973)
Schneider (10 June 1966)
        (20 Oct. 1972)
Schneidersohn (30 Nov. 1956)
Schnittman (19 Nov. 1965)
Schnur (10 Oct. 1952)
Schoen (18 Sept. 1964)
Schoenbaum (28 Sept. 1973)
Schoenberg (10 Jan. 1958)
        (20 July 1962)
Schoenhals (12 Apr. 1946)
Schoenholtz (12 Apr. 1946)
Schoer (7 Sept. 1956)
Schonbrunn (4 May 1951)
Schor (7 Sept. 1956)
Schorr (13 May 1949)
        (18 Aug. 1950)
        (11 Mar. 1955)
Schoss (8 Aug. 1969)
Schotenstein (8 Nov. 1963)
Schotte (1 Dec. 1961)
Schottenfeld (1 Dec. 1961)
Schramm (11 Sept. 1964)
Schreiber (5 Jan. 1968)
Schrenk (23 Oct. 1970)
Schreter (27 July 1973)
Schrift (27 May 1966)
Schroeder (27 July 1973)
Schroit (15 Feb. 1957)
Schuchart (17 Nov. 1972)
Schuchat (17 Nov. 1972)
Schulman (5 July 1946)
        (18 May 1956)
Schumer (5 Dec. 1969)
Schupak (14 Feb. 1969)
Schwam (2 June 1961)

Schwartz (1 Apr. 1966)
Schwartzberg (2 July 1954)
Schwarz (21 Dec. 1956)
       (1 Mar. 1957)
       (21 Sept. 1962)
Schwarzberg (2 July 1954)
Schwarzman (1 Mar. 1957)
Schweber (26 Aug. 1966)
Schweid (4 Mar. 1966)
Scoler (10 Jan. 1964)
Secher (21 Oct. 1966)
Seckel (6 Aug. 1954)
Sedlis (11 May 1973)
Seelenfreund (26 Oct. 1956)
Segal (19 Sept. 1952)
      (10 Jan. 1964)
      (9 Nov. 1973)
Segaller (10 Jan. 1964)
Seidelman (25 Jan. 1952)
Seidenmann (25 Jan. 1952)
Seidman (29 Nov. 1968)
Seidner (20 Feb. 1976)
Seinfeld (3 Mar. 1967)
Seldes (11 May 1973)
Seldin (21 Feb. 1958)
Selechnik (21 May 1976)
Selig (23 Jan. 1976)
Seltz (28 May 1971)
Seltzer (20 Apr. 1973)
Sender (8 Feb. 1946)
Sendrowitz (29 July 1960)
Senelnick (11 June 1971)
Senior (26 Nov. 1971)
Senturia (30 Jan. 1953)
Serbin (7 Oct. 1960)
Serksner (23 July 1971)
Serota (23 Sept. 1966)
Sesicki (4 May 1973)
Sesitsky (4 May 1973)
Shabselowitz (18 Aug. 1967)
Shabshelowitz (18 Aug. 1967)
Shachman (10 Sept. 1976)
Shachne (10 Sept. 1976)
Shaffran (9 Feb. 1968)
Shafran (9 Feb. 1968)
Shagam (6 Oct. 1967)
Shagan (6 Oct. 1967)
Shaiewicz (16 Apr. 1971)
Shaiewitz (16 Apr. 1971)
Shainsvet (24 Sept. 1976)
Shainsvit (24 Sept. 1976)
Shalit (19 Sept. 1969)
Shamanski (7 Nov. 1969)
Shames (11 Jan. 1957)

Shandalov (16 Sept. 1949)
Shapiro (11 Mar. 1949)
Sharf (10 Sept. 1971)
Shatsky (15 Sept. 1972)
Shatz (8 July 1955)
Shavitz (16 Apr. 1971)
Shebshaievitz (9 Feb. 1951)
Sheffshinsky (31 Mar. 1972)
Shein (31 Oct. 1952)
Sheps (18 June 1976)
Sherbell (23 Feb. 1973)
Sherer (24 June 1955)
Shereshefsky (20 Oct. 1950)
Sherman (24 June 1955)
        (10 June 1966)
        (4 Oct. 1968)
Shevel (13 Nov. 1970)
Shifrin (10 Feb. 1950)
Shigon (9 May 1969)
Shkolnik (18 May 1956)
Shladovsky (14 Dec. 1951)
Shlensky (17 June 1955)
Shlonsky (17 June 1955)
Shmelkin (28 Nov. 1969)
Shmigelska (18 Aug. 1972)
Shnitke (26 Feb. 1954)
Shoen (31 Oct. 1952)
Sholcow (5 Aug. 1955)
Sholk (13 Jan. 1967)
Shomer (5 Dec. 1969)
Shotenstein (8 Nov. 1963)
Shraber (5 Jan. 1968)
Shterenshis (21 Mar. 1969)
Shtull (21 Apr. 1950)
Shufler (17 Feb. 1950)
Shuldiner (12 Dec. 1958)
Shulevitz (29 May 1970)
Shulman (5 July 1946)
Shuman (8 June 1951)
Shunman (8 June 1951)
Sicherman (22 Nov. 1963)
Sicman (22 Nov. 1963)
Siegel (24 Dec. 1948)
       (19 Sept. 1952)
       (9 Nov. 1973)
Siegelbaum (9 Nov. 1973)
Siegelovich (24 Dec. 1948)
Siegfried (14 Jan. 1955)
Siekierka (12 Aug. 1960)
Siemandel (11 Jan. 1974)
Sik (24 Jan. 1964)
Silberberg (18 Apr. 1952)
Silberfarb (25 Dec. 1959)
Silberherz (10 Nov. 1950)

Silberman (8 Apr. 1955)
Silbermintz (25 Nov. 1960)
Silbersher (4 June 1976)
Silberstein (23 Dec. 1960)
Silbiger (23 Nov. 1945)
Silna (7 Dec. 1973)
Silpe (5 Oct. 1962)
Silverberg (18 Apr. 1952)
Silverstein (23 Dec. 1960)
Simandl (11 Jan. 1974)
Simkin (19 Nov. 1948)
Simonovics (19 Dec. 1952)
Simonowitz (19 Dec. 1952)
Simonsky (1 Feb. 1957)
Simonson (19 Dec. 1952)
Sinaiko (19 Oct. 1951)
Singer (16 Nov. 1945)
Sinilnik (11 June 1971)
Sinnreich (16 Jan. 1970)
Sirkes (27 Apr. 1951)
Sirota (23 Sept. 1966)
Sirotinsky (2 Sept. 1960)
Siskin (6 Dec. 1968)
Sissel (24 Mar. 1961)
Sisselman (19 Oct. 1956)
          (24 Mar. 1961)
Sitnik (27 Dec. 1968)
Sitrick (27 Dec. 1968)
Sivitz (8 Aug. 1952)
Skier (11 Feb. 1949)
Sklar (25 Sept. 1953)
Sklluta (11 May 1973)
Sklut (11 May 1973)
Skoler (10 Jan. 1964)
Skolnick (18 May 1956)
Skolnik (5 July 1946)
Skudin (22 July 1955)
Skui (15 Sept. 1950)
Skuja (15 Sept. 1950)
Skyer (12 June 1959)
Sladowski (14 Dec. 1951)
Slava (7 Dec. 1945)
Slavin (25 Dec. 1970)
Sleppin (6 Oct. 1967)
Sliva (7 Dec. 1945)
Slobodin (13 Oct. 1967)
Sluve (7 Dec. 1945)
Smilansky (20 Feb. 1953)
Smissman (30 Sept. 1949)
Smoler (12 Nov. 1971)
Smolian (11 Oct. 1963)
Smorgansky (17 Sept. 1954)
Smulian (11 Oct. 1963)
Sobolofsky (25 Sept. 1959)

Sofan (25 July 1958)
Sokol (1 Apr. 1955)
Sokolofski (18 Jan. 1946)
Sokolow (3 July 1959)
Sokolsky (25 Nov. 1949)
Solarz (28 Sept. 1956)
Solechnik (21 May 1976)
Solganik (21 Sept. 1973)
Solinger (8 Sept. 1972)
Sollender (5 Mar. 1971)
Solodar (1 Mar. 1963)
Solomin (20 Dec. 1963)
Soloveichik (9 Oct. 1964)
Soltz (15 Sept. 1967)
Soroka (18 Oct. 1963)
Sourkes (27 Apr. 1951)
Span (2 Oct. 1970)
Spector (7 Nov. 1952)
Spektor (7 Nov. 1952)
Spenadel (15 Feb. 1946)
Spener (2 Oct. 1970)
Sperling (7 Apr. 1950)
Spett (27 Feb. 1959)
Spialter (29 Sept. 1967)
Spiegel (18 June 1954)
        (10 Oct. 1958)
        (1 Sept. 1967)
Spiegelberg (4 Aug. 1967)
Spiegler (1 Sept. 1967)
Spielberg (4 Aug. 1967)
Spierer (21 Apr. 1967)
Spiesman (8 Jan. 1971)
Spindel (15 Mar. 1968)
Spinner (2 Sept. 1960)
Spiro (13 Mar. 1970)
Spitalny (28 Apr. 1967)
Splaver (14 Mar. 1969)
Spodek (7 Mar. 1958)
Sprachman (23 Dec. 1966)
Sprayregen (20 Sept. 1963)
Springer (14 Jan. 1949)
         (19 Nov. 1954)
Sroloff (1 Mar. 1963)
Srolov (1 Mar. 1963)
Stampfer (26 June 1970)
Stanislawski (10 May 1968)
Starobin (16 Nov. 1956)
Stauber (2 Aug. 1968)
Stauver (2 Aug. 1968)
Stavitsky (8 May 1959)
Stawitsky (8 May 1959)
Stechman (4 Apr. 1969)
Steckel (25 Apr. 1952)
Stehman (4 Apr. 1969)

Stein (18 Apr. 1952)
Steinberg (21 Sept. 1951)
        (24 Apr. 1959)
Steiner (1 July 1955)
        (5 June 1964)
Steinhorn (13 Mar. 1964)
Steinitz (16 Sept. 1949)
Steinlauf (30 Jan. 1970)
Steinschneider (10 Mar. 1961)
Stelzer (4 May 1962)
Stember (13 Feb. 1970)
Stempelmacher (10 Mar. 1961)
Stengel (12 Aug. 1960)
Sterin (2 May 1969)
Stern (22 July 1949)
Sternberg (20 June 1952)
Sternschuss (21 Mar. 1969)
Stertz (9 Feb. 1962)
Stier (18 Aug. 1950)
Stodtman (8 Oct. 1971)
Stoller (25 Feb. 1966)
        (27 Apr. 1973)
Stolnitz (15 June 1973)
Stolper (14 July 1972)
Stoper (22 Oct. 1954)
Storch (26 Nov. 1954)
Stotland (17 May 1968)
Strassheim (1 Jan. 1960)
Straus (26 Nov. 1954)
Strausberg (26 May 1972)
Strausenberg (26 May 1972)
Strenger (15 June 1951)
Strickowski (21 July 1972)
Strikman (20 Oct. 1972)
Strim (18 May 1951)
Strisover (13 Dec. 1963)
Stroh (6 Nov. 1953)
Strom (1 Apr. 1955)
Strumpf (15 Feb. 1952)
Strykowski (21 July 1972)
Strysower (13 Dec. 1963)
Sturm (18 May 1951)
        (1 Apr. 1955)
Stutman (8 Oct. 1971)
Suarsky (20 Dec. 1963)
Suchowiecki (11 July 1975)
Sudalter (7 Mar. 1969)
Sudater (7 Mar. 1969)
Sudawsky (5 Nov. 1948)
Sudberg (31 Mar. 1950)
Suesskind (6 Dec. 1968)
Suffis (16 Apr. 1971)
Sufrin (22 May 1953)
Sumbul (6 Jan. 1961)

Surasky (20 Dec. 1963)
Susskind (26 Mar. 1954)
        (6 Dec. 1968)
Sutin (19 Feb. 1954)
Sverdlov (7 Jan. 1949)
Swack (8 Feb. 1957)
Swak (8 Feb. 1957)
Swarsenski (29 July 1955)
Swerdlow (7 Jan. 1949)
Szacki (15 Sept. 1972)
Szajka (24 Feb. 1967)
Szaladjewski (16 May 1969)
Szalaszin (15 Dec. 1972)
Szczeciniarz (29 Apr. 1955)
Szewczynski (31 Mar. 1972)
Szmuk (14 May 1971)
Sznapsik (26 Sept. 1969)
Sznitman (19 Nov. 1965)
Szolewicz (29 May 1970)
Szpialter (29 Sept. 1967)
Szpielberg (4 Aug. 1967)
Szpilka (11 July 1952)
Szpilkarz (11 July 1952)
Szpitalny (28 Apr. 1967)
Szrojt (15 Feb. 1957)
Szupak (14 Feb. 1969)
Szyper (21 Feb. 1969)

Tabachin (19 June 1953)
Tabachnik (6 Sept. 1968)
Tabak (14 Sept. 1962)
Tabakin (19 June 1953)
Tabas (6 Sept. 1968)
Tadlis (20 Apr. 1973)
Tajs (5 May 1967)
Taksen (25 Sept. 1970)
Taksin (25 Sept. 1970)
Talisnik (14 July 1972)
Tallas (12 Feb. 1960)
Tam (2 Dec. 1966)
Tamarkin (10 Oct. 1958)
Tambor (23 Jan. 1953)
Tamsky (2 Dec. 1966)
Tandler (20 Jan. 1950)
Tannenbaum (31 Mar. 1967)
Tannenblatt (22 Aug. 1969)
Tantny (10 Nov. 1967)
Tanyzer (3 Jan. 1958)
Taradash (15 Aug. 1969)
Tarakanski (15 June 1973)
Tarakinsky (15 June 1973)
Tarfon (10 Mar. 1967)
Tarler (10 Feb. 1967)
Tarlo (27 Nov. 1959)

Tarran (29 Nov. 1968)
Tarshish (9 July 1976)
Tarutz (20 Aug. 1976)
Tatkin (23 May 1958)
Taub (5 May 1972)
    (16 Apr. 1976)
Taube (5 May 1972)
Taxin (25 Sept. 1970)
Tcbrich (12 Oct. 1956)
Tedalis (20 Apr. 1973)
Teig (2 May 1958)
Teitelbaum (1 Mar. 1946)
    (14 July 1950)
    (11 Dec. 1953)
    (31 Mar. 1967)
Teller (9 Dec. 1949)
Temkin (20 May 1960)
Tendler (20 Jan. 1950)
Tenelson (8 Oct. 1954)
Tennenblatt (22 Aug. 1969)
Teplitz (27 Mar. 1964)
Tepper (22 May 1964)
Tersch (22 Jan. 1971)
Tessel (8 Aug. 1969)
Tesser (3 June 1966)
Tessler (25 Feb. 1966)
Theumim (17 Mar. 1967)
Thomashow (16 Feb. 1973)
Thurim (10 Oct. 1975)
Ticktin (7 Aug. 1970)
Tiktin (7 Aug. 1970)
Tilbor (30 Dec. 1966)
Tishler (25 Feb. 1966)
Tismonetzky (7 Feb. 1964)
Titman (15 Dec. 1972)
Tittman (15 Dec. 1972)
Tobias (9 Sept. 1949)
    (30 Dec. 1955)
Tochterman (12 Dec. 1969)
Tockman (7 Apr. 1967)
Toder (27 Apr. 1956)
Todress (30 Aug. 1963)
Toepfer (22 May 1964)
Tokar (21 July 1950)
Tolmach (15 July 1966)
Tolokonsky (18 Nov. 1960)
Tolusciak (6 Mar. 1970)
Tomaszow (16 Feb. 1973)
Tomim (17 Mar. 1967)
Tompakov (19 May 1961)
Tonelson (8 Oct. 1954)
Tontak (10 Nov. 1967)
Topper (19 Mar. 1954)
Torgove (5 May 1950)

Torno (25 June 1954)
Torsch (22 Jan. 1971)
Tosk (19 Jan. 1951)
Traeger (17 June 1949)
    (21 July 1950)
Tragarz (24 Sept. 1971)
Tragash (24 Sept. 1971)
Trainin (27 Aug. 1976)
Trainoff (4 June 1954)
Traki (10 Jan. 1964)
Trattner (10 Feb. 1967)
Trazenfeld (23 Feb. 1951)
Treiger (17 June 1949)
Treistman (27 Jan. 1956)
Treu (13 Apr. 1956)
Tribus (17 Dec. 1954)
Tribuswinkel (17 Dec. 1954)
Triebwasser (26 Jan. 1968)
Triffon (10 Mar. 1967)
Trifon (10 Mar. 1967)
Trilling (8 Mar. 1957)
Trillinger (8 Mar. 1957)
Tringler (8 Mar. 1957)
Tritsch (7 Feb. 1958)
Trivsch (17 Dec. 1954)
Trock (4 July 1958)
Trocki (2 June 1972)
Troeger (21 July 1950)
Troki (4 July 1958)
    (2 June 1972)
Trostman (27 Jan. 1956)
Trotsky (2 June 1972)
Truebwasser (26 Jan. 1968)
Trustinetzky (14 Jan. 1966)
Trzcina (21 Oct. 1949)
Tshernin (17 Apr. 1968)
Tsolik (5 Sept. 1958)
Tsvi (7 May 1971)
Tuchman (29 Jan. 1954)
    (7 Apr. 1967)
Tuerkel (29 Jan. 1971)
Tullman (24 Nov. 1972)
Tulman (24 Nov. 1972)
Tumpowski (6 Dec. 1963)
Tunick (7 Apr. 1961)
Tunik (7 Apr. 1961)
Turansky (26 Aug. 1960)
Turchik (21 Nov. 1952)
Turkel (29 Jan. 1971)
Turman (14 Sept. 1973)
Turowitz (21 Mar. 1958)
Tygel (7 Oct. 1949)
Tyk (28 Oct. 1966)
Tyka (28 Oct. 1966)

Tysmienicki (7 Feb. 1964)
Tzchina (21 Oct. 1949)
Tzelnik (19 Nov. 1971)
Tzinman (26 Jan. 1951)

Uchitel (26 July 1968)
Udashin (31 Jan. 1969)
Udasin (31 Jan. 1969)
Udelson (21 Feb. 1964)
Ulkowitz (7 Jan. 1966)
Ullmo (10 July 1970)
Ulma (3 Feb. 1961)
Ulman (3 Feb. 1961)
      (10 July 1970)
Ulmer (3 Feb. 1961)
Ulmo (10 July 1970)
Umansky (28 Apr. 1961)
Ungar (21 Oct. 1960)
Ungerleider (8 Oct. 1971)
Unk (4 Oct. 1968)
Unka (4 Oct. 1968)
Unterberger (5 Oct. 1973)
Urbach (2 Jan. 1959)
Urdang (6 July 1956)
Urevich (1 Mar. 1946)
      (9 Nov. 1973)
Urinsky (2 Oct. 1959)
Uritzky (19 Mar. 1976)
Urkansky (7 June 1957)
Usem (24 Dec. 1971)
Ushkow (24 Dec. 1954)
Uzdanski (23 Oct. 1959)

Vaisrub (12 May 1972)
Varanc (22 Apr. 1966)
Vardi (30 Mar. 1951)
Varon (31 Dec. 1954)
Vasen (27 Oct. 1967)
Vaynshtock (28 Aug. 1953)
Veitel (14 June 1968)
Veleschin (23 Feb. 1973)
Velikov (17 Jan. 1958)
Vernikoff (20 Aug. 1976)
Victorson (14 June 1960)
Vidrovitz (28 Nov. 1958)
Viernik (20 Aug. 1976)
Viertel (23 Mar. 1956)
Viertenteil (14 July 1961)
Vigdorchik (2 Mar. 1956)
Vigoda (25 Sept. 1953)
Vilkomirsky (16 Dec. 1960)
Vinikour (5 Mar. 1954)
Virshup (2 Apr. 1976)
Viski (29 Dec. 1967)
Vital (26 May 1950)

Vitznodel (22 July 1960)
Vizansky (12 Feb. 1971)
Vladislavovski (3 Jan. 1964)
Vodicka (16 Dec. 1966)
Vogel (5 Sept. 1969)
Volitzky (13 June 1958)
Volkomirsky (16 Dec. 1960)
Voloski (28 Feb. 1969)
Volotsk (23 June 1950)
Volozhyn (23 Feb. 1973)
Von Treuenberg (13 Apr. 1956)
Vrum (24 June 1966)

Wachutinski (26 May 1972)
Wacker (12 May 1961)
Waghalter (19 Nov. 1971)
Wahnish (10 Nov. 1972)
Wahrman (18 Aug. 1972)
Walachinski (3 Aug. 1951)
Wald (14 June 1968)
Waldman (20 Feb. 1953)
Walecki (13 June 1958)
Waletzky (13 June 1958)
Walfand (17 Dec. 1971)
Walfisch (27 Aug. 1976)
Walker (28 Sept. 1956)
Wallerstein (16 June 1950)
Waltuch (30 Jan. 1959)
Wandel (1 Feb. 1974)
Wank (20 Aug. 1954)
      (13 May 1960)
Wapner (4 Dec. 1953)
Waranch (22 Apr. 1966)
Warmbrand (27 Sept. 1963)
Warnick (20 Apr. 1973)
Warnik (20 Apr. 1973)
Wartelski (29 Oct. 1954)
Wasel (19 Nov. 1948)
Wasserman (4 June 1954)
Wasserstein (7 Aug. 1970)
Wassertrilling (8 Mar. 1957)
Waxman (4 Nov. 1960)
Waxstein (6 June 1958)
Weber (21 Mar. 1951)
Wechsler (24 May 1957)
Wecker (12 May 1961)
Wedro (24 Sept. 1971)
Weger (27 July 1962)
Weidenfeld (27 Nov. 1970)
Weil (25 Feb. 1949)
      (16 Jan. 1953)
Weiler (25 Feb. 1949)
      (16 Jan. 1953)
Weilerstein (16 June 1950)

Weill (25 Feb. 1949)
  (16 Jan. 1953)
Weiman (22 Feb. 1952)
Weinberg (29 Apr. 1949)
Weiner (22 Feb. 1952)
  (4 June 1954)
  (26 Nov. 1954)
  (3 Feb. 1967)
  (28 Nov. 1975)
Weinfeld (6 Dec. 1968)
Weingarten (29 May 1964)
Weinglass (20 Apr. 1956)
  (22 Feb. 1957)
Weinherr (22 Feb. 1952)
Weinlaub (28 Aug. 1953)
Weinles (9 May 1952)
  (20 Apr. 1956)
  (22 Feb. 1957)
Weinman (3 Feb. 1967)
Weinraub (22 Feb. 1946)
Weinreb (22 Feb. 1946)
  (28 Aug. 1953)
Weinsaft (31 July 1964)
Weinsoft (31 July 1964)
Weinstein (28 July 1950)
  (1 Mar. 1957)
  (3 Feb. 1967)
Weinstock (22 Feb. 1946)
  (28 Aug. 1953)
Weisberger (21 Sept. 1962)
Weisbrod (8 Sept. 1950)
Weisel (19 Nov. 1948)
Weiskabonick (3 May 1946)
Weiskopf (25 Oct. 1968)
Weiss (21 Dec. 1956)
  (1 Mar. 1957)
  (21 Sept. 1962)
  (1 Apr. 1966)
Weissenberger (21 Sept. 1962)
Weisskopf (25 Oct. 1968)
Weissman (1 Mar. 1957)
Weissruebe (12 May 1972)
Weker (12 May 1961)
Weller (1 Mar. 1968)
Wellikoff (15 Apr. 1949)
Wember (4 Feb. 1966)
Wembor (4 Feb. 1966)
Wendorf (25 Apr. 1952)
Wendriner (16 Nov. 1956)
Wendroff (25 Apr. 1952)
Wener (4 June 1954)
Werben (21 Nov. 1975)
Werbin (21 Nov. 1975)
Werblowski (18 Apr. 1958)

Wernikoff (20 Aug. 1976)
Wertenteil (14 July 1961)
Wesel (19 Nov. 1948)
Westerwelle (26 May 1961)
Westerweller (26 May 1961)
Wickler (14 Dec. 1973)
Widder (13 June 1952)
Widetzky (5 Jan. 1951)
Widro (24 Sept. 1971)
Widrow (28 Nov. 1958)
Wieder (13 June 1952)
Wieland (28 July 1972)
Wiesel (19 Nov. 1948)
Wieser (4 Aug. 1950)
Wiezanski (12 Feb. 1971)
Wiklor (14 Dec. 1973)
Wildman (20 Feb. 1953)
Wilfand (17 Dec. 1971)
Wilfant (17 Dec. 1971)
Wilk (28 July 1972)
Willenzik (12 June 1959)
Wincig (23 May 1969)
Windner (2 Aug. 1968)
Winick (3 Aug. 1956)
Winkel (13 Aug. 1954)
Winkelman (19 Sept. 1958)
Winkenfeld (29 Dec. 1950)
Winkler (19 Sept. 1958)
  (14 Dec. 1973)
  (3 Sept. 1976)
Winna (7 June 1968)
Winnik (3 Aug. 1956)
Winograd (7 Oct. 1955)
  (21 July 1967)
Winokur (21 Dec. 1951)
  (5 Mar. 1954)
Wintner (9 Feb. 1951)
Winzig (23 May 1969)
Wirszub (2 Apr. 1976)
Wishnevetsky (1 June 1973)
Wiski (29 Dec. 1967)
Wisniowiecki (1 June 1973)
Wisser (4 Aug. 1950)
Witkin (28 Sept. 1951)
Witten (28 Dec. 1956)
Witwin (14 Oct. 1955)
Wodlinger (2 June 1967)
Wolf (13 Dec. 1968)
Wolfand (17 Dec. 1971)
Wolfant (17 Dec. 1971)
Wolfish (27 Aug. 1976)
Wolfman (22 Nov. 1963)
Wolgast (9 Apr. 1976)
Wolikov (21 Nov. 1958)

Wollman (1 Jan. 1960)
Wolochow (10 June 1955)
Woloski (28 Feb. 1969)
Wolozynski (3 Aug. 1951)
Wolpe (25 Dec. 1959)
Wolper (31 May 1946)
Wolpin (4 May 1973)
Wortelski (29 Oct. 1954)
Woskoboinik (3 May 1946)
Wovsaniker (20 Sept. 1963)
Wulwik (10 Aug. 1973)
Wunsch (29 Aug. 1975)
Wurmbrand (27 Sept. 1963)
Wygoda (25 Sept. 1953)

Yaabetz (11 July 1952)
Yabez (11 July 1952)
Yablonsky (26 Oct. 1973)
Yachnin (20 Apr. 1956)
Yachnitz (12 June 1964)
Yachnovitz (7 Sept. 1962)
Yagoda (20 June 1958)
       (10 July 1964)
       (12 July 1968)
Yagodnik (16 Apr. 1954)
Yakir (27 July 1962)
Yalkut (4 July 1952)
Yampolsky (21 Nov. 1975)
Yanes (30 Apr. 1954)
Yankauer (4 Dec. 1953)
Yanowitch (12 Oct. 1951)
Yantian (23 Feb. 1962)
Yares (26 Jan. 1951)
Yarin (26 Jan. 1951)
Yarnitzki (20 Feb. 1970)
Yashnitz (12 June 1964)
Yasinow (11 June 1971)
Yasnyi (13 Jan. 1956)
Yatkeman (7 July 1961)
Yawitz (11 July 1952)
Yedashkin (21 Nov. 1969)
Yegelwel (2 Oct. 1953)
Yegidis (10 July 1964)
Yekusiel (17 Jan. 1964)
        (29 Aug. 1975)
Yermak (14 Apr. 1961)
Yevdashkin (21 Nov. 1969)
Yoffee (15 Apr. 1949)
Yolleck (27 Apr. 1956)
Yolles (11 Sept. 1959)
Yosowitz (15 Sept. 1967)
Ytkin (22 Sept. 1950)
Yudel (21 Feb. 1964)
Yudelson (21 Feb. 1964)

Yudin (20 June 1958)
Yulish (6 Sept. 1963)
Yurman (27 Apr. 1962)
Yusem (24 Dec. 1971)

Zabarka (20 Nov. 1953)
Zabaroff (20 Nov. 1953)
Zabielski (18 Oct. 1968)
Zachariash (30 Sept. 1955)
Zackheim (25 Nov. 1966)
Zacuto (14 May 1954)
Zadok (15 Feb. 1974)
Zaenkel (10 Feb. 1961)
Zafrani (9 Jan. 1970)
Zager (20 Feb. 1959)
Zagerinsky (30 June 1950)
Zagor (3 Dec. 1954)
Zagorodny (26 May 1961)
Zaichik (30 Mar. 1956)
        (5 Oct. 1956)
Zaidman (29 Nov. 1968)
Zajac (8 Sept. 1972)
Zajdman (29 Nov. 1968)
Zak (13 July 1962)
Zakem (5 Mar. 1976)
Zaks (13 July 1962)
Zalkind (18 Feb. 1972)
Zalzin (18 Feb. 1972)
Zamek (28 May 1976)
Zanaretsky (10 July 1959)
Zander (12 Oct. 1956)
Zanger (30 Mar. 1973)
Zangwill (3 Mar. 1967)
Zankel (10 Feb. 1961)
Zanvil (3 Mar. 1967)
Zanville (3 Mar. 1967)
Zapf (9 Feb. 1973)
Zapp (9 Feb. 1973)
Zarankin (13 July 1951)
Zarch (15 May 1964)
Zareikin (12 Aug. 1955)
Zarmati (1 May 1970)
Zarobnik (9 Feb. 1973)
Zatilna (5 Dec. 1969)
Zausmer (1 July 1960)
Zauspartmer (1 July 1960)
Zebelman (14 July 1967)
Zeff (19 Oct. 1956)
Zegelbaum (9 Nov. 1973)
Zehner (10 Mar. 1961)
Zeichick (5 Oct. 1956)
Zeidner (20 Feb. 1976)
Zeitlin (11 Nov. 1949)
Zeitman (21 Oct. 1960)

Zeitz (30 Mar. 1956)
Zelden (21 Feb. 1958)
Zelicovitz (23 Jan. 1976)
Zelik (23 Jan. 1976)
Zelmati (1 May 1970)
Zelnick (19 Nov. 1971)
Zelvin (27 Sept. 1963)
Zendel (19 May 1967)
Zengebott (28 Feb. 1958)
Zepf (9 Feb. 1973)
Zermati (1 May 1970)
Zerobnick (9 Feb. 1973)
Zev (19 Oct. 1956)
Zeveluk (23 Aug. 1957)
Zfansky (14 Nov. 1952)
Zfass (14 Nov. 1952)
Zhlementinovski (25 Sept. 1970)
Zhurzhinsky (23 Dec. 1955)
Ziblat (29 Sept. 1967)
Ziehblatt (29 Sept. 1967)
Zieve (5 Mar. 1976)
Zif (8 Nov. 1968)
Ziffer (7 July 1950)
Zifkin (27 Oct. 1967)
Zimmerman (4 Sept. 1964)
Zimmerspitz (25 Oct. 1963)
Zimmet (28 Feb. 1964)
Zimring (28 Feb. 1964)
Zinneman (28 Feb. 1964)
Zinnreich (16 Jan. 1970)
Zionts (8 Sept. 1972)
Zipperstein (13 Oct. 1972)
Ziskin (6 Dec. 1968)
Ziskind (26 Mar. 1954)
        (6 Dec. 1968)
Ziv (8 Nov. 1968)
Zlatkin (1 Aug. 1958)
Zodikov (2 July 1971)
Zohn (20 May 1949)
      (8 Feb. 1957)
Zotilna (5 Dec. 1969)
Zolotarev (23 Oct. 1964)
Zolotoreff (23 Oct. 1964)
Zryb (9 Apr. 1971)
Zubres (23 May 1969)
Zuckerbrod (4 Mar. 1955)
Zuckerman (26 Nov. 1971)
Zudick (10 May 1957)
Zulauf (28 Mar. 1958)
Zunder (16 June 1972)
Zupnick (8 Mar. 1963)
Zurachov (31 July 1959)
Zurawin (17 Jan. 1969)
Zurik (3 Mar. 1961)

Zusmir (1 July 1960)
Zwerin (22 Dec. 1972)
Zwerman (23 Sept. 1949)
Zwi (7 May 1971)
Zwickler (15 July 1960)
Zwiebach (15 Dec. 1950)
Zwillenberg (5 Aug. 1949)
Zyblat (29 Sept. 1967)
Zyskind (6 Dec. 1968)

Index of Authors and Selected Subjects

Goetze, A., 0530
Goitein, S.D.F., 1010, 1077
Gold, D.L., 0105, 0996
Goldberg, A.D., 0531
Goldberg, H.E., 1011-1012
Goldberger, I., 0595
Golde, M., 0411
Goldin, H.E., 0003
Goldman, I.M., 1074
Goldschmidt, M., 0811
Goldsmith, M., 0812
Goldziher, I., 0493
Golomb, Z.N., 0995
Gonzalo Maeso, D., 0205
Gordon, A., 0626-0628
Gordon, B.L., 1151
Gottheil, R.J.H., 0965
Gottlieb, N., 0056
Gottschald, M., 0749
Gouldman, M.D., 1050
Gowen, H.H., 0293
Grandon, A.F., 1125-1126
Gray, G.B., 0179, 0182, 0206,
    0215, 0294, 0373, 0525, 0532
Greenfield, E., 1190
Grelot, P., 0533
Griffiths, J.G., 0481
Grimme, H., 0471
Grodner, A., 0921
Grohne, E., 0750
Gross, M.D., 1051
Grosser, D., 0751
Grünberg, S., 0207
Grünwald, Moriz, 086A, 0106, 0985
Grunwald, Max, 086B, 0208, 0295,
    0657, 0667, 0813
Güdemann, M., 0209, 0752, 0814,
    0933, 0942
Guenzburg, D., 0381
Gumpertz, Y.G.F., 0107
Gustavs, A., 0517
Gygès, 0697-0698

Haarbleicher, M.H., 0753
Haes, F., 0870
Ḥagiz, J., 0629
Halberstam, Ḥ., 0630
Halévy, J., 0415
Hall, B.L., 0996
Hall, R.M.R., 0996
Hamet, I., 1013
Hamilton, E.N., 0159
Hanson, A., 0367
Hanson, R.P.C., 0364

Harduf, D.M., 0160-0161, 0596-0597,
    1052
Ha-Reubeni, E., 0109
Harkavy, A.E., 0943-0944
Harkavy, Alexander, 0997
Harris, J.R., 0353
Hasson, A., 0880
Haupt, P., 0459
Hazan, E.B., 0631
Hazan, S., 0631
Heilig, O., 0816
Heinisch, P., 0442
Heintze, A., 0754
Heitz, F.-J., 0719
Heller, B., 0587
Heller, J., 0296, 0416, 0418
Hemerdinger, G., 0720-0721
Hengel, M., 0567
Henkin, Y.E., 0623
Henriquez Pimentel, M., 0986
Hertel, E., 0755
Hervé, J., 0057
Herzog, D., 1157, 1173
Hessen, I.I., see Gessen, ÎÛ. I.
Hieronymus, Saint, 0210, 0255, 0350
Hiller, M., 0211
Hirschberg, H.Z., 1014
Hirschfeld, H., 0466
Historia Judaica, 0023
Hitzig, F., 0396
Hölscher, G., 0212
Hösl, I., 0472
Hoffmann, A., 0405
Hogg, H.W., 0297
Hohlenberg, M.H., 0213
Hommel, E., 0214
Hommel, F., 0206, 0215, 0456
Honeyman, A.M., 0298, 0510
Horovitz, J., 0586-0587
Horovitz, M., 0633
Horowitz, C.M., 1093
Horowitz, J., 0598
Horwitz, L., 0817-0821
Hulst, A.R., 0429
Human, A., 0756
Humbert, P., 0468
Hunsberger, D.R., 0216
Hurwitz, E.S., 1095
Hyamson, A.M., 0017, 0110

Ibn Habib, Moses b. Solomon, 0634
Ikhilov, M.I., 0945
Imber, N.H., 0111
Ingholt, H., 0354

122

123

127

Index of Individual Names

Aaron, 0134, 0380, 0472
Aba, 0134
Abel, 0315, 0328
Aben (Ibn), 1157-1158
Abigail, 0369, 0371
Abraham, 0104, 0251, 0252A,
  0376-0384, 0414
Abram, 0376, 0378, 0384
Abravanel, 1132-1133
Adam, 0385-0387
Adlai, 0388
Adon, 0387
Agee, 0389
Ahab, 0370, 0390
Ahikar, 0369, 0391
Amminadab, 0392
Anna, 0104
Ariel, 0393
Asaph, 0454
Ashur, 0394
Avigdor, 1178
Badchan, 1134
Balaam, 0394A
Ballin, 1135
Balthasar, 1174
Baneth, 1136
Barhun, 1137
Bar Kochba, 1138
Bar Kozeba, 1138
Barnabas, 0373, 0395-0396
Baron, 1159
Barsabas, 0396
Bartholomew, 0397
Bartimaeus, 0396
Barzillai, 0398
Bathsheba, 0104
Benjamin, 0104
Berfet, 1139
Berlin, 1168
Bettsack, 1166
Bildad, 0399-0400
Brandes, 1140
Breslau, 1141
Breslauer, 1141
Cain, 0315, 0328, 0401
Caleb, 0402
Chaim, 0104, 1142
Chelbo, 1143
Cohen, 1144
Daniel, 0304, 0371, 0403
David, 0104, 0404-0407
Deborah, 0104, 0408-0409
Dreyfus, 1145-1146
Elhanan, 0406

Elihu, 0410
Elijah, 0104
Elizabeth, 0411
Elymas, 0375
Ephraim, 0370, 0498, 0855
Ephron, 0498
Esau, 0412
Esther, 0104, 0334, 0413
Eve, 0104, 0387, 0414-0416
Falk, 1147
Farisol, 1148
Franco, 1149
Gaspar, 1174
Gershon, 0104
Gittel, 0104
Goetz, 1150
Gordon, 1151-1153
Gutmann, 1154
Guzmán, 1154
Hagab, 0370
Hai Gaon, 1155
Hanani, 0417
Hananiah, 0417
Ḥayim, see Chaim
Helen, 0104
Hirsch, 0104
Hitler, 1156
Hosea, 0268, 0317
Ibn (Aben), 1157-1158
Ibn Baron, 1159
Ida, 0104
Isaac, 0104, 0268, 0418-0420
Ishbosheth, 0338
Ishmael, 0421
Isidore, 1160-1163
Israel, 0422-0437, 0439, 0442,
  0444-0446
Issachar, 0304
Ithiel, 0499
Jacob, 0104, 0419, 0438-0446
Jehoiachin, 0308
Jehoiakim, 0308
Jehu, 0447
Jephthah, 0370
Jeroboam, 0506
Jesus, 0448-0450, 0570
Jethro, 0451
Jezebel, 0369
Joash, 0452
Job, 0369
Joseph, 0370, 0419, 0440, 0453-
  0454
Joshua, 0455
Josiah, 0456

131